Living, Studying, and
Working in

France

Living, Studying, and
Working in

Everything You Need to Know to
Fulfill Your Dreams of Living Abroad

Saskia Reilly and Lorin David Kalisky

AN OWL BOOK
HENRY HOLT AND COMPANY   NEW YORK

Owl Books
Henry Holt and Company, LLC
Publishers since 1866
175 Fifth Avenue
New York, New York 10010
www.henryholt.com

An Owl Book® and 🄷® are registered trademarks of Henry Holt and Company, LLC.

Distributed in Canada by H. B. Fenn and Company Ltd.

Library of Congress Cataloging-in-Publication Data
Reilly, Saskia.
Living, studying, and working in France: everything you need to know to fulfill
your dreams of living abroad / by Saskia Reilly and Lorin David Kalisky.—
1st Owl books ed.
p.   cm.
"Owl books."
Includes index.
ISBN-13: 978-0-8050-5947-2
ISBN-10: 0-8050-5947-4
1. Americans—France—Handbooks, manuals, etc.   2. France—Social conditions—
20th century—Handbooks, manuals, etc.   3. Visitors, Foreign—France—
Handbooks, manuals, etc.   I. Kalisky, Lorin David.
DC34.5.A44R45   1999   99-11623
944—dc21   CIP

Henry Holt books are available for special
promotions and premiums. For details contact:
Director, Special Markets.

First Edition 1999

Designed by Paula Russell Szafranski

Cartography by Jeffrey L. Ward

Photographs courtesy of Joshua Lippard, Monica Larner,
Lorin David Kalisky, and Saskia Reilly
The Henry Holt Living, Studying, and Working Series originated with
Living, Studying, and Working in Italy by Travis Neighbor and Monica Larner.

Printed in the United States of America

5   7   9   10   8   6   4

For Trudy and Mo, whose love for France clearly rubbed off

—L.D.K.

For David and Annelies Reilly, who made everything possible

—S.S.R.

Contents

Contents

Acknowledgments

We would like to thank our editor, Jen Charat, for her support, enthusiasm, and patience. Thanks also to Monica and Travis for paving the way, and to Monica for thinking of us.

It is not often enough that I have the opportunity to express the gratitude I feel for all that my parents have done for me. With them I traveled to France for the first time, was left speechless by the beauty of Paris, and nibbled my first croissant-au-beurre in a French hotel. They taught me to explore the world around me and gave me the courage to take off and follow my dreams. For all this and more I am grateful. I would like to thank my brothers, Brian and Justin, and my sister, Melissa, who remind me that home is where they are. For his love, support, patience, and never-ending faith, I thank Antonio Corsano Leopizzi. Also special thanks to all the dear friends who made Paris magical and those who share my love for France, especially, Marion and Carla Broekhuizen; Marcus Mabry; Daniela Tafi; Carol and Chris Dickey; and Laure Klemm.

—Saskia Reilly
Boxborough, 1999

Acknowledgments

When I was fifteen, I spent the summer prancing around France with my mother and my sister. That summer, with all the passion and fascination of adolescence, I fell in love with France. I thank my parents for giving me such a wonderful gift, and in general for their love and support. Later, when I went to France to live, I was lucky enough to find some wonderful people with whom to share my life. Thanks to Jim and Roselyne, Sam and Rob, Mick and Fabienne, Christophe and Valerie, Amy and Fred, Tim, Caitlin, Barb, Anthony, Dominique, Eric Lee, and (of course) the Human Cannonballs. A special thanks to Gillian for sharing a crazy and formative year of her life with me, living in the swanky 15th, and for being so damn cool; to Mana for her tolerance, support, and love under the stress of my deadlines, and in general; and to all my other friends in France and friends from France in the United States.

—Lorin David Kalisky
San Francisco, 1999

Preface

France has a magic all its own. Whether you're *en Provence* or in Paris, there is something wonderful about being in France. If you've spent time there, perhaps you understand. Sometimes you recognize it only when you return to France after being away, but it is a distinct and familiar feeling, a feeling that France is your home. That may be why we ended up living in France, and it's certainly why we keep going back.

We became good friends while living in Paris for many reasons, but one powerful connection was the realization that we shared this passion, this understanding, and this love for our adopted home. That is not to say that, for us, living in France was all fun and games. No matter where you live, it is easy to take places for granted. We worked hard and struggled at times, and you probably will too if you are moving to France. But France doesn't let you forget where you are for long. Its magic is always there to save you, to take your mind off a bad day at work, or to lift your spirits when you're feeling down. One quiet walk by yourself through the empty streets of Paris on a Sunday night is all you will ever need to understand.

This book is a culmination of our lives and experiences in France, along with many days and nights of research. It is not meant as a tourist guide; it is intended to be a handbook for people heading to France to live, as students and professionals, and to help them make the most of the time they spend there. And although the information contained in this book may be useful to a broad range of people, including tourists and even French people, it offers a view of living, studying, and working in France from our perspective as Americans.

We've tried to focus this book on the unique challenges and needs of Americans moving to France to live, study, and work. We've intentionally left out details about French monuments and museums. There are plenty of guidebooks and tourist handbooks for that. This book is intended to help you navigate through the labyrinth of life in a new culture; it will provide you with insight and practical knowledge that you will likely find helpful as you're thinking about moving to France, while you're in transit, and after you've arrived. This is the book you will have on the bookshelf of your home in France; it will be your reference manual as you adapt and grow into your new culture.

This is also a book about our experiences as two individuals living, studying, and working in France. When relevant, we've tried to include anecdotes and stories to illustrate our points and to help you gain a fuller understanding of what life is actually like in France. To avoid confusion, we use the pronoun "I" when one of us describes a personal story or anecdote, and "we" when we're giving more general advice. It's also important to keep in mind that your life in France may differ significantly from our experiences. People are different and places are constantly changing, and while our stories may provide you with a certain insight, France is yours to discover and experience on your own. In addition, it's important to note that information is constantly changing, and you may find that details we give you in this book have become inaccurate. While we've tried to provide you with the most up-to-date information possible, you should always double-check phone and fax numbers, addresses, prices, and other information. This is especially true when it comes to the volatile and evolving world of the Internet. Because Internet addresses are constantly changing, we've created a Web site to complement the information in this book. At **www.liveinfrance.com** you can find current information about many of the companies and organizations that we've listed.

We hope that you find the book useful and informative. While there's no way we can ensure that your life in France is free of pitfalls and challenges, we can try to help you find ways to smooth out the bumps. And we hope that the magic of France is there for you, the way it has been there for us. *Bon courage!*

Living, Studying, and
Working in

France

Before You Go

CHAPTER ONE

A Place to Call Home

It is now more than a half century ago, back in the opening 1920s, that for the first time Paris began being included in the memories of a small contingent of youngish American expatriates, richer than most in creative ambition and rather modest in purse. For the most part we had recently shipped third class to France across the Atlantic, at that date still not yet flown over except by migratory sea birds. We had settled in the small hotels on the Paris Left Bank near the Place Saint-Germain-des-Prés, itself perfectly equipped with a large corner café called Les Deux Magots and an impressive twelfth-century Romanesque church, with its small garden of old trees, from whose branches the metropolitan blackbirds sang at dawn, audible to me in my bed close by in the rue Bonaparte.

—JANET FLANNER, *Paris Was Yesterday,* 1972

Americans have long had a love affair with France. In the 1920s, young writers and artists were drawn to France in search of inspiration. Today there are still some Americans who move to France in hopes of retracing the path to literary success taken by such writers as Ernest Hemingway and F. Scott Fitzgerald. But these days, not only artists and writers move to France. American expatriates living and working in France run the full spectrum of professions and cultural groups. Thousands of American businesspeople, lawyers, journalists, soldiers, diplomats, teachers, doctors, nurses, and entrepreneurs have all moved to France in search of that special French *je ne sais quoi,* and the numbers are ever rising.

In 1997, nearly 26,000 Americans were registered as permanent residents in France, not to mention the expatriates that are not on the books. More than 14,000 of them live in and around Paris, making up one of the largest communities in the world of Americans abroad.

All Roads Lead to Paris

One of the first things newcomers discover is that France is far more centralized than the United States and more than many of its European neighbors. Public education is controlled from Paris and all French schoolchildren follow the same curriculum. All social services and policies are conceived and coordinated in the capital. Even the network of trains that crisscross the country use Paris as a hub. It is nearly impossible to travel from Brittany to Provence without passing through Paris.

For much of its history, France was a monarchy. Louis XIV, better known as the *Roi Soleil* (the Sun King) for whom Versailles was constructed, epitomized the centralization of power when he declared, *l'État, c'est moi* (I am the State). Much of this centralization survived during the French Revolution, long after Louis XIV's death, and was strengthened under the rule of Napoléon Bonaparte.

By the late 1700s discontent had swept across France. The Sun King's extravagance had nearly bankrupted the State. A group of philosophers and writers led by Denis Diderot published the *Encyclopédie*, which challenged many widely held beliefs. The nobles, the middle class, and the peasants were all dissatisfied for different reasons. In 1789, the combination of new ideas, social unrest, and the financial ruin of the government exploded into the Revolution and the following ten years were a time of bloody struggle and turmoil in France. Thousands of French aristocrats—including King Louis XVI and his queen, Marie-Antoinette—lost their lives on the guillotine. Later, when the tide turned, thousands of revolutionaries lost their lives as well.

Much of French culture was destroyed. The revolutionaries decided to dispossess the nobles and the Catholic Church of their property. Monasteries and abbeys were burned or desecrated. Their contents were often destroyed, including thousands of books and manuscripts. Any intellectuals who spoke out against the Revolution were killed.

This mayhem was not destined to last. During the French Revolution, Napoléon Bonaparte rose through the ranks of the army. In 1799, ten years after the Revolution had started, he overthrew the revolutionary French government and took control of France. He remained in power until 1814 and then returned to power again for a hundred days in 1815 before he was defeated at Waterloo and sent into exile on an island off the coast of Africa.

During his time in power, Napoléon set up a very well organized system of governance that relied heavily on a centralized administration and set the stage for the modern French state. His government drafted and implemented groundbreaking legislation, including the Civil, Penal, and Commercial—Napoleonic—codes that have lived on not only in France but in other countries as well. He divided France into the administrative *départements* that still exist today and appointed prefects to manage them. He also redesigned and centralized France's educational system.

After Napoléon, later regimes including absolute monarchies, parliamentary monarchies, and the current Fifth Republic have all, for different reasons, preferred to maintain the centralization of power.

France and Her Colonies

France grew in strength and prosperity until World War I began in 1914. By then, French explorers and soldiers had claimed an enormous colonial empire in Africa and Asia. Their colonial dominance lasted through World War II and included a vast measure of cultural imperialism as well. French remains the second language in many Southeast Asian and North African countries.

The disintegration of this empire would cause French leaders headaches for decades to come. The first colonial revolt began in French Indochina in 1946 and the territory was eventually divided into Cambodia, Laos, and North and South Vietnam. The French withdrew from Indochina in 1954, after suffering heavy losses and leaving behind four unstable countries. This instability would eventually lead to the Vietnam War.

Several months after France's withdrawal from Indochina, revolution broke out in the French colony of Algeria, the home of close to a million French settlers. France granted Morocco, Tunisia, and other

Charming towns, like Pont-Aven in Brittany, dot the French countryside.

French colonies in Africa their independence to prevent further revolutions but refused to give up Algeria. The French Army fought a costly revolutionary war in the territory until 1961, when it became clear that only Algerian independence would end the war. Under President Charles de Gaulle, France and Algeria agreed to a cease-fire and French voters approved Algerian independence in the spring of 1962.

France has not been able to escape its colonial heritage. The country's responsibilities vis-à-vis its former colonies have been a source of conflict both within France, as waves of immigrants from North Africa attempt to make their way in French society, and with other countries that oppose preferential trade agreements that France has granted both to former colonies and its current overseas territories.

France Today

Today France is a country of contrasts. Newcomers are constantly surprised by the differences between the sophistication of Paris and the simple life of the countryside. The French have pushed to structure the European Union's agricultural regulations to ensure that they can continue to produce wine in the traditional ways, yet they pioneered the high-speed train. As a people, the French are at the same time strongly independent as individuals but fiercely patriotic as a group. Yet it was a Frenchman, Jean Monnet, who conceived of the European Union, and the French have been among the staunchest backers of European integration.

France's Role in the European Union

Under the guidance of Robert Schuman, Jean Monnet, and Charles de Gaulle, France was one of the six founding members of the European Economic Community in 1957, along with Belgium, Luxembourg, the Netherlands, Germany, and Italy. Two of the most vocal supporters of European unification—Jacques Delors, who held the European Commission presidency for nearly a decade, and François Mitterrand, who was president of France from 1981 to 1995—were Frenchmen.

These days the French see France as leading Europe toward economic and political union. Despite national pride, they have endorsed the Maastricht Treaty for European integration and are poised to participate in the common currency at the turn of the millennium.

Immigration

Thanks to favorable policies toward residents of former colonies and current territories, France has seen a marked increase in immigration in recent years. Immigrants from North Africa, the Caribbean, the South Pacific, and Asia have changed the face of French society. Paris alone has absorbed several hundred thousand immigrants. Some neighborhoods are filled with North African and Caribbean shops, restaurants, and night clubs, contributing to the truly international flavor of the city.

But the increase in immigration has not been a uniquely positive trend. Many French have felt threatened by the differences, particularly by the rise in prominence of Islam. The sight of young women wearing head scarves to high school and the construction of minarets and mosques in one-church towns have provoked a group of traditional French to organize in protest of immigration. Jean-Marie Le Pen, the head of *le Front National* (the National Front [FN]), has created an entire political party by rallying people's nationalist spirit and calling for tightening immigration controls and limiting the rights and civil liberties of many immigrants. It is not a side of the country that most French are proud of, but it exists and is gaining power. At the time of publication, the FN held two mayorships and had a handful of seats in the National Assembly.

Religion

France is primarily a Roman Catholic country although there are small Protestant, Jewish, and Muslim minorities. About 90 percent of the French consider themselves Catholic. From 1801 to 1905, the French government recognized Catholicism as the religion of the majority of the people. Bishops and priests were state officials and the government paid their salaries. Today, although most holidays and festivals are closely connected to the Catholic Church, young people are moving further and further away from the Church. Churches are half-empty, filled with aging congregations. That said, France is being forced to adjust to a rapidly changing religious identity. Immigrants from former colonies around the world have transformed the French religious landscape.

The Economy

France is one of only four West European countries to have a trillion-dollar economy. In 1997, the gross domestic product, which measures purchasing power parity, was close to $1.5 trillion. At the same time, the French government has retained control over a number of industries including the railways, airlines, electricity, and telecommunications. The inefficient management of these state-owned monopolies has led to high prices in these segments for French consumers. At the time of publication, there were plans to privatize some of these industries, namely, telecommunications and air transportation, but powerful union opposition has made the transition a slow one.

Farming and agriculture still comprise a very important component of the French economy. France is largely self-sufficient in agricultural products and is a major exporter of wheat and dairy products—selling anywhere from 20 percent to 70 percent of its production abroad. The French treasure their agricultural landscapes and the government has consistently provided high subsidies to farmers in order to enable them to preserve their way of life.

Although at one time France was heavily dependent on OPEC countries for oil imports, it has been a pioneer in developing nuclear power plants that now cover nearly 70 percent of domestic needs.

When it comes to work, persistently high unemployment is France's most challenging economic problem. Currently at 12.7 percent, French unemployment has proven difficult to reduce. The young make up the largest segment of the unemployed and the government has taken steps to create an environment that would make young workers more hirable, through special youth contracts and other incentives for French companies. France must reduce unemployment still further in order to be able to qualify for the European Economic and Monetary Union, which launched the euro, the common European currency, on January 1, 1999.

Making France Your Home

I was in love with the idea of France before I had ever even visited the country. Perhaps the images I had seen of French art, monuments, and the countryside inspired me. Or perhaps it was the thought of French food, culture, and traditions. Or perhaps it was a love of the language

A place to call home

and French literature. Whatever it was that moved me to pick up and start a new life in France, I was not alone. All the Americans and other expatriates that preceded me had created an incredibly helpful network of resources to make the transition to a new life and culture easier. And while there are some Americans who move to France and become more French than the French themselves, most find themselves living divided between both cultures, constantly contrasting and comparing the two and choosing the best of both to create a world as unique as France itself. *Bon voyage et bon séjour!*

CHAPTER   TWO

Getting Ready for Takeoff

*I have always thought that one man of tolerable abilities
may work great changes and accomplish great affairs
among mankind, if he first forms a good plan.*

—BENJAMIN FRANKLIN, *Autobiography*

Congratulations! You've taken the first step. It may not have been easy
but you have decided to move to France. Benjamin Franklin, the first
American ambassador to France, knew that one way to avoid a lot of
hassle, anxiety, and expense was by thinking ahead. With a little planning, you can make leaving home and dealing with your affairs a lot less
complicated.

It may seem obvious but before you can even contemplate a move
abroad, you must be sure that you have a valid passport. In the United
States, you can file passport applications at most local post offices, with
U.S. Passport Agencies, and in some state and local courts. It is a good
idea to make several photocopies of your passport and keep them in
different places. It can make a world of difference in the time it takes to
process the application for a replacement passport if yours gets lost or
stolen.

Visas

With a valid passport in hand, you can now begin to think about your
visa. As with most European countries, France and the United States
have an agreement whereby Americans traveling to France as tourists
for a period of less than three months do not need to apply for a visa.

Paris

Your passport will usually suffice, although the authorities have the right to ask for a return ticket, proof of hotel accommodations, proof of health insurance, and/or proof of financial means (cash, traveler's checks, or credit cards). If you have decided that you would like to live in France for more than three months, or you plan to come to France for reasons other than tourism, you must have what is known as a *visa de long séjour*. This visa does not in itself give you the right to work or study, but it is during this application procedure that you will decide what type of work or study privileges will best suit your needs. You will learn the likelihood of obtaining your desired visa.

This is the time when planning ahead really matters because according to French law, it is not possible for an American (or any non-EC national for that matter) to come to France as a tourist and then change his or her status to that of a student, worker, or long-term resident. As many of my friends have been discouraged to find out, the

French authorities will require you to return to your country of residence to apply for the relevant visa, which can prove to be both inconvenient and costly. Thus, if you know you are planning to make France your home for some time, think ahead and request a *visa de long séjour*.

To obtain a visa, you will need to go in person either to the French Embassy located in Washington, D.C., or to one of the eleven consular offices located across the United States. There are French consulates in the following cities: Atlanta, Boston, Chicago, Honolulu, Houston, Los Angeles, Miami, New Orleans, New York, San Francisco, and San Juan, Puerto Rico. France also maintains consular agents or honorary consuls in many cities in the United States. The closest French consulate can provide you with addresses. These agents can perform certain consular services, which sometimes includes the processing of visa applications.

The consulates are generally open in the morning, but accept telephone calls in the afternoon and are also often very busy. It is best to come prepared with all the necessary supporting documents and avoid the miserable prospect of queuing up multiple times.

At the consulate, an official will ask you to fill out an application form in which you state where in France you plan to go, for how long, and your reasons for going, among other things. You will also need to bring a number of documents with you. Although the specific requirements for each visa differ, the following general documents will certainly be required:

- Your completed application from the French consulate (six copies).
- A valid passport.
- A certified copy of your birth certificate.
- Passport-sized photos (four identical, in black and white).
- Proof of residency in the consular district.
- Proof of financial resources while in France. (This can take the form of bank statements, letters from banks confirming arrangements for regular transfers of funds from a U.S. bank account to an account in France, letters from family or friends guaranteeing regular support, or a *certificat d'hébergement* from a French family or friends with whom you will be staying. These documents should be notarized.)
- A medical exam certificate and a copy of your health insurance

plan. (Medical exams must be conducted by a physician approved by the French consulate. Ask the consulate for a list of doctors in your area.)

◆ A written authorization from parents or guardian, if you are under eighteen and traveling alone.

◆ Cash—to pay the visa processing fees.

Applying for a visa to France is just the first step on the long road to obtaining the elusive *carte de séjour*, which is the document that actually allows you to live in France (see Chapter 4, "Understanding Paperwork"). Again, it is how you manage the visa application procedure that determines how your request for a *carte de séjour* will be evaluated.

At times, the visa application process can really drag on. Be forewarned and apply well in advance. Applicants for certain kinds of visas may have to wait up to three months before their application is approved. It goes without saying that some visas are harder to get and that it is more difficult for residents from some countries to obtain visas to live in France than others.

SPECIAL REQUIREMENTS FOR WORKERS

In France, the concept of "working papers" does not technically exist. Rather, you are issued a certain category of *carte de séjour* that permits you both to reside in France and to work. The two concepts are then inseparable under French law. Thus, if you later want to change your status, you will need to start the immigration process over again. To apply for a visa that will enable you to receive a *carte de séjour* with worker status, you must have a work contract that has been approved by the French Ministry of Labor. This means that the French employer is required to present the signed contract to the Ministry requesting its approval. Once the Ministry has approved the contract, it forwards it to the immigration office (Office des Migrations Internationales) to be sent to the French consulate where you presented your application.

If indeed you are fortunate enough to have already found a job in France, in most cases the company will handle the visa application process for you. If you plan to be accompanied by your family, you will generally have to pursue the visa application process for them on your own. It is worth knowing that your visa may very likely be processed before theirs are.

Unfortunately, the need for an approved contract can lead to somewhat of a Catch-22 situation: in order to obtain a working *carte de séjour*, you must have a job offer in hand, but all too often employers will not extend an offer unless you can furnish the appropriate *carte*. At the same time, indicating in your application for a visa with worker status that you would like the visa in order to begin a job search in France is a sure way to be turned down (very quickly). More information on how to overcome these hurdles can be found in Chapter 4, "Understanding Paperwork," and throughout Part 4, "Working."

SPECIAL REQUIREMENTS FOR STUDENTS

In many ways, applying for a visa as a student is the easiest way to enter France. In addition to the general requirements, you must also obtain in advance an admission letter from the university or school in France. For French universities this letter is called an *attestation de préinscription*, if you are registering for the first time, and a *certificat d'inscription* or an *autorisation d'inscription* if you have previously studied in France. A French cultural affairs officer generally reviews this admission or registration letter before the consulate can issue the student visa. As with other categories of applicants, students will have to submit proof of financial resources. In this case, however, a letter from a study abroad program guaranteeing board and lodging, evidence of a fellowship or scholarship, or a letter from one's parents or guardians guaranteeing to pay the student's expenses may also be submitted.

SPECIAL REQUIREMENTS FOR AU PAIRS

Under French law, au pairs fall into a separate category of visa applicants. Not officially working for a French company and yet not fully financially independent, au pairs have unique contractual status. In addition to general requirements, an au pair must present a copy of a work contract signed by the applicant and the French family and approved by the French Ministry of Labor. For more information on au pair work, see Chapter 22, "Freelance, Part-Time, and Temporary Work."

SPECIAL REQUIREMENTS FOR MARRIAGE

If you are planning to move to France to marry a French resident and plan to stay more than three months, there is a special category for you in the visa application process. Before leaving home, you must apply for a *visa de long séjour pour mariage*. In France, according to the prefectorial authorities, the civil status of American citizens married to French citizens is different for marriages of less than one year and those of more than one year. If you have been married for more than one year and are American, you must apply for a long-stay visa for spouse (*pour conjoint:* type D visa) at the French consulate before your arrival in France.

If you are an American citizen and have been married to a French citizen for less than one year, you must enter France on a long-stay visa, as French law has no provision for extending tourist visas. You must then apply for a *carte de séjour*.

Preparing to Go

In addition to the formal bureaucratic preparations, you will have quite a lot of loose ends to tie up in the weeks and months before you leave. The leitmotif of this chapter is preparation, and once again, a little foresight before you board that plane will make your new life that much more hassle free.

FINANCIAL PREPARATIONS
Money! Money! Money!   Not so long ago, ensuring a regular cash flow while overseas was a cause of great stress and concern for American travelers. Nowadays, many of those concerns have diminished greatly with the advent of the ATM. In preparing for your trip, the first thing to bear in mind is that if you have an ATM card with an American bank, cash will almost always be available to you through French ATM machines. At least at the beginning, this is a wise way to proceed. It generally takes some time to set up a French bank account and this way you can rest assured that you will not be without money, provided you have funds in your American account.

Before leaving, you should check with your bank to find out what fee they charge for each withdrawal, how many withdrawals you can make per week or per month, and for what amount. If possible, try to see if you can increase the maximum amount of each withdrawal. This will save you money in transaction fees in the long run. You should also request a listing from your bank of all the compatible ATM outlets in

France. In the major cities almost every automatic teller accepts American bankcards with the international Visa or MasterCard symbols. The bank's listing will prove more useful if you find you will be moving or traveling to some of the smaller towns or more rural areas.

One thing to bear in mind is that French ATMs (and phones, for that matter) do not have the alphabet on the keypads. Before leaving you should be sure you have converted all your PINs and passwords to numeric form. For example, if your PIN is P-A-R-I-S, you would need to enter the numbers 7-2-7-4-7. In most cases, I have found that even in the smallest towns, the ATM machines offer a multiple language menu. You should not have to worry about misunderstanding the prompts.

Traveler's checks are also a safe option. If you plan to bring them along, be sure to stop by the bank or the local American Express office and order them before leaving. I brought a portion of funds in traveler's checks with me to France and after a year had passed, found that I did not really use them and ended up having to cash them in at a lower exchange rate than I would have received for cash. It is a question of personal preference but traveler's checks are no longer as indispensable as they once were.

Credit cards, on the other hand, are extremely useful. Most French stores now accept American credit cards. Indeed, while the French were once the people in Europe who depended most heavily on personal checks for everyday transactions, credit and debit cards are fast taking over, and it is not uncommon to find a credit card machine behind the counter at the local butcher shop!

It is probably a good idea to arrive in France with a few francs (between $50 and $100 worth) in your wallet, just to be able to pay for your first taxi and, in some airports and train stations, for a luggage cart. However, it is not essential because exchanges and ATM tellers can be found in almost all French airports.

Paying Your American Bills   If you have a lot of regular monthly expenses, such as mortgage, utility, or student loan payments, you should take some time to think about how you want to deal with them. You may want to set up a system whereby the bank or a trusted friend or relative pays them for you. Or, in the case of utility payments, you may want to estimate what the monthly payments should be and

17

prepay them. It is possible to overpay your utility bills and use the accumulated credit to pay off each successive month's charges. In any case, you should pack your checkbook in order to be able to pay regular bills, credit card bills, and other unforeseen American expenses from France.

Taxes   It is useful to know that Americans living in France can both file and pay their taxes through the U.S. Embassy or consulates. I found the IRS office at the American Embassy in Paris to be incredibly helpful and well informed. They are used to dealing with Americans living overseas and have all the necessary forms and information at their fingertips. If you prefer to file your taxes from the United States, you will need to be sure that someone has access to your W-2 forms and can get you the additional required forms. Remember that if you want to enable another person to access your bank account and make payments in your name, you need to ensure that you provide them with a "power of attorney," which can be taken care of at your bank.

For more information on money and taxes, look in Chapter 5, "Money, Banking, and Taxes."

CLOSING YOUR HOME

Household Expenses   If you own your home, you may want to consider terminating your utility contracts, unless you plan to make regular trips back to the United States. If your home will be standing empty for long periods of time, you may also want to give a set of keys to a trusted friend or pay someone to look in on your house at regular intervals to check for burglary attempts and/or damage (from water, storms, etc.). If you plan to rent your home while you are gone, be sure to transfer all utility contracts to your tenants; otherwise you may find yourself responsible for the charges they have run up.

Mail   Before leaving you should also establish what will happen to your mail. If you know your new address before leaving, for a fee, you can ask the U.S. Postal Service to forward it for up to one year. The post office will also hold mail for up to three months. Alternatively, you could ask a friend to collect it for you and forward it to you in France.

PLANNING TO KEEP IN TOUCH

Before taking off, you should be sure that you have compiled a list of all the people and companies you want and need to keep in touch with (insurance companies, doctors, shipping companies, and of course friends). It may be helpful to bring your local phone book with you, if you think you may need to be in touch with people and companies back home on a regular basis. You cannot directly dial American directory assistance from France and calling the French equivalent is very often a completely frustrating experience.

Telephones   Most of Europe has been following the international trend of privatizing nationalized telecoms. Needless to say, France Télécom did not lead the way although at publication, it was moving in that direction. As a result, phone calls both within France and abroad are rather pricey. There are currently two ways to sidestep the steep international charges. The first and easiest way initially is with an American telephone credit card. The rates with companies like AT&T or MCI are still expensive when compared to calling France from the United States, but are cheaper than a direct call.

Another option that has become available in recent years is to use one of the many call-back services. A number of companies, seeking to make a profit by undercutting the French rates, have set up systems whereby as a subscriber, you call a toll-free number in the United States and then hang up the phone. Within thirty seconds, you receive a phone call back that gives you an American dial tone and enables you to call the United States and any other country in the world at rates that are as much as 60 percent lower than the France Télécom direct rates. These programs operate in the United States as well, but it is usually cheaper to set up the contract once you have arrived in France and have a phone number.

E-mail   French Internet service providers abound, but if you are going to be in France for less than a year and do not want to deal with changing addresses, you may want to consider setting up an account with America Online or CompuServe, or with one of the many companies that enable you to access your E-mail through a site on the World Wide Web. E-mail has become an essential means of communication for people living abroad. It is the only way I could afford to keep in touch with most of my friends.

For more information on French telecommunication, see Chapter 6, "Setting Up House," and Chapter 11, *"La Vie Virtuelle."*

What to Bring Along

No matter what you decide to pack, you should check with the French Embassy or consulate to find out the latest customs regulations. You should be allowed to bring most of your belongings provided that they are for personal use and you do not plan to sell them. If you plan to bring your pet, you will need to obtain an official certificate from a state-certified veterinarian.

PERSONAL

Medicine and Toiletries It goes without saying that before leaving, you should schedule a full round of routine checkups (general practitioner, gynecologist, and dentist). You should also check with your insurance company and ensure that you are covered abroad. If you are not, you may want to consider switching to a plan with international coverage. That said, you also probably want to plan ahead and bring an extra supply of both prescription medication and over-the-counter medications or at least arrange for someone to send you refills. Some standard pain relievers like Tylenol and Advil do not exist in France. Their equivalents are expensive medicines that come in packages of ten or twelve tablets that you must ask the pharmacist for, and that do not necessarily work the same way. You should also ask your doctors for the generic names of any prescription medication to make it easier to find equivalents in France.

Finally, you should be sure to pack an extra supply of any name-brand toiletries that you are especially attached to (including deodorants, contact lens solution, etc.). Many American products have made it onto French counters, but a large number are still hard to come by.

American Gourmet Although you may have decided to move to France to immerse yourself fully in its renowned cuisine, many Americans often grow homesick for certain basic American items. Bringing along a little supply of your favorite treats and cookbooks can be a good way to cure the blues. A package of brownie mix or the chocolate chips and baking soda (these are both hard to find in France) you need to make your favorite cookies can go a long way to getting through culture shock. It might also be useful to bring along a set of American measuring cups and spoons as France uses the metric system for all measurements (see the appendix for conversion tables).

Electronics   In France, electrical appliances operate on a 220-volt, 50-hertz system. Before leaving, you should purchase a number of 110-to-220-volt, 50-hertz AC adapters. It is not difficult to find them in France but it is helpful to have some on hand when setting up house. It may be easier to purchase some small appliances directly in France, like hair dryers, curling irons, and toasters, as they can have difficulty adapting to the European currents. Hot rollers, on the other hand, are nearly impossible to find in France, so if you are attached to them, bring them along. For more information on electricity, see Chapter 6, "Setting Up House," and the appendix for electrical standards.

French videocassette recorders operate on the SECAM system, while American cassettes are recorded on NTSC, so unless you plan to pack your American VCR, don't pack a lot of movies. France is basically the only country that uses the SECAM format; the rest of Europe is more or less standardized on the PAL format.

PROFESSIONAL

If you know you will be working in France, there are a number of items you should consider packing, especially if you are going to be doing any kind of independent freelance or consulting work.

The Basic Tools   If you know that you need certain tools to operate efficiently in your profession, you should bring them along. Do not count on being able to find and repurchase everything once you have moved to France. If you are a photographer, pack your cameras, lenses, and at least a small supply of developing solutions and other essentials. If you are an accountant, bring your American calculator (French calculators use commas in the place of decimal points and can be confusing) and all necessary software. If you are a journalist, bring an American dictionary, a thesaurus, and an encyclopedia on CD-ROM if you have a computer. If you know that you will need certain business guides or journals, bring them along or arrange to have a subscription sent to you. Many of these tools that seem so obvious and necessary to you in conducting your daily professional life are either not used or available in France or are available only at exorbitant prices. Be prepared to hit the ground running and bring your basics with you.

Computer Supplies   Pack any software that you know you will use (as well as games) because English versions are not always easy to come by and are very pricey. French printers use A4 paper, which is slightly narrower and longer than American 8½-by-11-inch paper. While American printers can work with A4 size paper, it can be annoying if you need to send reports home or fit printed sheets into American-size binders. It is a good idea to bring extra paper and print cartridges along, as well as diskettes (floppies and Zip disks), which can be expensive.

Student Needs

Students moving abroad have special concerns to address as well. If you are enrolled in an American university and are planning to study abroad with a French program, be sure to discuss your leave of absence with your dean and try to establish exactly how and on what basis credits will be transferred. To avoid heartache on your return, it's better to understand how the courses you take will be evaluated beforehand.

If you plan to apply to American universities, graduate schools, or summer internship programs while in France, be sure to bring along all the necessary documents, including official copies of your transcript and recommendation letters as well as application forms, school catalogs, and test information. Most national exams can be taken in France but you should look into registration and buy any study books you might need beforehand.

Useful Addresses

EMBASSY OF FRANCE
4101 Reservoir Road, NW
Washington, DC 20007
Tel: (202) 944-6000
Fax: (202) 944-6166

FRENCH CONSULATE GENERALS
ATLANTA:
Marquis 2 Tower, Suite 2800
285 Peach Tree Center Avenue
Atlanta, GA 30303
Tel: (404) 522-4226 or 522-4423
Fax: (404) 880-9408

BOSTON:
Park Square Building, Suite 750
31 St. James Avenue
Boston, MA 02116
Tel: (617) 542-7374
Fax: (617) 542-8054

CHICAGO:
Olympia Center, Suite 2020
737 North Michigan Avenue
Chicago, IL 60611
Tel: (312) 787-5359/60/61
Fax: (312) 664-4196

HONOLULU:
2 Waterfront Plaza, Suite 300
500 Ala Moana Boulevard
Honolulu, HI 96813
Tel: (808) 599-4458/59/60
Fax: (808) 599-4751

HOUSTON:
777 Post Oak Boulevard, Suite 600
Houston, TX 77056
Tel: (713) 572-2799
Fax: (713) 572-2911

LOS ANGELES:
10990 Wilshire Boulevard, Suite 300
Los Angeles, CA 90024
Tel: (310) 235-3200
Fax: (310) 312-0704

MIAMI:
1 Biscayne Tower, 17th Floor South
Biscayne Boulevard
Miami, FL 33131
Tel: (305) 372-9799
Fax: (305) 372-9549

NEW ORLEANS:
1340 Poydras Street, Suite 710
New Orleans, LA 70112
Tel: (504) 523-5772
Fax: (504) 523-5725

NEW YORK:
934 Fifth Avenue
New York, NY 10021
Tel: (212) 606-3688
Fax: (212) 606-3620

SAN FRANCISCO:
540 Bush Street
San Francisco, CA 94108
Tel: (415) 397-4330
Fax: (415) 433-8357

SAN JUAN, PUERTO RICO:
Mercantil Plaza Building, Suite 720
Ponce de Leon Avenue, Stop 27½
Hato Rey, San Juan, PR 00918
Tel: (809) 753-1700/1701
Fax: (809) 754-1492

CALL-BACK PROVIDERS

Global Access Direct
Tel: (01) 39 07 01 01
Fax: (01) 39 07 00 77
First Telecom
Tel: (0801) 37 66 66
AXS Telecom
Tel: (01) 53 00 37 10

STUDENT INFORMATION

Educational Testing Services (ETS) of
the College Board
Princeton, NJ 08541-6000
Tel: (609) 921-9000
(publications about the GRE, MCAT, etc.)
Council on International Educational
Exchange (CIEE)
205 East 42nd Street
New York, NY 10017
Tel: (212) 822-2600

Living

CHAPTER THREE

Bienvenue en France:
Making the Adjustment

Moving to France will likely be one of the most exciting transitions of your life. You will learn a new language, meet new people, and have a host of experiences while getting to know a new culture. And yet it is precisely that new and different culture that may make some parts of your transition to living in France difficult and at times even painful.

Learning a new language takes time and you may have trouble making yourself understood. It is difficult to accept that while you might improve your vocabulary and pronunciation, it's going to be pretty tough to lose all vestiges of that American accent.

Living without certain basics of American life can begin to seem unbearable, as can getting used to certain basics of French daily living. Before moving to France, you drove to work. Now you take the *Métro* or the bus and live without a car. Your favorite breakfast in the world is bagels and Philadelphia cream cheese. The French have five hundred kinds of cheese—what would it cost them to import Philadelphia cream cheese? In your hometown, even complete strangers smile at each other when their paths cross. Why do Parisians wear a permanent scowl? Is smiling so difficult?

Many of these feelings are related to culture shock, the humps and hurdles a foreigner has to go through when trying to adapt to a new culture.

The Phases of Culture Shock

Often newcomers are able to anticipate many of the differences between home and their new French life. They read about France and French culture and study the language. When they arrive, they do their utmost to understand everything going on around them. Yet while these individuals are undoubtedly better prepared, they too experience many of the feelings associated with culture shock. From our experience, there are four main phases from introduction to acclimation.

INITIAL EXCITEMENT AND ENTHUSIASM

When you first arrive in France, everything seems so, well, French. You are thrilled to be here. The food is wonderful. Better still, you love that it takes hours to do your food shopping as you skip from one quaint specialty shop to the next. You don't mind that your building does not have an elevator because "the exercise is good for me, and who needs all that American technology anyway?" And even though it's kind of hard to understand, people's French accent when they speak English is charming and you decide you will spend the rest of your life in France. Actually, you decide you are going to do everything you can to become as French as possible, hiding all signs that you are American. You even think about buying a beret.

DISBELIEF, FRUSTRATION, AND LOSS

After some time, you begin to miss certain things about home and start to notice things about France that you don't like. This often happens after a certain amount of time passes in a frustrating job search or after an hour-long wait at the *préfecture de police* while trying to get your papers in order. You can't believe how poorly foreigners are treated. Americans would never treat immigrants this way, you think, and you begin to miss things from home. Your favorite snack, your favorite television show, or even your king-size mattress. You wonder why the French use bolster rolls instead of pillows to sleep on.

You begin to wonder what on earth it was that made you decide you wanted to move to France anyway. This is the most difficult phase and the one that most genuinely feels like culture shock. It can last a few days, a few weeks, or even a year, as you evaluate the pros and cons of life in this new place. If there are enough things you like about your

Celebrating France on Bastille Day

new home, you will gradually cross into the next phase. If there are not, you may end up moving home if you have the option.

RENEWED EFFORTS TO LEARN

If you can get through the separation from your native culture, you enter a phase in which you begin to approach learning about France from a new and more balanced perspective. Aware that the country and its people are not postcard perfect and that it is okay to miss certain things from home, you take a new attitude to learning about France. You branch out, make new friends, or sign up for a class. As your language skills improve, so do your relations with the bureaucracy and your local shopkeepers, and you even begin to read the local newspapers and magazines instead of always searching for news from home.

ACCLIMATION AND BELONGING

All of these efforts lead to the final phase of culture shock, one of well-being, in which you appreciate French culture as different but now also feel part of it. While you still miss home, you feel comfortable and at ease in France. You have made French friends, but may also have strong ties to the American expatriate network that help you feel connected to home. It may surprise you, but you have now adjusted so well to French culture and society that if you ever decide to move home, you will likely experience another difficult transition known as reentry culture shock. Who would have ever imagined?

Cultural Differences That Contribute to Shock

Culture shock is an intense experience and your perceptions of French cultural differences are not imaginary. A number of factors can contribute to your sense of displacement and loss.

SOCIAL INTERACTION

The French have fairly strict rules that govern social interaction, many of which can make them seem cold or aloof to the newly arrived American.

Manners   Etiquette is quite important in France. Children learn from a very early age what kind of behavior is acceptable. Little French girls and boys are often very poised and when in the company of adults rarely scream or run around playing in any way that could be disturbing. French parents and adults are often astonished when they see how free American children are to do as they please, no matter how irritating their behavior may be to others around them. In French schools, the same policy holds. Creativity and spontaneity are not encouraged and for better or for worse, this can also carry through to adult life.

As a whole, the French are not a population of risk takers and are not very spontaneous. In cities, for example, you would never just drop in on your neighbor; you always call first. Even developing a friendship takes longer. The French take friendship very seriously and recognize that it comes with certain obligations. They therefore take their time before establishing strong bonds. Once you become someone's friend, however, you will find the friendship to be a lasting one. It is also important to know that being invited into a French person's home is a significant occasion. While many Americans would take new guests for a tour of the home, this is not customary in France. You should not follow your host around, unless you are very close friends, although you can offer to help.

This strict adherence to certain customs also carries over to professional life. France is a country with a fairly low incidence of entrepreneurship, a result of bureaucratic complications, high interest rates, and the unwillingness to take risks. For more information on appropriate office behavior, see Chapter 19, "Business Etiquette."

Public Smiling One common complaint Americans have about the French, especially Parisians, is that they are so unfriendly and seem to have permanent scowls on their faces. While occasionally you may encounter a friendly smiling French person in a public place, what you are more likely to experience is a kind of scowling stare. With the exception of residents in a few large cities, most Americans are fairly open and friendly. We are taught to believe that smiling at strangers is a polite and disarming act and we do it quite often. We smile when we enter a shop. We smile when we speak to the teller at the bank and we smile at complete strangers when our paths cross on the street.

To the French, public smiling is a sign of stupidity, and in fact they do not understand why Americans are constantly walking around with a stupid smile on their face. The best way to deal with this is to understand that the lack of a smile is not a sign of unfriendliness and go about your business not taking this seeming initial coldness personally.

Physical Contact Apart from the cheek-to-cheek double air kiss known as *la bise*, there is very little physical contact in French relationships. Typically both men and women will shake hands when first introduced. After a friendship has developed, both when greeting friends and parting company, the men continue to shake hands with each other and exchange *la bise* with the women. Women also exchange *la bise* with each other. In Paris and some other cities, the standard number of kisses to be exchanged is two, while in the provinces, three and sometimes up to four kisses are exchanged. Losing track of the appropriate number can lead to bumping noses and cheeks, if you are not careful.

Americans who are used to hugging their friends when they say good-bye may be surprised to find that this simply is not done in France. Though Americans are by far not as comfortable with touching and other physical contact among friends as some other cultural groups, the hug as a sign of affection is hard to leave behind. That said, even though I knew that hugs were not the norm, I had managed to introduce some of my closest friends to the hug by the end of my stay. You will have to play it by ear.

LANGUAGE SKILLS

The degree to which you speak French fluently will greatly impact the ease with which you understand and become part of French culture. Until you can read the newspaper, understand the news, and begin to "get" French humor (which, to some, is notoriously unfunny), you will remain on the outskirts of the culture. Do your best to learn the language. Contrary to the stereotype, the French genuinely appreciate it when foreigners (especially Anglophones) make an effort to speak their language. You will find salesclerks, bureaucrats, and neighbors alike more willing to converse and help you if you just begin your conversation in French. For information on where to improve your French, see Chapter 15, "Language Schools."

BUREAUCRACY AND LONG LINES

The French bureaucracy can often be overwhelming to Americans, whose most frustrating experience with American bureaucrats is at the Registry of Motor Vehicles. In France, you can expect to come up against state employees who have not been trained in customer relations, who cannot be fired, and who have no real desire to help you solve your problem. You can also expect to find long lines in most public services including the post office and the bank. Most likely, the line will not be an orderly queue but rather a mass of people gathered around the teller. Privacy is not the rule. To deal with long waits, it is best to come prepared with a book, a newspaper, or something to do to avoid the inevitable feeling of wasting time.

FRENCH PERCEPTIONS OF AMERICANS

It can also often be frustrating to constantly encounter French people who seem to know more about the United States than you do and who resist all arguments that don't jibe with their own perceptions. The French have something of a love-hate relationship with the United States and all things American, which has evolved over time as a result of history and of American movies and television programs. The French, who would like to consider themselves the only "other super-power," perceive a sense of direct competition with the United States in international affairs, business, and culture. The French like to refer to Americans as cultural or McDonald's imperialists, exporting all things mass-made and dominating the world market. They criticize American dominance of the film industry and heavily subsidize French producers and directors with an unimpressive hit or miss record. They call Americans naive and simple. Yet at the same time, they crave American imports. American films regularly outsell French films. The latest American sitcoms and soap operas are translated into French overnight. And almost every Frenchman and woman owns at least one pair of Levi's, drinks Coke, and loves McDo (McDonald's). There is little you can do to change the negative attitudes you encounter, other than be yourself and make a positive impression. It's not worth all the energy you would expend in trying.

Networking

Although many companies and school programs provide training and advice on how to deal with culture shock before sending employees and students abroad, the best way to get over the hurdle is to begin meeting people and making friends. A rather impersonal word that describes this process is *networking*. Newcomers to France, and especially Paris, will be pleasantly surprised at the vast resources available to American expatriates in particular as well as to residents in general. One invaluable French resource is the Accueil des Villes Françaises (AVF)—literally the French City Welcome Organization—which has offices throughout France and serves to welcome new arrivals of all nationalities and familiarize them with the area (schools, sports, social, and cultural activities).

ENGLISH-SPEAKING EXPATRIATE NETWORK

When living overseas, it can be extremely helpful to be part of the English-speaking expatriate network. Many of these people have lived as expatriates in France for years and already know all the shortcuts. They are often great sources of advice on how to solve problems, find a lawyer, a plumber, an accountant, and even how to make life more enjoyable. There is really no reason to reinvent the wheel. Americans with experience living in France will prove to be invaluable contacts.

In Paris alone, there are more than eighty American organizations, literally something for everyone. Often, the organizations are linked to a central institution such as a school, a hospital, or a church. But many organizations exist independently. The U.S. Embassy does not sponsor many events for the general American public (there are just too many Americans living in France). They do, however, have a free guide for U.S. citizens residing in France that contains a list of American groups and associations, and is filled with other helpful information.

Many organizations also publish newsletters or hold events, classes, lectures, or even concert series. Churches are a particularly valuable networking resource. Each October, for example, the American Church in Paris holds a *Bloom Where You Are Planted* orientation program for all newcomers to Paris. The American Cathedral also houses numerous cultural and service organizations. Many organizations are designed to serve the American or French communities in some way but there are also many opportunities to volunteer and do other service work. A list of American organizations can be found at the end of the chapter.

AMERICAN BARS AND RESTAURANTS

Many Americans gather in the dozens of American bars and restaurants that cover Paris and can be found throughout France. Tex-Mex cuisine hit Paris hard in the 1980s and American south-of-the-border restaurants are filled with American expatriates, but also with French diners. There are now restaurants that serve all kinds of American cuisine from bagels to steak. These restaurants can do wonders for curing a bout of homesickness. Many Americans also gather for drinks at the famous Harry's Bar and other American pubs around the city. To find American restaurants in Paris, just open a copy of *France-USA Contacts (FUSAC)* or the *Paris Free Voice* (described below).

ENGLISH-LANGUAGE RESOURCES

You may be surprised at how easy it is to find local and international publications in English.

International Publications   Most newsstands carry at least one of the following English-language newspapers: *The International Herald Tribune, The International Financial Times, The Wall Street Journal Europe,* and *USA Today.* Many also carry a weekly English-language newspaper, *The European.* In Paris especially, it is fairly easy to find American and British periodicals, including *Time* and *Newsweek* international editions, as well as home and fashion magazines.

Local English-Language Publications   In Paris, there are a number of English-language publications that may become indispensable. Most of these publications are free and can be found in any American restaurant, bar, bookstore, cinema, or specialty shop. One helpful exception is *Pariscope,* a French guide to happenings in Paris published weekly and sold in newsstands. The last few pages are filled with condensed information on movies, theater, exhibitions, and other events in English put together by *Time Out,* an international publication. Some of the free English-language publications include *France-USA Contacts (FUSAC),* which is filled with advertisements directed at Americans and classified ads for apartment rentals and moving sales, as well as employment opportunities. Another free publication is the *Paris Free Voice,* a color tabloid filled with movie reviews, restaurant reviews, and other articles on life in Paris and France, as well as some classified ads. The *Paris Free Voice* is also available on the Internet.

English-Language Bookstores   There are dozens of English-language bookstores in France. Some of the American ones can be invaluable for networking, as most have bulletin boards with handwritten ads from American expatriates. See Chapter 17, "Bookstores, Libraries, and Research," for addresses.

English-Language Movies   In Paris, most cinemas offering showings of foreign movies (including American) are either dubbed in French or in the original language with French subtitles. Many cinemas in the rest of the country do this as well. To understand whether a movie will be shown in English, check the listing for the letters *v.o. (version originale),* after the time. The letters *v.f. (version française)* mean that the film has been dubbed into French. Most video rental shops also have a section for films in *v.o.*

GAY RESOURCES

From a political standpoint, France is quite friendly to gays. At publication, the National Assembly was discussing the *Pact d'Union Sociale*, and there were many demonstrations in favor and against. Gay couples enjoy the same social, tax, and inheritance rights as married couples. The SNCF, the railway, has been giving gay couples the same discount as heterosexual couples for several years.

That said, there is a real distinction between Paris and the rest of the country when it comes to resources for homosexuals. Paris is extremely welcoming to gays and there is even a neighborhood (le Marais) where gay restaurants, bars, and clubs are the norm rather than the exception. Outside of Paris, the resources are more limited and the mind-set can be less tolerant. *Gai Pied Hebdo* is a magazine dedicated to covering the relatively vocal gay and lesbian community in Paris. It is a great source for political and social information.

RESOURCES FOR PEOPLE WITH DISABILITIES

In France, services for disabled people are somewhat limited. Although most sidewalks and pavements have been adapted and contoured to allow wheelchair passage, most public buildings including hotels, restaurants, shops, and museums are poorly equipped. There are a number of national organizations and support groups, both American and French, that lobby on behalf of disabled residents and visitors. Contact information can be found at the end of this chapter's address list.

Useful Addresses

ACCUEIL DES VILLES
FRANÇAISES (AVF)

Regional Office
Région Île-de-France
62, rue Tiquetonne
75002 Paris
Tel: (01) 44 76 00 25
Paris Office
167, avenue Victor Hugo
75116 Paris
Tel: (01) 47 27 45 62

CHURCHES AND RELIGIOUS
INSTITUTIONS

American Cathedral in Paris
(Episcopal)
23, avenue George-V
75008 Paris
Tel: (01) 53 23 84 00
American Church in Paris (Protestant)
65, quai d'Orsay
75007 Paris
Tel: (01) 40 62 05 00

Baptist Church
48, rue de Lille
75007 Paris
Tel: (01) 42 61 13 95
Church of Christ
4, rue Déodat-de-Séverac
75017 Paris
Tel. (01) 42 27 50 86
First Church of Christ, Scientist
36, boulevard St-Jacques
75014 Paris
Phone: (01) 47 07 26 60
Second Church of Christ, Scientist
58, boulevard Flandrin
75116 Paris
Tel: (01) 45 04 37 74
Third Church of Christ, Scientist
45, rue de La Boétie
75008 Paris
Tel: (01) 45 62 19 85
Church of Jesus Christ of Latter Day
Saints (Mormon)
64-66, rue de Romainville
75019 Paris
Tel: (01) 42 45 28 57
Great Synagogue
44, rue de la Victoire
75009 Paris
Tel: (01) 45 26 95 36
Liberal Synagogue
24, rue Copernic
75116 Paris
Tel: (01) 47 04 37 27
Mosquée Abu Bakr As Siddiq
39, boulevard de Belleville
75011 Paris
Tel: (01) 48 06 08 46
St. John's Lutheran Church
147, rue de Grenelle
75007 Paris
Tel: (01) 47 05 85 66
Saint Joseph's Church (Roman Catholic)
50, avenue Hoche
75008 Paris
Tel: (01) 42 27 28 56
Saint Michael's Church
5, rue d'Aguesseau

75008 Paris
Tel: (01) 47 42 70 88
The Unitarian Universalist Fellowship
of Paris
7 bis, rue du Pasteur-Wagner
75011 Paris
Tel: (01) 30 82 75 33

GAY AND LESBIAN

Gai Pied Hebdo
45, rue Sedaine
75011 Paris
Tel. (01) 43 57 52 05

AMERICAN CLUBS AND
ORGANIZATIONS

American Chamber of Commerce
21, avenue George-V
75008 Paris
Tel: (01) 40 73 89 90
Association of American Residents
Overseas (AARO)
Pavillon Balsan
40, rue Worth
92150 Suresnes
Tel. (01) 42 04 09 38
Fax: (01) 42 04 09 12
(protects rights of Americans overseas)
American Cathedral Club
23, avenue George-V
75008 Paris
Tel: (01) 53 23 84 00
American Club of Paris
34, avenue de New-York
75016 Paris
Tel: (01) 47 23 64 36
Fax: (01) 47 23 66 01
American Tax Institute
184, rue de Faubourg-St-Honoré
75008 Paris
Tel: (01) 42 89 49 50
Fax: (01) 42 56 00 45
Berkeley Club/France
9, avenue Franklin-D.-Roosevelt
75008 Paris
Tel: (01) 46 07 00 43 c/o Futur Vision
Fax: (01) 46 07 09 50

LIVING

Boston University Alumni Association
91, avenue Gambetta
75020 Paris
Tel: (01) 44 62 20 53
Business Development Network
Mrs. Elizabeth de Vulpillières
Parc Croix Marie 4, avenue des
Jonchères
78121 Crespières
Tel: (01) 30 54 94 66
(information on business, networking,
and starting a business in France)
Harvard Business School Club
c/o France-Amérique
9-11, avenue Franklin-D.-Roosevelt
75008 Paris
Tel: (01) 42 56 20 98
Harvard Club of France
c/o France-Amérique
9-11, avenue Franklin-D.-Roosevelt
75008 Paris
Tel: (01) 60 72 43 78
Princeton Alumni Association
6, rue des Bauches
75016 Paris
Tel: (01) 45 27 30 44
Stanford Club of France
79, avenue de la République
75011 Paris
Tel: (01) 45 23 28 84
The Travelers
25, avenue des Champs-Élysées
75008 Paris
Tel: (01) 43 59 75 00
(British/American men's club with
lodging and restaurant service)
Yale Club
c/o Allin C. Seward
16, rue Vieille-du-Temple
75004 Paris
Tel. (01) 48 04 51 75
Fax: (01) 48 04 51 17
YMCA
22, rue de Naples
75008 Paris
Tel. (01) 45 22 23 49
Fax: (01) 42 94 81 24

WOMEN'S CLUBS
Association of American Wives of
Europeans
B.P. 127
92154 Suresnes Cedex
Tel: (01) 47 28 46 39
American Catholic Women's Association
Saint Joseph's Church
50, avenue Hoche
75008 Paris
Tel: (01) 42 27 28 56
American Women's Group in Paris
22 bis, rue Pétrarque
75116 Paris
Tel: (01) 47 55 87 50
Junior Guild/American Cathedral
23, avenue George-V
75008 Paris
Tel: (01) 47 20 17 92
Junior Service League of Paris
The Mona Bismarck Foundation
34, avenue de New-York
75016 Paris
Tel: (01) 53 23 84 00
La Leche League
B.P. 18
78620 L'Étang-la-Ville
Tel: (01) 39 58 45 84
("Good mothering through breast-
feeding")
Message
c/o Sallie Chaballier
Tel: (01) 39 65 79 29
(mother support group; publishes "The
ABCs of Motherhood in Paris")
Saint Anne's Guild
American Cathedral
23, avenue George-V
75008 Paris
Tel: (01) 42 67 26 74
Sister
MBE 108, 117, boulevard Voltaire
75011 Paris
Fax: (01) 46 71 12 77
(organization of black American women
living in France)

Women of the American Church
65, quai d'Orsay
75007 Paris
Tel: (01) 40 62 05 00

SOCIAL SERVICES

The Counseling Center at the American Cathedral
23, avenue George-V
75008 Paris
Tel: (01) 47 23 61 13
Fax: (01) 47 23 95 30
FACTS
190, boulevard de Charonne
75020 Paris
Tel: (01) 44 93 16 32
Factline: (01) 44 93 16 99 (Monday, Wednesday, Friday 6–10 P.M.)
(AIDS counseling and treatment information)
Foundation Foch
40, rue Worth
92150 Suresnes
Tel: (01) 46 25 20 00
(service organization affiliated with the Hospital Foch)
International Counseling Service
65, quai d'Orsay
75007 Paris
Salvation Army
76, rue de Rome
75008 Paris
SOS—English-Speaking Crisis Line
B.P. 239.16
75765 Paris Cedex 16
Tel: (01) 47 23 80 80

VETERANS AND PATRIOTIC ORGANIZATIONS

American Legion
22-24, boulevard Diderot
75012 Paris
Tel: (01) 44 74 73 42
American Overseas Memorial Day Association
34, avenue de New-York

75016 Paris
Tel: (01) 42 61 55 77
Society of the Cincinnati
2 bis, rue Rabelais
75008 Paris
Tel: (01) 45 61 45 40
Comité La Fayette
177, rue de Lourmel
75015 Paris
Tel: (01) 45 58 34 19
Children of the American Revolution
c/o Mrs. Alain Maitrot
118, avenue Félix-Faure
75015 Paris
Tel: (01) 45 54 64 19
Daughters of the American Revolution
c/o Mrs. Alain Maitrot
118, avenue Félix-Faure
75015 Paris
Tel: (01) 45 54 64 19
Inter-Allied Club
33, rue du Faubourg-St-Honoré
75008 Paris
Tel: (01) 42 65 96 00
Fax: (01) 42 65 70 34
Ladies Auxiliary to the VFW
15, rue Rémusat
75016 Paris
Tel: (01) 42 24 10 64
Sons of the American Revolution
52, avenue des Champs-Élysées
75008 Paris
Tel: (01) 43 59 10 31
USO
20, rue de La Trémoille
75008 Paris
Tel: (01) 40 70 99 68 (7 days a week)
Fax: (01) 40 70 99 53

CULTURAL AND EDUCATIONAL ORGANIZATIONS

Academic Year Abroad
Reid Hall
4, rue de Chevreuse
75006 Paris
Tel: (01) 43 20 91 92

39

American Center for Students and
Artists
51, rue de Bercy
75012 Paris
Tel: (01) 44 73 77 77
American Friends of Blérancourt
34, avenue de New-York
75016 Paris
Tel: (01) 47 20 22 28
American Library in Paris
10, rue du Général-Camou
75007 Paris
Tel: (01) 53 59 12 60
Boy Scouts of America
c/o American Embassy
2, avenue Gabriel
75382 Paris Cedex 08
Tel: (01) 43 12 27 66
Council on International Educational
Exchange
(CIEE)
1, place de l'Odéon
75006 Paris
Tel: (01) 44 41 74 74
Fax: (01) 43 26 97 45
The Culture Club
2, rue Gounod
75017 Paris
Tel: (01) 47 66 52 11
(classes and cultural visits)
English Language Library for the Blind
35, rue Lemercier
75017 Paris
Tel: (01) 42 93 47 57
Fax: (01) 42 93 47 57
France-Amérique
9-11, avenue Franklin-D.-Roosevelt
75008 Paris
Tel: (01) 43 59 51 00
France-États-Unis
6, boulevard de Grenelle
75015 Paris
Tel: (01) 45 77 48 84

Franco-American Commission for
Educational Exchange—Fulbright
9, rue Chardin
75016 Paris
Tel: (01) 44 14 53 60 (administration)
Tel: (01) 45 20 46 54 (documentation
center)
International Association of American
Minorities
3, rue de Chaufour
78270 Cravent
Tel: (01) 34 76 18 75
Les Arts George V
23, avenue George-V
75008 Paris
Tel: (01) 43 23 84 00
(development of art and music at the
American Cathedral)
Mona Bismarck Foundation
34, avenue de New-York
75016 Paris
Tel: (01) 47 23 38 88
Fax: (01) 42 86 94 07
Paris Choral Society
American Cathedral
Contact: Chris Bell
23, avenue George-V
75008 Paris
Tel: (01) 40 50 05 21
Reid Hall
4, rue de Chevreuse
75006 Paris
Tel: (01) 43 20 33 07
(fosters Franco-American university
exchange; many overseas academic
programs are based here)
WICE
20, boulevard du Montparnasse
75015 Paris
Tel: (01) 45 66 75 50
Fax: (01) 40 65 96 53
(nonprofit educational and cultural
association)

POLITICAL ORGANIZATIONS

Democrats Abroad
68, avenue Victor-Hugo
92100 Boulogne
Tel: (01) 48 04 51 75
Fax: (01) 48 04 51 17
Republicans Abroad
Ms. Phyllis Morgan
67, Rue Pascal
75013 Paris
Tel: (01) 43 31 00 80

ASSOCIATIONS FOR INDIVIDUALS
WITH DISABILITIES

**Comité national français liaison
réadaptation handicapés (CNFLRH)**
236 bis, rue Tolbiac
75013 Paris
Tel: (01) 53 80 66 66
RATP Voyages Accompagnés
21, boulevard Bourdon
75004 Paris
Tel: (01) 49 59 96 00
(free door-to-door service; book 48 hours
ahead)

SPRINT (Sharing of Professional
Resources, Ideas and New Techniques)
Contact: Mrs. Frances Ryan
Tel: (01) 42 22 90 62
(offers specialized care and advice for
parents of children with physical and
mental handicaps and learning
disabilities)
FAVA (Franco-American Volunteer
Association for the Mentally Retarded)
24, rue d'Alsace-Lorraine
75019 Paris
Tel: (01) 42 45 17 91
Alcoholics Anonymous
American Church of Paris
65, quai d'Orsay
75007 Paris
Tel: (01) 46 34 59 65
American Aid Society
2, rue St-Florentin
75001 Paris
Tel: (01) 42 96 12 02
(helps U.S. citizens who encounter
serious problems while in France)

Understanding Paperwork

Dealing with bureaucracies and wading through paperwork can be a challenge at home, in your native language, when you know the ropes. In a foreign country, the same process can seem like an insurmountable task. In France, where bureaucrats are not known for their friendliness, you may begin to believe you will never see the light at the end of the tunnel in your quest for a residency permit and other kinds of documents. This chapter should help you navigate some of the bureaucratic hurdles.

Residency and Work Permits

Possessing French residency has a number of advantages. In addition to simplifying your daily life by making it easier to apply for a bank account, install a telephone, get utilities in your apartment, and apply for a driver's license, it also entitles you to *la sécurité sociale* (French social security, which includes health care and unemployment benefits) and many other benefits otherwise reserved only for French citizens. Not to mention that you are required by law to establish residency of some sort, if you remain in France for more than ninety days.

French police are legally entitled to stop anyone they like to per-

Navigating your way through the French bureaucracy without help can be as challenging as finding the exit of a boxwood labyrinth.

form a *contrôle d'identité*. They can also hold you without charging you with a crime for up to forty-eight hours. The police are particularly vigilant in running controls on nonwhite immigrants. While you are in France, you should carry identification with you at all times. Though there are certainly thousands of foreigners living in France without the proper credentials and documents, if you are serious about making your stay a long one, you would be wise to get your paperwork in order. If you are deported, the French government may limit your possibilities to return to France for several years.

Anyone who plans to live in France for more than three months must go through immigration procedures and apply for a *titre de séjour* (residence title). There are two kinds of *titres de séjour*. The first is the *carte de séjour*, which is essentially a temporary residence permit, valid for up to a year and renewable, that may or may not include the right to work. This is usually the first *titre* most foreigners receive.

The second is the *carte de résident*, which is a long-term residence permit, valid for ten years and automatically renewable. The *carte de résident* is issued automatically to spouses of French nationals and is in itself a work permit. Foreigners who can show proof of at least three years of residency in France can often trade up to receive a *carte de résident*.

HOW TO APPLY FOR RESIDENCY

Americans who wish to apply for residency must process their residence and work permit applications before coming to France. If you are being expatriated by an American company, the company will generally take care of the paperwork before your departure. If you have found a position with a French company after conducting a job search in France, you will have to return to the United States to request a *visa de long séjour* and to have the required medical exam. It may take up to three months for the *visa de long séjour* to come through. Once it arrives, you will have to face the French bureaucracy.

If you arrive in France with the required long-stay visa, within eight days of your arrival you should present yourself and your passport at the local police station or, in Paris, at the *centre d'accueil des étrangers* for your arrondissement. Students holding student visas are given a bit more leeway and have up to thirty days to present themselves to the authorities. In Paris, all students should go to the *centre de réception des étrangers* in the fifteenth arrondissement.

At the police station or *centre d'accueil*, you will be asked to fill out a questionnaire and provide a local address. Before leaving you will be given a convocation for an appointment two weeks to three months later at the *préfecture de police*, which is essentially the police headquarters for a particular administrative area. The convocation will include the date, time, and location of the office where you should appear. You should bring the convocation with you when you go to the *préfecture*.

When you go to the *préfecture*, you will be required to submit the following basic documents:

- Valid passport with long-stay visa and a photocopy of the title and visa pages
- Three black-and-white passport photos
- Proof of residency (*justicatif de domicile*), which could be a copy of a lease or a utility bill
- Proof of financial resources
- Proof of medical insurance
- One stamped, self-addressed envelope

All documents in English must be translated into French by a sworn translator (*traducteur-juré*). The American Embassy or consulate nearest you can provide lists of sworn translators. Depending on the category of the *carte de séjour* you are requesting, you may be required to submit additional documents.

WORKERS

Those expecting to work in France must submit a copy of their contract with their employer. There are several categories of *cartes de séjour* that are granted to those who hope to work in France.

- *Carte de séjour de détaché*, which covers transferred individuals who will be working for a subsidiary of a foreign company in France for up to eighteen months.
- *Carte de séjour salarié*, a long-term permit for people who will be hired by a French company to work in the category of *cadre* (executive). The individual will be on the payroll of the French company and may stay indefinitely.
- *Carte de commerçant étranger*, for those who are self-employed or are trying to set up a business in France. The application for this *carte* takes the longest to process as you must demonstrate your ability to earn enough money to live.

STUDENTS

When they go to the *préfecture*, students must bring along a copy of a letter of admission into a school, proof of registration, proof of independent financial support, and proof of a French bank account where funds from the United States may be deposited.

Students are in the unique position of being able to work part-time, for up to twenty hours per week during the academic year and up to thirty-nine hours per week over the summer holidays. However, the time spent in France on a student visa does not generally count toward a permanent residence visa.

Au Pairs

Individuals who plan to work in France as au pairs must present themselves at the *préfecture* with an au pair visa and a copy of a contract approved by the French Ministry of Labor.

Residency and Work Permits

Titres de Séjour		*Work Permits*
Carte de séjour	♦ Valid for one year ♦ Renewable ♦ May or may not include the right to work	♦ Worker *détaché*—transferred employees *salarié*—long-term executive hires *commerçant*—self-employed or business owner ♦ Student ♦ Au pair
Carte de résident	♦ Valid for ten years ♦ Automatically renewable ♦ Issued automatically to spouses of French nationals ♦ May be issued automatically after three years of proven residence ♦ Includes the right to work	

If you meet all the requirements, your *carte de séjour* will be mailed to you after processing. Generally, you will be issued a temporary *carte* known as the *récépissé de demande de carte de séjour*, which is valid for up to three months and serves as proof that you have applied for a residence permit. You should carry the *récépissé* with you as evidence of your legal status until your receive your *carte*.

Marrying a French Citizen

If you want to marry a French citizen while you are both in the United States, you should contact your nearest town or city hall and ask which documents are required (generally a passport and the results of some blood work). You must also then notify the local Immigration and Naturalization Service (INS) office to ensure that you have completed all the steps necessary to enable your spouse to remain in the United States without problems. There are INS offices at the Embassy and consulates in France if you need more information before leaving for the United States.

If you plan to marry in France, the process is not so different. Many couples are married in a church, as in the United States, but in France the marriage is not recognized until the civil ceremony has been performed. The civil ceremony, which must be performed in the *mairie* (town hall) by a deputy, must be completed before the church ceremony. To arrange a marriage, you or your partner must submit an application at least one month in advance to the town hall in the area where you normally live. You must have been a resident for at least forty days. This requirement cannot be waived. You will be expected to provide birth certificates, proof of residence in France, and a medical certificate of good health. Both the bride and groom must also provide the names of at least one witness each.

Couples married in France are automatically issued a *livret de famille*, a family book which serves as an official record of the marriage and subsequent births, deaths, divorces, and other family events. The *mairie* can also provide a marriage certificate, the *extrait d'acte de mariage*.

As an American, if you marry a French citizen you will be entitled to French citizenship after two years of marriage. If you are an American marrying a French national, you should contact the American Embassy or consulate nearest you for additional guidance.

The U.S. Embassy and Consulates

Benjamin Franklin was the first American ambassador to France. While he was there, he worked out of his own residence. Today the 26,000 Americans officially residing in France, as well as the thousands of American tourists who pass through France each year, have an embassy, two consulates, and a consular agency to turn to. The U.S. Embassy is in Paris. There are consulates in Marseille and Strasbourg that provide consular services for the south and west of the country respectively. There is a consular agency, which can handle some consular duties, in Nice.

The U.S. Embassy in Paris is located in a beautiful neighborhood, adjacent to the Champs-Élysées, just down the street from the Élysée Palace, the residence of the French president. If you are invited to attend a reception at the Embassy it would be worth your while just to see the gardens and some of the artwork. Unfortunately, although the Embassy occasionally agrees to host functions sponsored by American social and business groups, because so many Americans live in France, it does not generally have events that are open to the general public, as many other smaller embassies occasionally do.

While there are a number of very helpful services that the Embassy and consulates provide for U.S. citizens, they will not help find housing, employment, obtain your *carte de séjour*, or intervene on your behalf with the French government in any way. They will help you in times of emergency, and can provide assistance with paperwork, taxes, and finding other American resources in France.

REGISTRATION

As soon as possible after arriving in France, you should register with the U.S. Embassy or consulate nearest you. Registration will enable the Embassy to contact you in case of an emergency, although your whereabouts will not be revealed without your permission. Another advantage of registering is that it can make it easier to apply for a replacement passport, should yours be lost or stolen.

EMERGENCIES

The Office of American Services at the Embassy and the consulates is available to help U.S. citizens in France and their families in times of emergency. If you are hospitalized, they will come to visit you. If a relative or a loved one dies while in France, they will help you make arrangements to send the body home. While they will not intervene on your behalf if you are imprisoned, a representative will come visit you, ensure that your family is notified, and make sure you are not being discriminated against as an American.

The U.S. Embassy in Paris also has access to funds to help Americans who are destitute, through the American Aid Society. The Society, which is funded entirely through donations, helps Americans in temporary difficulty in France and has a limited number of grants for elderly, disabled, or sick Americans residing in France.

PAPERWORK

The Embassy and consulates can provide a number of related services for U.S. citizens. If your passport is lost or stolen, they can issue you a new one. If your passport expires while you are in France, they can renew it for you. Contact the Office of American Services to know what you should bring with you before going.

Most children born abroad to a U.S. citizen parent or parents automatically acquire U.S. citizenship at birth. If you have had a child while in France, you should contact the Embassy or consulate nearest you as soon as possible after the birth. When your child has acquired U.S. citizenship, the Office of American Services can register the birth and help you obtain a first passport and social security number for the newborn.

The Embassy and consulates also provide notarial services, which are available to all U.S. passport holders and to foreigners with documents that will be used in the United States. To have a document notarized, you should come in person to the Notarial Services office with your passport, the document, approximately ten dollars (at publication) per document in cash, and witnesses if necessary.

Occasionally the French authorities require a copy of your police record, known as an *extrait de casier judiciaire*. The Notarial Services office can provide you with a police record in the form of your own affidavit or a sworn statement on a form they provide.

FINANCIAL INFORMATION AND SUPPORT

The Embassy has offices to help U.S. citizens with taxes and federal benefits. Even though you may be living in France, you are still required to report your worldwide income on your federal income tax returns. You are not relieved of your responsibility to file tax returns although you may be entitled to various deductions, credits, and exclusions. For information, you should contact the Internal Revenue Service office at the Embassy.

If you are currently receiving monthly benefits from a federal or state agency (social security, state pensions, etc.), you should contact the Embassy or consulate nearest you to find out about the procedures for having your benefits checks sent overseas. The people best equipped to help you in this area can be found in the Federal Benefits Unit of the Embassy.

AMERICAN NETWORKS AND RESOURCES

The Embassy and consulates also have information in the form of lists meant to help Americans living in France. The Office of American Services has lists of English-speaking doctors, dentists, attorneys, tax consultants, insurance agents, shipping companies, translators, private detectives, genealogists, religious institutions, schools, banks, and U.S. and Franco-U.S. organizations.

Voting in U.S. Elections from France

Even though you reside in France, in most cases, you are still eligible to vote in U.S. elections using an absentee ballot. You must request a ballot at least sixty days before the election although requirements and deadlines vary from state to state. You can contact the Embassy or nearest consulate for more information and in the case of presidential elections, you can request the ballot at the American Embassy. Otherwise, from France you can call the Federal Voting Assistance Program using their toll-free number found at the end of the chapter.

Useful Addresses

U.S. EMBASSY
2, avenue Gabriel
75008 Paris Cedex
Tel. (01) 43 12 22 22
Embassy Information Lines
On Passports:
Tel: (01) 43 12 49 42 (in service between
3 and 6 P M.)
On registering births, notarizing
documents, and citizenship concerns.
Tel: (01) 43 12 23 47

U.S. CONSULATES AND CONSULAR AGENCIES

Marseille—Consulate
12, boulevard Paul-Peytral
13006 Marseille
Tel. (04) 91 54 92 00
Strasbourg—Consulate
15, avenue d'Alsace
67000 Strasbourg
Tel. (03) 88 35 31 04
Nice—Consular Agency
31, rue du Maréchal-Foch

06000 Nice

Tel. (04) 93 88 89 55

OTHER U.S. RESOURCES

Federal Voting Assistance
Toll-free number from France
Tel: (0800) 90 01 56
American Aid Society
c/o United States Consulate
2, rue St-Florentin
75001 Paris
Tel: (01) 43 12 48 07

CENTRES D'ACCUEIL ET
RÉCEPTION IN PARIS

Centre de Réception des Étrangers
(1st, 2nd, 3rd, 4th, 5th, 6th, 14th, and
15th arrondissements)
114, avenue du Maine
75014 Paris

Centre de Réception des Étrangers
(11th, 12th, 13th, 20th arrondissements)
163, rue de Charenton
75012 Paris
Centre de Réception des Étrangers
(8th, 9th, 16th, 17th arrondissements)
19-21, rue Truffaut
75017 Paris
Centre de Réception des Étrangers
(10th, 18th, 19th arrondissements)
90, boulevard de Sébastopol
75003 Paris
Centre de Réception des Étrangers (for
all students)
13, rue Miollis
75015 Paris
Préfecture de Police de Paris
Service des Étrangers
1, rue de Lutèce
75195 Paris RP (4th arrondissement)

51

CHAPTER FIVE

Money, Banking, and Taxes

One of the most important, often time-consuming, and sometimes frustrating experiences of your life in France is dealing with finances. French banking regulations and tax laws are quite different from those in the United States, and this is often a source of frustration for foreigners, especially newcomers. The best thing that you can do is to do your homework—learn the basic vocabulary of accounting, read up on the ins and outs of the system, and, when in doubt, seek professional advice. While the information presented here, especially on tax law in the United States and France, will give you an understanding of the basics, laws and regulations are always changing. Before you leave for France, it is a good idea to enlist the services of an accountant or lawyer who has the latest information and can advise you based on your individual financial and legal situation. There are many accountants and lawyers, both in the United States and in France, who specialize in helping foreign nationals deal with the intricacies of each system.

Generally speaking, the French pay less tax than their counterparts in other European nations, but quite a bit more than Americans are used to paying. Throughout the country, there is a value-added tax (*taxe à la valeur ajoutée* or TVA in French), a sales tax that is common throughout Europe, of about 19 percent. In addition, if you find yourself in the highest tax bracket, income tax can run more than 50 percent. That, combined with the 18 to 20 percent that you pay toward social security, is usually the bigger half of what you earn each year in salary. As an American, this amount of tax may seem usurious, but the tax rates are higher in most of the rest of Western Europe, especially the Scandinavian countries.

Regardless of that fact, the French do love to complain about taxes. In fact, they do more than complain—they downright rebel. Tax evasion is rampant. The French are notorious for their organizational skills and the country is rife with bureaucracy, but the people have a revolutionary spirit to the core and find many excuses to rebel against the system. The crime of not paying or avoiding taxes does not carry the same stigma as it does in the United States, and although the penalty can be severe if you're caught (the tax courts can almost arbitrarily name your fine), the government's record on enforcement has been shoddy, at best. As information technology takes over more and more of the traditionally manual tasks associated with taxation and enforcement, there will likely be a crackdown, but that will probably go hand in hand with public outrage. It's all part of that unique contradictory romanticism that comes with being French.

Banking

If you're planning on staying in France for any significant length of time, you will probably need to set up an account in a French bank. Even if the bulk of your financial resources are kept at your bank in the United States, having French checks and a French bankcard *(Carte Bleue)* can open up a lot of doors for you. If you're renting or buying a house you will almost certainly be required to have an account at a French bank from which your monthly rent or mortgage payment can be automatically debited. Most landlords won't consider you unless you have a French bank account. The only exception is if you're renting a short-term apartment from one of the dozens of rental property companies catering to business professionals and tourists. In addition, it is generally a good idea to have a French bankcard to use for payment on the off chance that you encounter a problem having your U.S. bankcard or credit card accepted. For some time French banks have been using "smart cards"—cards with a microchip (or *puce*) embedded in them— so transactions do not always involve a time-consuming bank network approval process. Using a French bankcard, therefore, will generally be easier and faster than using an American one.

Another contrast to the American system is that checks are almost universally accepted in France. They are literally almost as good as cash. This is because bouncing checks is virtually unheard of. Writing a check for insufficient funds is a crime and can turn into a major hassle. Check bouncers are quickly declared *interdit bancaire*, or put on a blacklist, and no French bank will do business with you for a year or more. If you accidentally bounce a check, and it's your first time, it is possible to avoid the ordeal of *interdit bancaire* if you quickly make amends and continue to keep your account in good standing.

USING YOUR U.S. BANK

That said, there are several advantages to keeping money in a U.S.-based bank account. The French embraced the world of plastic early, for Europe, and Visa and MasterCard are widely accepted in France. In addition, if you have an ATM card that is accepted by one of the major cash machine networks, like Cirrus, NYCE, or Star, most French ATMs will accept your card and give you better exchange rates than any bank teller or exchange window. ATM and credit card transactions are based on bank-to-bank exchange rates, usually fractionally better than the highest rates you find advertised in bank and exchange agent windows. ATMs can be found all over France, even in some of the smallest towns, and are just as prevalent in metropolitan areas as they are in the United States. You should remember to ask your bank if your account is charged for withdrawing money or using ATMs not associated with their network—these fees can add up quickly, and may make it expensive if you need to access your account often. Do remember to have your PINs memorized by their numerical values, as French bank machines often do not have letters associated with the numbers.

Most American banks offer service to customers residing abroad, and some of the largest U.S. banks even have a branch in Paris or another large city. Although these outlets are generally set up for business accounts, they sometimes have an ATM or provide some consumer services. Before you leave the United States, it is a good idea to check with your local bank to see if they can provide some services to you while living abroad. Many banks will forward your statements and correspondence to your French address for an additional fee. As the

A sidewalk post box

Internet becomes more pervasive and more banks offer Web-based banking services, it will become easier to access your accounts from wherever you happen to be.

Using a French Bank

French banks, like many of the institutions of French society, do not adhere to the standards of customer service that many Americans are used to. In fact, doing business with your French bank can be downright frustrating at times. You'll probably experience frequent long lines, grumpy tellers, and shorter hours of operation than at banks in the United States. At the same time, however, banking is often much more "personal," and this can sometimes make the business of banking more pleasurable. When I opened a checking account at a local branch of Banque Nationale de Paris, the branch manager sat down with me and helped me through the application, then later continued to formally greet me by name whenever she saw me walk into the branch.

The "personal" aspect of French banking, however, can sometimes make obtaining an account a challenge. In most cases, you will need to have proof of residence in France and proof of employment. Sometimes you'll need other documentation such as your passport or even a letter of "recommendation" from your U.S. bank or your employer. If you're following a job at an American company to France, your company may be able to provide you with the necessary documentation and help you get an account at the bank with which it does business. If you are employed by a large French corporation, opening an account is usually not a problem. Otherwise, you may find that you'll only be able to open a savings account or will be required to deposit a substantial sum in order to convince a bank to give you a checking account.

Many French banks have a presence on the Internet, and some have even begun to let you do some of your banking on-line. More will likely be launching Internet banking programs in the coming years. If you have a computer, you can also get software to help you prepare your taxes, such as TurboTax.

Taxes

It is important to give careful consideration to how you plan to deal with taxes while living in France. The decisions you make impact your financial status both at home and in France, and mistakes can be frustrating and costly. Tax laws and regulations change often; it is strongly advised that you consult an accounting or legal professional when deciding how and to whom you are required to pay taxes. This is particularly important if your financial status is not completely straightforward or if it is likely that you will need to pay a substantial sum in taxes.

If you are working or doing business in France, you are required to make yourself known to the French tax authorities. At the same time, living in France—or anywhere outside the United States—does not exempt you from paying U.S. taxes. France and the United States do have an agreement whereby you are not required to pay taxes in both countries. If you are paying French taxes, it is unlikely that the IRS will require you to pay U.S. taxes, but regardless you'll have to file a tax return each year and state your argument for exemption.

DEALING WITH THE IRS FROM FRANCE

The IRS maintains an office in the U.S. Embassy in Paris that can answer your questions, and where you can file your tax return. They also have a supply of tax forms and are adept at handling the questions and intricacies of Americans living abroad. In addition, the IRS has established an extensive presence on the Web, and if you have Internet access, many of your questions can probably be answered on-line. A listing of useful Web addresses is in the listing section that follows this chapter.

As most people are well aware, U.S. taxes are due each year on April 15. Americans who have qualified for the IRS's nonresident status are automatically granted an extension until June 15, and can request additional extensions with IRS Form 4868. If you have not secured this status, use Form 2350. Generally speaking, if your move to France is for job- or business-related purposes, you'll probably be able to deduct much of the costs associated with your move.

If you make your "tax home" in France, you are allowed to exclude up to $70,000 of your French income each year on your U.S. tax return. The IRS will increase this exemption by $2,000 per year, beginning in 1998, until it reaches $80,000 in the year 2002. To claim this "earned income exclusion," use IRS Form 2555 or 2555EZ. For more information about this exclusion and other IRS regulations, refer to IRS Publication 54, "Tax Guide for U.S. Citizens and Resident Aliens Abroad." You can order this from the IRS by calling (800) 829-3676. To report interest you have earned on foreign bank accounts, you'll also need to file Form 90-22.1 from the U.S. Treasury before June 30 of the year in which you report these earnings. If you end up having to pay taxes on French-earned income both to the IRS and in France, you can claim a "foreign tax credit" from the IRS using Form 1116. More information about this credit and the U.S.-France tax treaty can be found in IRS Publication 514, "Foreign Tax Credit for Individuals."

If you do run into problems and end up paying more than you

should or have a conflict regarding your status and paying both U.S. and French taxes, you can seek assistance from an office the IRS maintains specifically to deal with these types of problems. Contact the Office for International Tax Problem Resolution, located in Washington, D.C. The address is in the listing at the end of this chapter.

IRS TAX FORMS AND PUBLICATIONS FOR EXPATRIATES

- Publication 776, "General Overseas Tax Package"
- Publication 901, "U.S. Tax Treaties"
- Publication 593, "Tax Highlights for U.S. Citizens and Residents Going Abroad"
- Publication 54, "Tax Guide for U.S. Citizens and Resident Aliens Abroad"
- Publication 554, "Tax Information for Older Americans"
- Publication 516, "Tax Information for U.S. Government Civilian Employees Stationed Abroad"
- Publication 4, "Student's Guide to Federal Income Tax"
- Publication 953, "International Tax Information for Businesses"
- Publication 514, "Foreign Tax Credit for Individuals"
- Publication 520, "Scholarships and Fellowships"
- Forms "Package X," two volumes of income tax forms and information
- Form TD F 90-22.1, "Report of Foreign Bank and Financial Accounts"
- Form 8822, "Change of Address"
- Form 888, "Direct Deposit of Refund"
- Form 2350, "Filing Extension"
- Form 2555 or 2555EZ, "Foreign Earned Income Exclusion"
- Form 5471 Schedule M, "Foreign Corporation Controlled by a U.S. Person"
- Form 5471 Schedule N, "Foreign Personal Holding Company"
- Form 3903F, "Foreign Moving Expenses"
- Form 1116, "Computation of Foreign Tax Credit: Individuals, Fiduciary, or Nonresident Alien Individual"
- Form 1118, "Computation of Foreign Tax Credit— Corporations"

THE TAX SYSTEM IN FRANCE AND THE MAIN TAXES TO WATCH FOR

Regardless of whether or not the Socialist Party holds the French presidency or a majority of the Parliament, socialism is a deep-rooted social and political tradition in France, and this translates, perhaps most noticeably, into high taxes. While the system is easily criticized, especially by Americans who are used to much lower tax rates, the high taxes do pay off in the form of decent national health care and other public services that are absent on the other side of the Atlantic. If you've decided to make France your tax home, the tax you pay will probably be quite a bit higher than what you pay in the United States, but there are many ways to lessen the impact. French tax law allows for a range of deductions and exclusions that, if you qualify, may make the tax you end up paying significantly less than what you expect. Do your best to understand the tax system and where you can reduce the amount you pay.

If you've come to France to work or do business, you are required to register with the *inspecteur des impôts*—the tax authority—when you arrive. This serves to notify the government of your status and will put you on the list to receive a tax return *(déclaration fiscale)* each year. In addition, if you live in France for more than half of the year, you are generally expected to pay French income tax on what you earn, regardless of where it was earned. Personal income tax, or *impôt sur le revenu des personnes physiques* (IRPP), ranges from about 12 percent at the low end of the scale, up to about 57 percent at the high end. Your taxable income includes earnings from your job, your business if you're a business owner, your investment earnings, earnings from letting and leasing property, and capital gains. Bonuses, commissions, and living allowances are also taxed. Generally, you can make deductions for dependent children, disabled dependents, alimony, and even university-attending dependents up to the age of twenty-five. French tax law encourages reproduction: the more children you have, the less tax you will pay. In addition, your social security contributions are deducted before taxes are calculated. There are many other deductions and personal allowances permitted—if you're expecting to pay a lot of tax, a professional accountant can help you sift through them all.

The main tax date to remember is February 28, at which time the main income tax return (Form 2042) is due. Income earned outside of

France must be declared on Form 2047. French employers do not generally withhold tax from French resident employees, but are more likely to for nonresidents. Social security tax is always withheld. You are not required to pay taxes during your first year living in France, but your tax will be assessed, and you'll be required to pay the second year of your residency, but even then you can request an extension. You can get tax forms from a local tax center or your local *mairie*. When, finally, you are required to pay you can opt to make installments, usually three payments over the course of a year.

When you're ready to leave the country, you'll need to get a *quittance fiscale*, or tax clearance certificate, before the authorities will let you move your stuff back to the United States. Other tax forms you may need include "Rental Income Statement," Form 2044, and "Capital Gains Income Statement," Form 2049.

The U.S. and French Social Security Systems

The system of national health care in France makes many Americans green with envy, but this may not be the case for long. In recent years, there has been tremendous public outcry over the cost to individuals for the system. French *sécurité sociale* is a system entirely separate from the income tax, and provides assistance in the form of medical insurance, unemployment benefits, sick pay, retirement benefits, death grants, maternity benefits, housing subsidies, and workers' compensation insurance. The costs for these benefits are shared between employers and employees and are high: as an employee, you'll pay 19 percent of your gross salary to the *sécurité sociale*, and your employer will contribute a whopping 38 percent. There are caps to social security contributions, so your rates will decrease as your gross salary increases. Both American and French social security systems are based on credits that accumulate as you work and make payments. You convert these credits into benefits when you retire, need medical assistance, or take advantage of the other benefits. If you choose to pay into the American system or are exempted from the French social security system, you can't receive benefits under the French system and must arrange for other forms of medical coverage. But, if you have been working in France and contributing to the *sécurité sociale* for a period of six months, you are entitled to the same benefits as a French citizen.

If you're a dual national, it is likely that you can choose which system you wish to adhere to. In theory, however, any work activity you do on French soil qualifies you to make social security payments, but there are agreements in place whereby Americans living in France can remain under the U.S. system. These agreements allow you to count credits across the systems and then claim partial benefits based on partial credits. For detailed information about this, it is important to contact the U.S. Social Security Administration at the address listed at the end of this chapter. Unless you are moving to France permanently or are employed by a French company, you will probably pay U.S. social security taxes and continue to be covered under the American system. If an American employer sends you to France for five years or less, you must continue to pay U.S. social security tax.

Useful Addresses

MONEY TRANSFERS

American Express Moneygram
Tel. (800) 926-9400 (in the U.S.)
French headquarters.
11, rue Scribe
75009 Paris
Tel· (01) 47 77 77 07
(for other American Express
offices in France, see
http.//www.americanexpress.com)
Western Union Money Transfer
Tel (800) 325-6000 (in the U.S.)
French headquarters:
228, rue du Faubourg-St-Martin
75010 Paris
Tel. (01) 53 35 90 53
Web site. http://www.westernunion.com

AMERICAN TAX ASSISTANCE IN
FRANCE

Arthur Andersen
Barbier Frinault & Associés
Cabinet d'audit et de conseil financier
41, rue Ybry
92576 Neuilly-sur-Seine
Tel: (01) 1 55 61 00 00
Web site: http://www.arthurandersen.com

Arthur Andersen
Barbier Frinault & Associés
Cabinet d'audit et de conseil financier
Tour Crédit Lyonnais
129, rue Servient
69431 Lyon Cedex 03
Tel: (01) 4 78 63 72 00
Web site: http://www.arthurandersen.com
Arthur Andersen
Barbier Frinault & Associés
Tour Europe
20, place des Halles
67000 Strasbourg
Tel: (01) 3 88 37 59 30
Web site: http://www.arthurandersen.com
Pricewaterhouse Coopers
32, rue Guersant
75017 Paris
Tel: (01) 56 57 58 59
Fax: (01) 56 57 58 60
Web site. http://www.pwcglobal.com
Pricewaterhouse Coopers
Tour AIG
34, place des Corolles
92908 Paris–La Défense
Tel: (01) 56 57 58 59
Fax: (01) 56 57 58 58

Web site. http.//www.pwcglobal.com
Pricewaterhouse Coopers
Francis Descubes
Immeuble Le Tauzia
11-19, rue de Tauzia
33800 Bordeaux
Tel. (05) 56 33 36 66
Fax: (05) 56 33 36 88
Web site: http://www.pwcglobal.com
Pricewaterhouse Coopers
Thierry Vassault
6, rue du Cap-Vert
21805 Dijon-Quétıgny
Tel: (03) 80 73 90 65
Fax. (03) 80 73 90 69
Web site. http://www.pwcglobal.com
Pricewaterhouse Coopers
Isabelle Rosset
Immeuble Grenat
3, avenue Doyen Weil
B.P. 1524
38025 Grenoble Cedex 1
Tel. (04) 76 84 33 50
Fax. (04) 76 84 33 51
Web site: http://www.pwcglobal.com
Pricewaterhouse Coopers
Yvan Lipovac
37, rue du Vieux Faubourg
59800 Lille
Tel: (03) 20 12 50 59
Fax. (03) 20 51 34 56
Web site. http·//www.pwcglobal.com
Pricewaterhouse Coopers
Bernard Rascle
177, rue Garibaldi
69428 Lyon Cedex 03
Tel: (04) 72 60 52 00
Fax: (04) 78 17 81 79
Web site: http://www.pwcglobal.com
Pricewaterhouse Coopers
Olivıer Auscher
1, rue de la République
69001 Lyon
Tel: (04) 72 98 98 98
Fax: (04) 72 98 98 99
Web site: http.//www.pwcglobal.com

Pricewaterhouse Coopers
Philippe Willemin
Les Docks—Atrium 10-1
10, place de la Joliette
B.P. 48
13472 Marseille Cedex 2
Tel: (04) 91 99 30 00
Fax: (04) 91 99 30 01
Web site. http://www.pwcglobal.com
Pricewaterhouse Coopers
Jacques Gallo
Le Palmeira
45, rue St-Philippe
B.P. 6
06001 Nice Cedex 1
Tel: (04) 93 37 20 20
Fax: (04) 91 99 90 01
Web site. http://www.pwcglobal.com
Pricewaterhouse Coopers
Jean-Marc Bresson
1, allée Baco
B.P. 41529
44015 Nantes Cedex 1
Tel. (02) 40 35 06 35
Fax: (02) 40 48 41 88
Web site: http://www.pwcglobal.com
Pricewaterhouse Coopers
Guy Issler
2, avenue de la Forêt-Noire
67000 Strasbourg
Tel. (03) 88 45 55 50
Fax: (03) 88 45 55 51
Web site. http://www.pwcglobal.com
Pricewaterhouse Coopers
Dominique Sourdois
15, rue du Languedoc
B.P. 836
31080 Toulouse Cedex
Tel: (05) 61 14 88 88
Fax: (05) 62 26 70 77
Web site: http://www.pwcglobal.com
Deloitte Touche Tohmatsu
185, avenue Charles-de-Gaulle
92200 Neuilly-sur-Seine
Tel: (01) 40 88 28 00
Fax: (01) 40 88 28 28

Web site. http.//www.dtonline com or
http.//www.deloitte.com
Merrill Lynch
96, avenue d'Iéna
75116 Paris Cedex 16
Tel: (01) 40 69 10 00
Fax (01) 40 69 11 90
Web site. http.//www.merrilllynch.com
(institutional and individual investors)
Merrill Lynch
Centre D'Affaires Paris Trocadéro
112, avenue Kléber
75761 Paris Cedex 16
Tel. (01) 53 65 55 55
Fax: (01) 53 65 56 00
Web site. http.//www.merrilllynch.com
(institutional investors)

THE INTERNAL REVENUE SERVICE

Web site. http.//www.irs gov
For technical questions about
international tax laws and treaties.
**Office of the Associate Chief Counsel,
International**
Internal Revenue Service
1111 Constitution Avenue, NW
Washington, DC 20224
Tel: (202) 622-3800
Fax. (202) 622-4484
For questions about international filing
and forms.
**Customer Service Division
International Taxpayer Service
Internal Revenue Service**
950 L'Enfant Plaza, SW
Washington, DC 20024
For tax problem resolution
**International Tax Problem Resolution
Internal Revenue Service**
P.O. Box 44817
950 L'Enfant Plaza, SW
Washington, DC 20024

To request forms by phone·
Tel. (800) 829-1040
To request forms by fax.
Fax: (703) 368-9694
To download forms via the Web:
Web site. http.//www.irs.gov
IRS Office at the U.S. Consulate in Paris.
United States Consulate
2, rue St-Florentin
75001 Paris
Tel. (01) 43 12 25 55
Fax: (01) 43 12 47 52

SOCIAL SECURITY

Web site. http.//www.ssa.gov
For general information from the United
States.
**Office of Public Inquiries
Social Security Administration**
6401 Security Boulevard
Baltimore, MD 21235
Tel· (410) 965-7700
To file a claim from the United States:
**Social Security Administration
Office of International Operations—
Totalization**
P.O Box 17049
Baltimore, MD 21235
Tel: (410) 965-3548
For information about the U.S.-France
agreement.
**Social Security Administration
Office of International Policy**
P.O. Box 17741
Baltimore, MD 21235
Tel. (410) 965-3564
To file a claim with French authorities.
Renseignements sur la Sécurité Sociale
69 bis, rue de Dunkerque
75453 Paris Cedex 09
Tel. (01) 42 80 63 67
Minitel. 3615 SEC SOC

Setting Up House

Many things will sculpt your life in France but few will have as great an impact on you as the place where you choose to live. There is a virtually limitless variety of accommodations in France. Perhaps you're moving to France to live out your retirement dream of restoring a thirteenth-century country farmhouse; or maybe you're a corporate executive who needs to find a Paris apartment with full modern amenities. Maybe you're a student looking for inexpensive shared housing or a young professional looking to buy a small Paris flat. Whatever your situation, your choice of living space is a very important one, and finding the right place, setting it up, and moving in can be a complex and frustrating task if you're unaccustomed to how things are done in France.

More so than in many other countries, life in France revolves around the home. This way of life persists even today. Many French people live their lives in and around their homes, sometimes the same homes in which they grew up, traveling outside of their village or neighborhood only for a summer vacation or other special occasion. In this way, France is a country of small villages, neighborhoods, and *quartiers*, and even the major cities are basically clusters of small communities.

Paris, in many ways a sprawling metropolis, is really a compilation of individual villages—the arrondissements that spiral out from the center of the city. Each has a unique personality, a center for commerce and culture, and even a mini city hall, or *mairie*. I lived in each of nine different Parisian neighborhoods, but never did I have to walk more than ten minutes to find a bank, a neighborhood grocery store, a café or brasserie where I could people-watch, or a city park or square. And I could always count on there being a *boulangerie* open nearby: a French law mandates that each square kilometer in urban areas must have an open bakery every day of the week. Unlike the residential subdivisions and "bedroom communities" increasingly common in the United States, even the most secluded neighborhoods in France are dynamic, living communities with shops, services, and places for social and cultural activities.

But while your life in France can be an immensely gratifying experience, the experience of finding a place to call home can be more than a little bit frustrating if you don't know what you're doing or are not prepared. Especially if you're planning to buy property, there is a formidable amount of paperwork to be filled out and many regulations to understand. To say the least, it can be overwhelming to get off a plane and almost immediately be forced to deal with French landlords, rental contracts, real estate agents, insurance, and all the other mundane tasks associated with securing living space.

Finding a home can also be a rewarding and pleasurable experience if you have a good attitude and know what to prepare for. Many people arriving in France stay in a hotel or hostel for the first days, or even weeks, while they go about the task of house hunting. If you are lucky enough to have a business sponsoring your move to France, it is a common practice that the company will hire a relocation service to take care of many of the bureaucratic and time-consuming tasks associated with your move.

The price levels of real estate and rental properties in France, as elsewhere, depend on market conditions and the national economy. In recent history, prices have fluctuated dramatically. The astronomical property prices of the 1980s largely melted away during the economic recession that took hold of France in the early 1990s. Throughout the 1990s property prices dropped dramatically, especially outside of Paris and the other urban areas, sometimes by as much as 50 to 60 percent. Today, housing prices have basically recovered but there are still many bargains to be found. Whether you are looking to rent or to buy, it is a good idea to research the real estate market thoroughly before you leave for France, so that you are not homeless or in a state of flux for an extended period of time after your arrival.

The options for accommodations in France are numerous. Many students choose to live with a French family or rent a *chambre de bonne*, the small maid's room that accompanies many French apartments. Professionals and those with more money to spend can find furnished rentals or sign a standard long-term lease. Still others might decide that the investment of buying a house or apartment is right for them. Finding accommodation is likely to be one of the first major tasks that you will undertake upon your arrival, and it's not something that you want to take lightly. It's important to prepare well for your home hunting and see as broad a range of housing options as possible before you sign a lease or agree to buy.

Rent or Buy?

One of the first things that you have to decide is whether you will be renting or buying a home. For most people, the decision is not a difficult one. Buying property in France requires more money in the form of a down payment, more red tape in the form of paperwork and bureaucracy, and higher monthly mortgage payments. Generally speaking, mortgages from French banks require at least a 20 percent down payment and are based on a fifteen-year term, as opposed to the thirty-year or longer mortgages standard in the United States. If you don't have a lot of money for a down payment and a large income for monthly payments, renting may be your only option. However, if you do have your heart set on that special country estate or quaint Parisian flat, investing in property is rarely a bad financial move. Get your money together and skip to the section on "Buying Property."

Temporary Accommodation

If you're only staying in France for a few months or need a place to stay while you continue your search for the perfect living space, there are several options for temporary accommodation. For example, you can find shared accommodation, live with a French family, or rent a short-

Setting up house in a château

term apartment. In Paris, there is a bevy of agencies that provide furnished apartments for tourists and executives. Some agencies charge a commission, usually of one month's rent, to help you find a suitable apartment and deal with the landlord. Other agencies own the apartments outright or have contracts with the landlords, and you pay a flat monthly fee for the rental. If your French is still not up to par and you have the money to spend, these agencies can help alleviate a lot of the headaches associated with apartment hunting yourself. Some agencies will even provide maid service and deal with setting up utilities such as telephone, cable, and electricity.

Leasing an Apartment

There are basically two types of residential leases in France. Short-term furnished apartments are rented for one-year terms and are renewable at the landlord's discretion. Rents for furnished apartments can be substantially higher than for equivalent unfurnished places.

This is not only because of the costs of furnishing the apartment, but also because these apartments are commonly rented by professionals and executives who don't mind paying a premium for the convenience. Landlords know this and routinely charge extra for furnished apartments. Unfurnished apartments are let for a period of three years, and leasing contracts are heavily weighted in favor of tenants' rights. Once you've signed a regular three-year lease for an apartment, it can be very difficult for your landlord to evict you. In addition, rent increases are regulated by the government, and are generally kept to only a few percentage points each year. For this reason, many landlords will buy a few appliances and bring in a few pieces of furniture and call the place furnished in order to have the option of leasing for shorter terms and to maintain greater control over the use of the property.

When you are deciding what type of apartment you are looking for, it is important to consider how long you're planning to stay in France as well as how much furniture and property you have to fill an apartment. If you're only planning on being in France for a year, or even a few years, a furnished place may be preferable to moving your entire household to France. On the other hand, if you're planning to move to France permanently or for several years, you might be better off with a long-term lease. With long-term leases, you also generally have the right to sublet your apartment for up to a year. It is also important to keep in mind that an unfurnished apartment in France means that the premises are entirely bare—there will be no curtains, no refrigerator, and often no oven or stove. Unless you're prepared to make a significant investment in household necessities such as these, go for a furnished apartment.

THE FORMALITIES OF RENTING

The real estate market varies from place to place in France. Among international cities, Paris has long had a reputation for being one of the most expensive rental markets. Getting a landlord to rent you an apartment often takes a special blend of charm, persuasion, and money. If you're doing it on your own, you will probably have to speak a reasonable amount of French and be able to convince the landlord (or *propriétaire*) that you are an upstanding citizen in every way, that you have a good, stable job, and that you will disturb no one. Sometimes you'll need a letter of recommendation from your employer that states your monthly income. In most cases, landlords will expect that your income is equal to at least four or five times the monthly rent. In addition to all this, you'll likely have to come up with a significant sum of money. Most landlords will require that you pay the first and last months' rent in addition to a security deposit (called a *caution*) equal to at least one month's rent and sometimes more. Foreigners are generally required to have established bank accounts and banking relationships, as most landlords require that rent be automatically debited from your bank account each month. As a tenant, you'll also have to pay a *taxe d'habitation*, or residential tax, that could amount to several thousand francs per year.

DEALING WITH REAL ESTATE AGENTS

Many properties are rented and sold through agents *(agents immobiliers)*, rather than handled by the landlord or the seller himself. There are real estate agencies located everywhere in France, and each has its own unique selection of properties. There are no multiple listings in France, so it is generally advisable to work with a number of different agencies to find suitable accommodation. Generally speaking, you'll have to pay half of the agency's fee for furnished apartments and the whole fee for regular unfurnished rentals, which normally is between 10 and 15 percent of the annual rent for the apartment. Most agencies list properties only in one specific location or locality, so if you're not sure about where you want to live, you'll have to work with agencies in each of the areas you're considering. In addition, some agencies handle only rentals, and others handle only properties for sale. Make sure that you understand all of the charges and fees that you will incur when you enlist the help of an agency. Sometimes agencies will charge you fees regardless of whether or not they are the ones who ultimately find you an apartment. It is important to be clear about what services will be performed and exactly what charges you'll be held accountable for.

RELOCATION CONSULTANTS AND AGENCIES

If you're not thrilled about the prospect of setting out on your own to find that perfect apartment, you can hire one of the many relocation consultants or moving agencies located in France to help you with the searching and moving process. Although this can be an expensive proposition, if you have the money to spare, these services can save you a tremendous amount of time and the hassle normally associated with finding a suitable place, negotiating the rental terms, and moving your belongings from overseas. These companies can be particularly helpful if you don't speak a lot of French and/or if you're moving with your family and a large household. Often, if you are moving to France with a job, your company will pay your moving expenses and may agree to pay for a relocation consultant as well. Even if you're not following a job to France, if you have the money to spare, a relocation service may be a good investment. These companies will help find you temporary or long-term accommodations, handle the shipment of your possessions, and interface on your behalf with the many bureaucrats, agencies, and businesses along the way. In addition, these agencies can acquaint you with the city or neighborhood where you'll be moving, advise you about schools, and generally help you get established—all of which will make your move more pleasant. Consult the address section at the end of this chapter for contact information for a variety of relocation agencies.

UNDERSTANDING FRENCH LISTINGS

There are several characteristics of French apartment and property listings that you should be aware of before embarking on your hunt for accommodation. In contrast to American listings, apartments and houses are listed by the total number of rooms *(pièces)*, rather than the number of bedrooms *(chambres)*. Therefore, you can assume that an *"appartement avec trois pièces"* is a three-room apartment, usually meaning that it consists of a bedroom, a living room, and a dining room. Basically, the number of *"pièces"* does not include the kitchen, toilet, or bathroom but does include everything else. Which brings us to another difference: most houses and apartments in France have a "toilet room," called the *toilettes* or the *WC*, separate from the bathroom, which is where the sink and bathtub exist. Properties are measured in square meters, with one square meter roughly equal to ten square feet. Rent is normally quoted by the month, rather than by the week as it is in the United Kingdom, and there may be *"charges"* to pay in addition to normal rent. *Charges* can cover a wide variety of costs associated with the apartment including maintenance, renovations, and/or concierge fees. When inquiring about a listing, it is always important to ask if there are *charges* in addition to rent, and how much they are. Refer to the short glossary we've provided to help you navigate the sometimes confusing world of property listings.

Buying Property

Purchasing property in France requires a bit more time and energy, and sometimes more money, than buying a home in the United States. However, as in the United States, it is often preferable to buy if you have the money because you'll be investing mortgage payments in your own property rather than sending rent payments off to a landlord. Even if you're not planning on making France your permanent home, property can be a good source of income and can usually be sold at a considerable profit. Although property values in France do not increase at the fanatical rates that they sometimes do in the United States, the real estate market is very good and continues to recover from the country's recent recession. Generally speaking, the recession of the 1990s made buying property in France more attractive and affordable than it had been in years.

That said, buying a home in France can be a much more expensive undertaking than it is in the United States. Down payments of at least 20 percent of the cost of the property are usually required, and there are also many fees associated with the buying transaction itself. In addition, most mortgages are based on a fifteen-year term, making mortgage payments roughly double what you would pay for the same value property in the United States, where most banks issue thirty-year loans.

> ### GLOSSARY
>
> **Agences immobilières**—real estate agencies
> **Bail**—lease
> **Caution**—security deposit
> **Chambre**—room or bedroom
> **Chaudière**—hot water heater
> **Cuisine**—kitchen
> **Cuisinière**—stove
> **Digicode**—coded entry system
> **Douche**—shower
> **Escalier**—stairway
> **Étage**—floor
> **État des lieux**—inventory
> **Facture**—bill
> **Frigo**—refrigerator
> **Location**—rental
> **Loyer**—rent
> **Meublé**—furnished
> **Non-meublé**—unfurnished
> **Pièce**—room
> **Rénouver**—renovate
> **Salle de bain**—bathroom
> **WC** or **toilettes**—toilet room

TAXES

Property tax, called *taxe foncière*, is payable by all owners of property in France. The tax is assessed by the Centre des Impôts of your region, based on the value of your property, and you are expected to pay on an annual basis. In addition to property tax, you will be obliged to pay the standard residential tax if you live in your property, or if you live in France in general. Usually, there are tax exemptions for new homes and newly renovated properties. For detailed information about what taxes you'll be liable for, you need to contact the Centre des Impôts in your area. These offices can answer all your questions and provide you with all the necessary tax forms.

HOME PROTECTION

In Paris and the other large cities in France, burglary and theft can be a big problem, especially if you live in a ground-floor or easily accessible apartment. Although many apartment buildings have, in recent years, implemented certain security measures such as a *digicode* (coded entry system), it is always a good idea to have a deadbolt or two on your door and windows that lock. The *digicode* systems have been only somewhat successful; as these electronic security systems have been installed, concierges and *gardiens* have been increasingly phased out, resulting in easier access to many buildings. There are many insurance agencies in France that will issue you policies to protect property; check your Yellow Pages for local agents.

FINAL SUGGESTIONS WHEN BUYING

You should be very careful when considering buying property in France, particularly if you are not well accustomed to the ins and outs of the real estate market or have not familiarized yourself thoroughly with the property in question. Buying property in France should always involve a lawyer, and you would be well served by employing various other property consultants as well. You should have an engineer look at the property in question and inquire around about the history of the property. Have a plumber and electrician assess the property and find out if it will need any repairs. Find out what manipulations or renovations have been done to the property, and if more construction or fixing up is necessary. If you're thinking of buying a place in which people other than the landlord are currently living, make sure you are well aware of the legalities involving their tenancy, should you want to evict. Generally speaking, it is very difficult to evict tenants, regardless of whether the property has changed ownership.

Useful Real Estate Publications

There are a range of publications and an increasing number of Web sites that cater to French real estate. Most publications have listings for both rentals and properties for sale. The best places to start are the weekly *De Particulier à Particulier* and *J'Annonce*, two newspapers dedicated to classified advertising for properties all over France. The major French dailies also have listings, notably *Le Figaro* and *Libération*. In addition, the Paris-based *France-USA Contacts (FUSAC)* has many apartment listings and advertisements geared toward Americans and the expatriate community.

Utilities and Housing Bills

As you're settling into your new French home, you'll need to set up service for electricity and gas (if you have appliances that require it), and for telephone. Usually, this is not a difficult process and generally requires only a phone call to the local Électricité de France/Gaz de France (EDF/GDF) office and to France Télécom. If you're moving into an apartment or house where the former tenants recently moved out, you'll probably have all of the outlets and sockets that you'll need, and setting up service will merely be a matter of changing the name and other information for billing. If you're moving into a new home or into a place that has not had service in some time, you'll likely need to schedule a visit from a technician.

In most, if not all, cases, you'll be able to set up an automatic debit system for your utility bills. You'll still get a bill each month, but the total will be subtracted from a bank account of your choice. This service can be set up when you make your initial call to establish service in your name, or can be set up at a later date.

TELEPHONE SERVICE

The state-run France Télécom provides telephone service, and although the telephone network is very modern, France Télécom may have you missing the benefits of American-style deregulation. Although France Télécom has been forced to become more competitive in recent years, its legacy of having a total monopoly has many French jaded. Telephone service is still overpriced compared to many Western nations, and France Télécom can be notoriously slow and bureaucratic when it comes to ordering new services and handling repairs. That said, there is a bevy of new, independent telephone service providers popping up to cater to the international calls market. So-called "call-back services" will provide you with a local phone number that you call up, dial an access code, and then hang up. The system will then call you back with a dial tone and you can make standard international calls to anywhere in the world at rates comparable to or lower than U.S. rates. For more information on France Télécom and communications services, see Chapter 11, "*La Vie Virtuelle:* Navigating French Cyberspace."

ELECTRICITY/GAS

Most of France's electricity is generated using nuclear power, and is sold and distributed by the state-owned Électricité de France. Electric supply is delivered at 220/240 volts with a frequency of 50 hertz. This means that most of your American electric appliances, which are geared to the U.S. system of 110 volts, will not work without a transformer. Some appliances—many computers, for example—have transformers that can accommodate both voltages, and will have either manual switches or switch automatically. Generally, appliances state their electric requirements and capabilities near their power cord or power supply. For appliances that work only with 110-volt current, you can usually buy a transformer at a local hardware store in the United States. In addition, plugs and outlets have a different shape in France, so you will need to buy a conversion kit to use them.

Gas is not as widely used for heating and cooking in France as it is in the United States, although in Paris and the larger cities, it is certainly possible to find apartments and homes with gas heat and stoves. Gas service is provided by Gaz de France (GDF, which is combined with EDF). When you move into a new property, you'll need to contact GDF to come and read your meter in order to bill you properly. Both gas and electric bills are normally sent to you every two months.

Useful Addresses

General information.
Tel: (202) 659-7779
Maison de la France
444 Madison Avenue, 16th Floor
(between 49th & 50th Sts.)
New York, NY 10022-6903
Fax (212) 838-7855
Web site http://www.francetourism.com
Maison de la France
676 N. Michigan Avenue
Chicago, IL 60611-2819
Fax. (312) 337-6339
Web site. http //www.francetourism.com
Maison de la France
9454 Wilshire Boulevard, Suite 715
Beverly Hills, CA 90212-2967
Fax. (310) 276-2835
Web site. http.//www.francetourism.com

AGS
9-11, boulevard Galliéni
92230 Gennevilliers
Tel: (01) 40 80 20 20
Mory Worldwide Moving
165, route de Bezons
78420 Carrière-sur-Seine
Tel: (01) 61 04 22 00
J.M. Freight
Tel. (01) 48 62 13 25 or 48 62 13 43
Fax. (01) 48 62 14 10
Access Self Storage
Tel: (01) 53 01 90 00
(locations in Paris, Nanterre, Courbevoie,
and Montreuil)
Excess International
Tel: (01) 48 62 73 05
Fax: (01) 48 62 73 01
Allship Worldwide
Tel. (01) 48 70 04 45

Homeship Worldwide
Tel. (01) 48 65 21 61
Transpaq International
116 bis, avenue des Champs-Élysées
75008 Paris
Tel. (01) 45 63 43 00
Fax. (01) 45 63 03 42
Neer Service Demenagements
2, rue Désiré-Lemoine
93300 Aubervilliers
Tel. (01) 48 35 47 00
Web site: http.//www.neerservice.fr
Desbordes International
12-14, rue de la Véga
75012 Paris
Tel. (01) 44 73 84 84
Fax. (01) 43 42 51 48
Executive Relocations France
30, rue de Lübeck
75016 Paris
Tel. (01) 47 55 60 29
Fax. (01) 47 55 60 86
Cosmopolitan Services Unlimited
113, boulevard Pereire
75017 Paris
Tel. (01) 55 65 11 65
Fax. (01) 55 65 11 69

Capitale Partners
11, rue La Boétie
75008 Paris
Tel. (01) 42 68 35 60
Fax. (01) 42 68 35 61
Apalachee Bay International
56, rue Galilée
75008 Paris
Tel: (01) 49 52 01 52
Fax. (01) 40 70 01 37
Web site: http //www.apalachee.com
France Appartements
116, avenue des Champs-Élysées
75008 Paris
Tel: (01) 44 21 80 20

Fax. (01) 44 21 80 21
Web site. http.//www.france-
apartment.com
De Circourt Associates
11, rue Royale
75008 Paris
Tel. (01) 43 12 98 00
Fax. (01) 43 12 98 08
Web site: http.//www.paris-
anglo.com/housing/decircourt.html
Paris Appartements Services
69, rue d'Argout
75002 Paris
Tel. (01) 40 28 01 28
Fax. (01) 40 28 92 01
Web site. http.//www.paris-appartements-
services.fr
France Lodge Locations
41, rue La Fayette
75009 Paris
Tel: (01) 53 20 09 09
Fax. (01) 53 20 01 25
Euro Service Immobilier
20, rue du Cirque
75008 Paris

Tel: (01) 47 42 35 35
Fax. (01) 47 42 35 36
NEXT Immobilier
116, avenue des Champs-Élysées
75008 Paris
Tel: (01) 44 21 80 28
Fax. (01) 44 21 80 29
Locaflat
Tel (01) 43 06 78 79
Fax. (01) 40 56 99 69
Web site. http://www.locaflat.com
Barnes & Naylor
Tel: (01) 45 74 24 21
Fax. (01) 45 74 60 12
Cattalan Johnson Agency
Tel. (01) 45 74 87 77
Fax: (01) 45 74 87 80
Rival Conseil Immobilier
59, rue Boissière
75116 Paris Cedex
Tel: (01) 53 70 04 53
Fax· (01) 47 04 24 79
Web site: http://www.rival-immo.com

Santé!: *Health and Health Care in France*

France has a very advanced health care system, both in terms of its national health insurance coverage and the quality of medical practitioners. Medical research and development in France have historically been at the forefront of the science, and are sometimes considered to be better than their counterparts in the United States and the rest of Western Europe. Medical research organizations such as the Institut Pasteur have led the way in the fight against diseases such as cancer, AIDS, and other world epidemics. The French national *sécurité sociale* provides health insurance coverage for every French citizen or resident who has made contributions to the system, and there are cross-coverage agreements with most of the rest of Europe. In addition, the *sécurité sociale* covers many nontraditional or alternative medical treatments, such as homeopathy and acupuncture, which have long been popular in France.

It seems sometimes that the French love taking pills even more than Americans. Regardless of whether you see a French doctor for a broken bone or a simple checkup, you will generally leave with at least one prescription. At the same time, the French are a very healthy people. The fashion of fitness that took America by storm over the last generation has taken hold in France as well, and gyms and health clubs have been popping up all over the country, especially in Paris.

A popular form of exercise in France is to go for a stroll.

and the bigger cities. Health foods and vitamins, many of which are available only in pharmacies, have also increased in popularity. France also has a very low incidence of heart disease, sometimes attributed to the large quantity of red wine that is consumed along with virtually every meal. Generally speaking, because health care is free or inexpensive, people are more likely to take advantage of medical services and the French medical system is therefore geared toward preventative medicine. Another cultural facet of interest: Don't be surprised if your "pills" are somewhat "waxy"; French doctors and pharmacists are particularly fond of handing out treatments in the form of suppositories, a practice that some Americans might find somewhat difficult to get used to.

Your health is not something that you want to take chances with, so it is important to understand the intricacies and differences of the French health care system, and how to get and pay for medical assistance should you or your family need it while living in France. It is important to note that for most medical services in France, including visits to a doctor's office, emergency services, and prescriptions, bills are generally payable when the services or treatments are rendered.

Insurance plans, including the national *sécurité sociale*, will reimburse you after you submit a copy of the bill you paid.

Emergency Medical Care

It is very important to know whom to call during a medical emergency and how the system works. Take some time once you arrive in France to familiarize yourself with the services provided in your area and how to access them. Emergency telephone numbers are generally provided in the informational section at the beginning of telephone directories, and your local police department can also tell you what to do in the case of a medical emergency. Once you are settled into an apartment or house, it is also a good idea to learn where the hospital nearest you is located. Note that not all hospitals are equipped to provide trauma care or other emergency medical services.

It is generally understood that in life-threatening situations, it is best to call the fire department, called *les pompiers*, first. French fire crews are usually the quickest to the scene of an accident or medical emergency, carry life-support systems in their vehicles, and many are also trained paramedics. Fire departments work closely with public ambulance services, the Service d'Aide Médicale d'Urgence or SAMU, and will transport you to the nearest hospital that can treat you. In Paris and other cities, the fire department can be reached by dialing 18 from any phone. Alternatively, the SAMU can be called directly in life-threatening situations as well. The SAMU operates a fleet of ambulances equipped with lifesaving gear and staffed by trained professionals. SAMU is reachable in Paris by dialing 15 from any phone; outside the capital you can find the number at the front of your phone book or on the instruction card in public phone booths. In Paris and other urban areas, there are sometimes phone boxes located in large intersections or public places with direct lines to emergency medical services.

There is a range of other on-call services that you can call on in an emergency. SOS Médecins is an organization that provides twenty-four-hour house calls by fully trained doctors. SOS Dentistes is a similar organization that can attend to dental emergencies. In addition, there are ambulance services that you can call in non-life-threatening situations that provide transport and care to and from hospitals and other health care facilities. Look in your phone book under ambulances for a complete listing of local companies. The local *mairie* can also provide a complete list of doctors on call in your neighborhood and other various specialists. See the listing at the end of this chapter for contact information.

The French Public Health Care System

The French national health care system, an element of the *sécurité sociale*, is one of the most encompassing public health insurance systems in the world, and the French pay a hefty price for it. The system is perpetually in hundreds of millions of dollars of debt, but the care is of unparalleled quality and virtually ubiquitous. Due to the economic recession that France has only recently begun to recover from, the government has been under the gun in recent years to reform the system, make cuts, and reduce excessive costs.

The *sécurité sociale* does not pay doctors, hospitals, or other health care establishments directly; rather, most bills are payable immediately by the patient, who will later be reimbursed for a proportion of the amount by the government's *caisse primaire d'assurance maladie*. The *sécurité sociale* generally covers about three-quarters of your medical expenses, depending on the type of product or service and whether it was administered by a doctor that adheres to a set of *sécurité sociale* guidelines. The social security health care system provides a list of common treatments and medicines and assigns each a value. Before choosing a doctor or agreeing to a particular treatment, you should check to see whether your doctor is *conventionné* (charges are based on the *sécurité sociale*'s fixed and agreed-upon amount for services) or *non-conventionné*. Doctors who are *non-conventionnés* may still be *agrées* (approved) by *sécurité sociale*, and a lesser proportion of your bill will be reimbursed. Generally, hospital stays are reimbursed up to about 80 percent, general doctor's services at 75 percent, and 65 percent for prescriptions and alternative treatments such as chiropractic, physical therapy, homeopathy, and acupuncture. Maternal care and services are 100 percent covered by *sécurité sociale*.

Mutuelles and Other Private
Insurance Companies

Because social security generally covers only a percentage of your medical bills, most people take out a "top-up" policy from private insurance companies, called *mutuelles*. If you get very sick or need surgery or a hospital stay, charges not covered by *sécurité sociale* can add up quickly. There is a wide range of plans available at a variety of costs, so it is important to review a number of policies from different companies before settling on one. If you're working for a French corporation, there may be a *mutuelle* with which your company is affiliated that offers employees group rates or other discounts. Otherwise, look in the Yellow Pages under *mutuelles d'assurance* for a complete listing of the companies in your area offering these policies.

You may want to take out other insurance policies to cover you immediately upon arrival in France, while you are looking for work, or if you are not eligible for coverage under national health care. There is a wide range of companies that offer coverage tailored to the needs of expatriates and foreigners living in France. The policies available differ tremendously; you should research various offers thoroughly before signing on the dotted line. You should ask about coverage limits, how you make and are granted payment of claims, and if there are premiums based on age, location, or preexisting conditions. We have listed several insurance companies at the end of this chapter; others place ads in the English-language press in Paris and other French cities, or can be found in the Yellow Pages of your phone book.

Foreign students will have to take out private health insurance policies, if not covered under arrangement from the college or university in which they have enrolled. The International Student Identity Card (ISIC), which can be purchased for $20 from the Council on International Educational Exchange (CIEE) or at various student travel offices both in the United States and in France, offers basic coverage for emergency evacuation, accidents, and sickness. In addition, Council Travel, the CIEE's sister travel agency, offers an insurance scheme that complements the ISIC coverage. If you're on a study abroad program from an American high school or university, your school may be able to cover you under your current student health plan. Check with your school and refer to the listing at the end of this chapter for contact information.

How to Become Eligible for Public Health Care

Medical and dental coverage is available for every French citizen and resident who makes *sécurité sociale* payments. If you are working in France under contract with an established company, it is likely that you will be automatically covered by the French *sécurité sociale*. To qualify for coverage, you need to have been employed in France for a period of at least three months. Regardless, it is always important to ask about your health care status before entering into a contract to work abroad.

Generally, an employee's family is covered under his or her plan. Once you're enlisted in the national health care system, you'll receive a *carte d'assuré social*, a social security card that includes information about where to send bills to be reimbursed. It will also list all members of your family included in your coverage. If you're a freelancer or independent contractor, you can qualify for coverage by electing to make social security payments on your own, although the system will generally pay a smaller percentage of your medical bills. In addition, most Western European countries have cross-coverage agreements with France. If you are a resident or national of another EU member nation, you can generally continue to make payments to your own social security system while in France.

Hospitals

In Paris, there are two hospitals that are fully bilingual in French and English, and more than a dozen others that offer excellent health care in French. If your French is not great, you may prefer to go to a hospital where information is explained to you in English. The American Hospital in Paris is substantially more expensive than its French counterparts, but will accept Medicaid and most American insurance policies. In addition, both the American Hospital and the American Embassy can provide you with a list of English-speaking doctors in France. The other English-language option is the Hertford British Hospital, which is partially subsidized by the French government and specializes in maternity care.

Like doctors, hospitals are either *conventionnés* or *non-conventionnés*, depending on whether they adhere to *sécurité sociale* guidelines and prices for care. Most cities in France will have at least one hospital that is *conventionné*. Hospitals usually have one or more specialties, and may or may not be equipped to handle trauma care or emergencies. Some specialize only in long-term care or convalescence, others are research hospitals associated with a university. You should get recommendations and research a hospital before you or a loved one is admitted for care.

Pharmacies, Prescriptions, and Medicine

French pharmacies, recognizable by the distinctive green first aid cross, carry a wide range of health-related products in addition to prescription medications. Some specialty items that you might normally find in a supermarket in America are available only in pharmacies in France, including items like medicated shampoo, common analgesics, and throat lozenges. Most pharmacies also carry a large selection of personal hygiene products, lotions, and powders. Pharmacists can answer many of your health-related questions and recommend doctors and treatments for many common maladies. In addition, in emergencies pharmacists are permitted to prescribe medication. French regulations governing medications are often different from those in the United States, and some medications that require a prescription in the United States are available over the counter in France, and vice versa. In addition, the brand names and, sometimes, generic names of many pharmaceuticals are different in France, so if you have specific medications that you use in the United States it is important to research their French counterparts.

Pharmacies are virtually everywhere, and every city and town in France will have at least several to choose from. In bigger cities, there is usually at least one pharmacy that is open late or around the clock. It is a good idea to know where these are located on the chance that you need a prescription filled after normal business hours. We list several of Paris's late-night pharmacies at the end of this section; if you're outside Paris, you can usually find the name and location of an after-hours pharmacy in the phone book or by calling your local *mairie*. All pharmacies list on their doors the one that is open.

Women's Health and Maternity Care

Many American women prefer to see a doctor who specializes in women's health, such as a gynecologist or obstetrician, as their personal care physician. You can do this in France as well, but keep in mind that the French medical profession in general has different attitudes toward the doctor-patient relationship. If you don't speak French well or have just arrived in France, you might be more comfortable seeing a doctor who speaks English and understands American "bedside manner." You should find a doctor with whom you are comfortable and who is sensitive to your concerns.

If you are pregnant, or planning to be, while in France, you should research your options thoroughly and choose your doctor carefully. Pregnant women's care and childbirth are covered 100 percent by the *sécurité sociale*. If you have private insurance, you should check to see how much of the prenatal care and delivery is covered under your plan. Most births in France take place in hospitals, and are sometimes attended to by midwives, or *sages-femmes*. Among other things, you should inquire about the birthing process at your hospital, including how long after delivery most mothers and newborns are kept, if classes or exercise lessons are given, and whether or not fathers are permitted in the delivery room.

Birth control is widely available in France, although, as in the United States, you will need to see a doctor for a prescription for birth control pills. Condoms, called *préservatifs*, and other birth control products can be purchased at pharmacies. In addition, there are condom machines all over France including in *métro* stations and many bar and café rest rooms. As an interesting note, the two highest-selling Paris *Métro* station condom machines are at St-Michel, in the Latin Quarter, and at Père Lachaise, the cemetery in the north of Paris. Do what you will with that information.

Useful Addresses

In an emergency, dial 18 from any telephone for the fire department, 17 for the police, or 15 for an ambulance.

AMERICAN INSURANCE AGENCIES
OFFERING OVERSEAS COVERAGE

Travel Guard International
1145 Clark Street
Stevens Point, WI 54481
Tel. (715) 345-0505 or (800) 826-1300
Travel Insured International, Inc.
52-S Oakland Avenue
P.O. Box 280568
East Hartford, CT 06128-0568
Tel: (800) 243-3174
Fax. (860) 528-8005
Travel Safe Insurance
Chester Perfetto Agency
40 Commerce Drive
Box 70510
Wyomissing, PA 19610
Tel. (610) 678-0373 or (800) 523-8020
Wallach & Co.
107 West Federal Street
PO. Box 480
Middleburg, VA 20117-0480
Tel. (800) 237-6615
Fax. (540) 687-3172

INFORMATION ABOUT FRENCH
MUTUELLES D'ASSURANCE

Fédération Nationale de la Mutualité Française
255, rue de Vaugirard
75015 Paris

MEDICAL SERVICES AND
INFORMATION

International Association for Medical Assistance to Travellers
417 Center Street
Lewiston, NY 14092
Tel: (716) 754-4883

Council on International Educational Exchange European Headquarters
1, place de l'Odéon
75006 Paris
Tel. (01) 44 41 74 74
Fax: (01) 43 26 97 45
SOS Médecins
Tel. (01) 47 07 77 77
SOS Dentistes
Tel. (01) 43 37 51 00

HOSPITALS CATERING TO ENGLISH
SPEAKERS

American Hospital of Paris
63, boulevard Victor-Hugo
92200 Neuilly
Tel (01) 46 41 25 25
Hertford British Hospital
3, rue Barbès
92300 Levallois-Perret
Tel (01) 46 39 22 22

ENGLISH-LANGUAGE AND LATE-
NIGHT PHARMACIES

British and American Pharmacy
1, rue Auber
75009 Paris
Tel. (01) 47 42 49 40
La Pharmacie Anglaise
62, avenue des Champs-Élysées
75008 Paris
Tel. (01) 43 59 22 52
Pharmacie Anglo-Américaine
6, rue de Castiglione
75001 Paris
Tel. (01) 42 60 72 96
Pharmacie Dhéry (open 24 hours)
84, avenue des Champs-Élysées
75008 Paris
Tel: (01) 45 62 02 41

CHAPTER EIGHT

Shops, Shopping, and Shopkeepers

The French have a term for window shopping—*le lèche-vitrines*. And it literally means "window licking." While I have yet to see chic Parisians with their tongues attached to the windows of the Chanel Boutique on avenue Montaigne or even to the windows of the local pastry shop, there are definitely some differences between shopping in France and shopping at home. True shopping malls do not really exist, nor do discount shops like T. J. Maxx and Filene's Basement. But the French countryside is dotted with hypermarkets (supermarkets that have more than 2,500 square meters of surface area), and towns and cities are filled with the kinds of delightful specialty shops that have been lost in the United States.

Shopping Etiquette

Shopping in Paris can be completely different from shopping in the rest of the country. Both experiences can be either delightful or frustrating beyond belief, depending on what you are looking for, your luck, and, most of all, how you behave.

Before heading out to hit the shops, it helps to have a bit of knowledge about shopping etiquette. It may seem undemocratic, but if you want to be taken seriously and treated well in most French stores (with the exception of food shops and supermarkets), you should literally put your best foot forward. The French dress up to go shopping. In fact they dress up just to leave the house. The casual, comfortable, grungy look that is so popular in the United States has not taken off here and it is rare to see a Frenchwoman, even in the supermarket, without lipstick. Wearing shorts, a T-shirt, and Tevas to shop in a nice boutique is simply not done here.

Dressing the part is half the battle to getting good service. The other half relates to your behavior in the shops. When you enter a small shop, with only a few salesclerks, you should greet the first person you make eye contact with with a polite *"Bonjour, Madame"* or *"Bonjour, Monsieur."* The formalities end there, however, as the French do not generally exchange further pleasantries with strangers. The common American "How are you?" or "How's it going today, Ma'am?" does not carry over into an exchange of *"Ça va?"* and *"Bien, merci."* When you leave a store you should say *"Merci, Monsieur"* or *"Madame."*

While you are in the store, you should feel free to browse, although the salesclerks are there to help. If you want assistance, just ask. In general, smaller stores frown upon customers who touch all the merchandise. In small food shops (especially fruit and vegetable stands, bakeries, cheese shops, etc.), you should ask first if you can serve yourself. In clothing shops, you should never unfold items that are displayed on the shelves. Those same items are almost always hung on display on one of the lower shelves. You may look at those items and then ask for help regarding sizes.

Store Hours

Because of French labor laws, stores are limited in the number of hours and days they can stay open. Few stores operate on the 9 A.M.–to–9 P.M., seven-days-a-week schedule Americans know and love, and most are closed on Sundays. Most stores in Paris are open from 9:30 or 10:00 A.M. until 7:00 P.M., although some close for lunch between 12 and 2 or 1 and 3. This lunch break closure is even more common outside of Paris, where shops may even close for three hours in the afternoon and stay open until 8 P.M. to compensate. In most cities and towns, stores are open later (until 9 or 10 P.M.) one night a week. As you become a more regular customer you will understand each store's hours better. A few shops that are family owned and operated (and thus not subject to the same labor laws) are also open on Sundays. In general these are primarily bakeries and food shops although some big international chains in Paris (especially on the Champs-Élysées) have started to keep Sunday hours as well.

In August, the month when most French go on vacation, you may find that many of your favorite shops close down for two weeks or a month at a time. Food shops should coordinate with their competitors to ensure that residents in their neighborhoods and towns do not go hungry. They generally plan to go on vacation in waves. In compensation, during the holiday periods, while the shops in the cities and towns are closed up tight, stores in the various resort towns (beach and mountain) are open seven days a week.

Payment

Paying for goods and services in France has become less and less complicated in recent years. It goes without saying that cash is always welcome, although the French do not like to carry large quantities of cash around. Almost all stores accept the Visa credit card and many accept MasterCard credit cards as well. American Express cards are generally accepted only in areas with a lot of international shoppers. Checks issued by American banks are not accepted in any French stores and you will be extremely hard-pressed to find a bank that will cash an American check in fewer than six weeks and without charging you at least half the check's value.

Checks issued by French banks, on the other hand, are accepted almost everywhere and for even the smallest denominations. I was surprised to discover that I was once able to pay for a baguette, worth about sixty cents, with a check, because I did not have any cash. *"Pas de problème, Madame,"* the baker told me—"No problem." French bankcards, with their famous *puce* (microchip), that serve as both credit and debit cards are also accepted almost everywhere.

Returns

Although stores are slowly moving toward more flexibility, it is still rather rare to find a shop that is willing to take back merchandise that

The water from French public water fountains, such as this one, is safe to drink.

has already been paid for. While in America, most stores offer a thirty-day money-back return policy, the best you can hope for with most French stores is store credit. Some of the larger department stores are beginning to change their ways and may offer you seven days to change your mind but it's always best to ask first. In general, it is wise to be very sure of what you are buying and not bring things home to decide.

Armed with this basic advice, you are now ready to hit the streets and shop till you drop. You know how to behave. You know when to go. And you know how to pay. Now you need to know where to go to get what you need.

Shopping for Food and Necessities

The French take food very seriously and shopping for just the right ingredients is a big part of daily life. Although supermarkets can be found in almost every French city and town, most people still prefer the quality of the products in the smaller specialty stores. Shopping in the specialty shops takes more time and can be confusing at first but with a little experience, you will begin to understand how food shopping is divvied up and will develop the relationships with the various shopkeepers that typify French shopping.

L'ÉPICERIE OR L'ALIMENTATION GÉNÉRALE

Literally the "spice shop," the *épicerie* is akin to the American mini-market. These shops are a bit like little grocery stores and carry everything from spices to laundry detergent, paper towels, and breakfast cereal. Some also carry a small selection of fruits and vegetables, butter and cheeses, and prepackaged bread. In Paris, a special category of *alimentation générale*, informally referred to as *Arabes* because many are run by families of North African origin, are open later in the evenings, usually until ten or eleven o'clock. These shops are invaluable when you come home late from work to an empty refrigerator, or realize, at nine o'clock on the night you are hosting a dinner party, that you have forgotten that key ingredient and guests will be arriving any moment.

BOUCHERIE

In the *boucherie* (butcher shop), you can find most kinds of meat except pork and cold cuts, which are sold in the *charcuterie*. Choosing the right cut can be confusing at first, as meat is cut differently in France, but your butcher can help with explanations and can usually provide you with cooking advice and recipes.

BOULANGERIE/PÂTISSERIE

My daily stroll to the neighborhood *boulangerie* (bakery) was one of the joys of my time in France. The *boulangeries* carry all kinds of bread, croissants, rolls, sweet rolls (brioches), and other sweet and salty treats. Although all *boulangeries* carry the classic baguette, other breads like the *pain de campagne* (literally countryside bread), which is a heartier loaf, made with a mixture of grains, are delicious as well. The smell of bread baking permeates the air around the *boulangeries* throughout the day, as many bake bread up to three times a day to ensure a constant fresh supply.

If you really have a sweet tooth, you should head to a *pâtisserie*, or a pastry shop, where you can find fruit tarts, cakes, and petit fours that at times seem too beautiful to eat.

CHARCUTERIE

The *charcuterie* is much like an American delicatessen and sells pork and other prepared meats and cold cuts, including ham, pâté, and *saucissons* (dried sausage) as well as some prepared foods like grilled potatoes, roast beef, ratatouille, soups, and other dishes.

FROMAGERIE/CRÈMERIE

The *fromagerie* (cheese shop) is another national treat. In 1962, French President Charles de Gaulle asked, "How can anyone govern a nation that has 246 kinds of cheese?" Today that number is on the rise. The local *fromagerie* is the place to go to begin tasting them. While most supermarkets sell cheese and other dairy products, the *fromagerie* ages cheese on the premises and generally sells only cheeses made with unpasteurized milk. A *crèmerie*, on the other hand, is the place to go for fresh milk, cream, yogurt, butter, and other dairy products.

POISSONNERIE

Seafood shops are called *poissonneries* in France. You can expect a large selection of different kinds of fish and shellfish, usually beautifully presented in colorful displays. The shopkeeper will also clean and scale your fish for you if you ask for it to be *préparé*.

TABAC

Though tobacco is not necessarily a basic, tobacco shops and the bars and cafés to which they are often attached are an essential part of life for most French. The tobacco shop is an official source of government forms (including tax forms), postage stamps, and lottery tickets, in addition to cigarettes, tobacco, matches, and cigarette lighters.

A tabac

KIOSQUES

Kiosques (newsstands) are found in most towns and all across Paris and other cities. They are the first place to look for the news of the day, as well as an enormous range of magazines. Most *kiosques* in Paris carry a range of international newspapers and magazines. In smaller towns, a newsstand may also be part of the local bookstore.

OTHER SHOPS

Some other shops that will make your life easier are the *pharmacie* (pharmacy), the *teinturier* (cleaners), the *pressing* (dry cleaners), the *fleuriste* (florist), the *coiffeur* (hairdresser), the *esthéticienne* (beautician), the *papeterie* (stationery shop), the *graveur* or *imprimeur* (engraver or printer), the *serrurier* (locksmith), and the *cordonnier* (shoe repairer).

Shopping for Clothes

France, land of haute couture, is an international Mecca for shoppers seeking the best selection of high fashion and brand names including Hermès, Louis Vuitton, Christian Dior, Chanel, and Yves Saint-Laurent. These designers make beautiful and expensive clothing and accessories, but where do average French people go to buy clothes?

Typically, the French prefer quality over quantity and will spend more for classic clothing that will last a long time and never go out of style. In Paris and most large cities, there are large department stores called *grands magasins*, including Galeries Lafayette, La Samaritaine, and Le Printemps among others. The *grands magasins* are often crowded but are very convenient because they carry clothing for the whole family and stock many brands and designers. They also often have cafeterias or tearooms where you can take a break.

Beyond the department stores, there are boutiques. Paris has several shopping neighborhoods, ranging from the very prestigious rue du Faubourg-Saint-Honoré and avenue Montaigne to the more moderate boulevard Montparnasse. Most cities and towns have at least one shopping area where clothing boutiques can be found. In addition, more and more American and British chains are making their way into the French market, including Marks & Spencer, the Body Shop, the Gap, and Esprit, which can make for more familiar shopping.

Markets

Most towns have at least one market a week, with vendors selling everything from fresh produce to running shoes. Most cities have several different markets a week. Paris has several daily produce markets, as well as a number of flea markets, a book market, a flower market, and an antique market that take place on different days across the city. Shopping at a market is a typically French experience and can be a lot of fun to observe, even if you don't plan to buy anything. For information about the markets scheduled in your town or city, contact the *mairie* (city hall).

Supermarkets, Hypermarkets, and Shopping Malls

Most towns have at least one supermarket. Cities usually have one per neighborhood and they make for convenient one-stop shopping, although they are often cold and impersonal when compared to the smaller specialty shops. The larger chains include Casino, Prisunic, Monoprix, and Franprix.

Hypermarkets, *les hypermarchés,* are giant supermarkets, usually found on the outskirts of town, with enormous free parking lots. To qualify as a *hypermarché*, the supermarket must spread over at least 2,500 square meters. Most *hypermarchés* sell everything from food to clothing, computers, appliances, furniture, books, and compact disks. Some of the best known are Auchan, Carrefour, Champion, and Leclerc.

I have not yet seen a truly American style shopping mall in France, although many *centres commerciaux* are trying to fill that gap. *Centres commerciaux*, usually found near or around a *hypermarché*, are often filled with shops selling inexpensive, low-quality clothing and accessories and have not become the social centers or meeting points that American malls have. That said, in Paris and some of the other cities, there are a number of beautiful old covered galleries where stores are clustered together in a protected space. Some of my favorites in Paris are the passage du Perron on rue de Beaujolais in the first arrondissement and passage Jouffroy on boulevard Montmartre in the ninth arrondissement.

Catalog Shopping

Catalog shopping is not quite the phenomenon it has become in the United States but several large mail-order companies provide convenient and at times inexpensive opportunities for catalog shopping. The two largest are La Redoute and Les Trois Suisses. They publish catalogs two times a year, which can be purchased at any newsstand. Like Sears and J. C. Penney, the companies refund the price of the catalog with the first purchase.

Bargains

The French are generally suspicious of bargains and really do not like to talk about how much they paid for something. Unless you are very close friends, it is really a faux pas to ask. Bargains are not easy to find but they are out there. Twice a year, at the end of January and the beginning of July, clothing shops hold sales (*les soldes*). Prices are cut up to 50 percent but beware: during *les soldes*, all sales are final.

Factory outlets are not common and discount clothing shops like T. J. Maxx and Filene's Basement do not exist but some good deals can be found. For some ideas, buy a copy of the latest *Paris Pas Cher* (published by Flammarion), which is filled with tips on how to save money in all aspects of daily life: where to shop, how to travel, where to eat, and so on. Although the book is directed at Parisians, many of the suggestions can be applied elsewhere in France.

American and International Food

Fortunately most supermarkets in France are beginning to carry a limited range of international products. So, if you are ever bored with French cuisine (I know it seems hard to imagine) or are just craving a taco or some hummus, most supermarkets now have sections with Asian, Middle Eastern, Mexican, Italian, and even American cooking ingredients (among others, pancake mix and baked beans for some reason). If you happen to live in one of the larger cities, there is usually at least one international food shop. Paris, a city filled with immigrants from all over the world, has dozens. Some of the exclusively American and English food shops are listed at the end of the chapter.

Tax Rebates for Non-EU Citizens

The value-added tax (TVA) in France, which is already included in the list price of any item, amounts to 19 percent, one of the highest rates in Europe. If you will be returning to the United States or any non–European Union member state within three months of making a large purchase or purchases (you must spend a certain amount, usually around $200, to be able to qualify), you may apply for a TVA rebate. To do so, you must request a special receipt from the store and then bring the receipt and the items purchased to the tax rebate counter at the airport before boarding the plane.

Useful Addresses

AMERICAN AND BRITISH FOOD
SHOPS IN PARIS

The Bagel Place
6, place Ste-Opportune
75001 Paris
Tel: (01) 40 28 96 40

Ben & Jerry's Ice Cream Les Halles
4, rue Pierre-Lescot
75001 Paris
Ben & Jerry's Ice Cream Drouot
18, boulevard Montmartre
75009 Paris

Ben & Jerry's Ice Cream Bastille
22, rue de la Roquette
75001 Paris
Coffee Shop
8, rue Perronet
75007 Paris
Tel: (01) 45 44 92 93
The General Store
82, rue de Grenelle
75007 Paris
Tel: (01) 45 48 63 16
The General Store
30, rue de Longchamp
75116 Paris
Tel: (01) 47 55 41 14

Marks & Spencer
35, boulevard Haussmann
75009 Paris
Tel: (01) 47 42 42 91
The Real McCoy
194, rue de Grenelle
75007 Paris
Tel: (01) 45 56 98 82
Thanksgiving
20, rue St-Paul
75004 Paris
Tel: (01) 42 77 68 29
Saveurs des Amériques
39, rue Letellier
75015 Paris
Tel: (01) 45 71 05 49

Les Transports:
Getting Around in France

As soon as you set foot in France, you will begin learning how to get around. The French, especially Parisians, are always on the go and France's transportation infrastructure is among the best in the world. You will be left to decide which of the many transport options is best for you. How you get around in France on a daily basis will have a lot to do with whether you live in a city or in a more rural area. On the other hand, how you decide to travel as you cross the country for business or pleasure will depend both on where you live and where you would like to end up.

Public Transportation

As it is in many other aspects, France is a highly centralized country with regard to public transportation. Not only is it true that (almost) all train routes lead to Paris but also that when one group of transport workers goes on strike, others around the nation tend to follow. Transportation strikes have been on the rise in recent years, becoming more and more frequent as the government tries to push toward privatization and trimming down of some of the very cushy benefit plans most public employees enjoy. One of the most debilitating strikes occurred in the fall of 1995, when subway, bus, and train employees went on a

A typical Paris Métro *station*

highly coordinated strike for nearly a month, leaving millions of French to travel on foot.

The impact was particularly felt in the capital where many millions of Parisians use the *Métro* each day to commute back and forth to work and school. In the traditionally intense pre-Christmas shopping weeks, the strike was estimated to have cost Parisian merchants and businesses billions of francs. The strike went on for so long that, in response to a desperate demand for a means to cross town, some of the famous tour boats opted to transport people up- and downriver on the Seine from the Eiffel Tower to the Bastille.

Yet when it works, much of French public transportation is incredibly efficient, particularly in the cities and especially in Paris.

Le Métro

The underground railway *(métro)* found in a number of French cities has entered into the national consciousness. *Métro, boulot, dodo* (subway, work, sleep)—a phrase coined to describe the daily grind—starts the day off with a subway ride. In Paris alone, at least four million people ride the subway each day. If you do live in Paris, I highly recommend you use the *Métro* to get around. With almost 150 miles of tracks, over 300 stations, and 15 lines, it is by far the fastest and easiest way to get to your destination. Within the city center, you are very rarely more than a few blocks away from a stop. Lille, Lyon, Marseille, and Toulouse are the four other French cities with underground railway systems, though none nearly as complex and far reaching as the Paris *Métro*.

In Paris, and in some other cities, the subway stops can usually be identified by a big yellow "M" in a yellow circle on a pole outside the station. Some of the older stops in Paris are decorated with beautiful art deco signs in green wrought iron and majolica, one of the few remaining relics of the first *Métro* line's grand opening in 1900. These signs are featured in many postcards. The capital's metro is run by the RATP (Régie Autonome des Transports Parisiens) and in Paris, as in many other French cities, tickets and passes for the subway are valid for other forms of transportation as well, including buses and regional rail services.

In discussing how the subway network operates, I base my description on the Parisian example. The *métros* in most other cities operate in a similar fashion. Trains run from 5 A.M. until 1 A.M. and in peak hours you can expect to wait no more than forty seconds for a train. Tickets for the *Métro* must be purchased in one of the subway stations or in a *tabac*, and can be bought individually *(un billet)*, in packs of ten *(un carnet de dix)*, or as some kind of pass. The most common pass is the *Carte Orange*, which is generally bought each month and is valid for the entire calendar month regardless of when you purchase it. To buy a *coupon mensuel* (monthly pass), you must first present a photo and application form to the counter at any station, where you will be issued an orange ID card and a carrying case for your coupon. The ID card also contains a pocket-sized *Plan de Poche* (map of the bus, *Métro*, and RER routes) and even the most seasoned Parisians are often seen studying the maps on sidewalks and on subway platforms trying to discover the best way to reach their destination. As the monthly passes are nontransferable, you should carry your ID with you whenever you use the *Métro*; police checks are frequent and the fines are steep if you are caught without a ticket or without your ID card.

You must insert all tickets into the turnstile and take them back with you, and hold on to them until you reach a sign that says, *Limite de Validité des Billets*. Lines are identified by number and end-point, and though the tunnel network can seem a maze at some stations, it is generally a fairly straightforward process to find the platform in the direction you want. Once you are inside the train, it helps to know that the doors do not open automatically at each stop. Rather, you must push a red button on the door or lift a small stainless steel lever to find your way out.

Subway maps of the entire city can be found in each station, at the entrance, in the tunnels, and on the platforms. Outside most stations, at street level, you can usually find a map of the neighborhood that can help you find your way.

In Paris, commuters can also take advantage of the RER (Réseau Express Régional), which connects the city itself to its many suburbs (les banlieues) and is a sort of cross between the Métro and a train. The four RER lines, labeled A, B, C, and D, service most of the surrounding communities. Tickets must be purchased at RER stations that sometimes overlap with Métro stations. In fact, a Métro ticket works on the RER for those stops that are within city limits.

Buses

In Paris, the network covered by green-and-white RATP buses (les bus) works very well in tandem with the Métro. More than two thousand buses crisscross the capital. Though the buses are often slowed down by traffic, they are also a very pleasant and comfortable way to travel and see the city at the same time. The buses use the same tickets as the Métro in Paris, though the total number of tickets to be canceled in the machine at the driver's side depends on the number of zones to be crossed. Bus stops are green-and-white shelters with benches; the inner wall of each stop lists the routes of the buses that pass in front of that stop. Inside each bus, there are also several maps of the route to be followed. Maps are also available free of charge in the Métro stations. Service is usually reduced on Sundays, holidays, and after 8:30 P.M. When traveling on the bus, you should push one of the signal buttons, located near the doors and windows, to indicate that you would like to get off.

In most other French cities and towns, the residents do not have the luxury of choosing between riding the métro or taking a bus. In the smaller cities, buses (known as les cars as opposed to les bus in Paris) and trams work quite well. Unfortunately, in small towns, the bus is all there is and often it is not worth much. If you are planning to live in a town or a village in a more rural setting, you will find that, much like in the United States, you cannot count on the bus network to get around. The lines are often designed around school hours and there may be one or two buses a day in each direction. I was once stranded in a small town in Brittany and had to wait four hours for a bus to take me to a town just a half an hour away. If you are going to be living somewhere *en provence*, it may be wise to think about acquiring some additional means of transportation, whether that be a bicycle, a scooter, or a car.

Trains

The French are very proud of their SNCF (Société Nationale des Chemins de fer Français)—the national railway, which covers every corner of *l'Hexagone*. The SNCF is the largest and farthest-reaching rail network in Europe with more than twenty thousand miles of rails. With the advent of the TGV *(trains à grande vitesse)*, France's high-speed trains that travel up to 300 kilometers per hour (kph) (190 mph), they have even more reason to be proud. Because France is so highly centralized around Paris, there are very few trains that cross the

Gare d'Austerlitz
Southwestern France, Spain, and Portugal
7, boulevard de l'Hôpital
75013 Paris
Tel: (01) 45 65 60 60
Gare de l'Est
Eastern France, Luxembourg, southern Germany, eastern Europe, northern Switzerland, and Austria
place du 8-mai-1945
75010 Paris
Tel: (01) 40 18 20 00
Gare de Lyon
Central, southern, and southeastern France, Italy, Switzerland, and the Alps
20, boulevard Diderot
75012 Paris
Tel: (01) 53 33 60 00
Gare Montparnasse
Western France
17, boulevard de Vaugirard
75015 Paris
Tel: (01) 40 48 10 00
Gare du Nord
Northern France, Belgium, Northern Germany, the Netherlands, and the United Kingdom
18, rue Dunkerque
75010 Paris
Tel: (01) 49 95 10 00
Gare Saint-Lazare
Northwestern France and the United Kingdom
108, rue Saint-Lazare
75008 Paris
Tel: (01) 53 42 00 00

country from city to city without passing through Paris. For example, to travel from Quimper in Brittany to Aix-en-Provence in the southeast, you must first go to Paris, change stations, and take another train for Aix. In fact, Paris is such a hub that it has no less than six railway stations *(gares)*, each serving a specific region of France.

All the stations are connected by *Métro*, of course!

There are three general categories of trains: local trains, *trains des grandes lignes* (long-distance trains), and the TGV high-speed trains.

You can recognize the record-holding TGV by its distinctive bullet shape and its bright orange or blue coloring. Because the TGV requires special tracks that enable the train to travel at an accelerated speed, it has taken some time to create a new network of railways. In fact, there was resistance to building the TGV in some of the wine-producing regions of France (like Bordeaux) because of fear that the high-speed train passing by would impact the aging of wine in many of the area's underground cellars. The SNCF has managed to overcome many such hurdles and the TGV now connects Paris to all the major cities in France, including Lille, Lyon, Marseille, and Bordeaux. It also connects Paris to Geneva and Lausanne, and in collaboration with a number of other private providers connects Paris to Brussels, Amsterdam, and—via the Channel Tunnel—to London (in just three hours). In fact many people prefer to take the train and arrive quickly and smoothly from one city center to the next, rather than fly and arrive in airports that are often inconveniently located on the periphery. It is important to remember, however, that to travel on the TGV, you must have a reservation in addition to your ticket.

BUYING A TICKET

You have several options when it comes to buying a ticket or making a reservation. The obvious option is to go to any train station, stand in the right line, and purchase your ticket and/or reservation. At most stations, you can also purchase tickets and reservations for shorter trips (under 100 km) by using the automatic ticketing machines, which accept coins and most credit cards.

Another extremely efficient option is to reserve or even purchase your ticket by Minitel. By dialing 3615 SNCF, you can access an automatic ticketing and reservation service that walks you through the process and leaves you with a code that you present at the station to pick up your ticket. In 1997, the SNCF introduced a service that enables travelers to receive train tickets delivered to their doorstep, if ordered at least four days in advance and paid for by bankcard. This is one of the safest ways to be sure that you have a seat and a ticket, if you do not have time to get to the station.

DISCOUNTS

Fares vary based on the day of the week and the hour of the day for all travel on the *grandes lignes*. Before planning a trip, take a look at the *Calendrier Voyageurs*, available at any train station, to plan your trip and save up to 50 percent on your fare. The SNCF also offers a number of impressive discounts for families, couples, young people, senior citizens, students, and those heading out on getaway weekends. It never hurts to ask the person helping you with your ticket if there is a less expensive way to make the same trip.

Before boarding, it is essential to remember to validate your ticket. In French this is called *composter le billet* and is done by inserting your ticket to be stamped with the date and time into yellow or orange boxes found at the beginning of the platform and in various other points in the station. The SNCF created this policy in response to a loss in profits as people were purchasing tickets, evading the conductor in the train if possible, and then requesting a refund with an unused ticket. If a conductor finds that you have not validated your ticket, you will have to pay a severe fine on the spot. As a foreigner, you may have some leeway by claiming ignorance, if you genuinely did forget to stamp your ticket, but I would not risk it intentionally. Eurail Passes are an exception to this rule and only need to be validated before the initial departure.

Planes

Air travel in France is still dominated by government-owned Air France and its internal sidekick Air Inter, though some international carriers have begun to make headway into the French national market in recent years. Though subject to sporadic but debilitating strikes, Air France and Air Inter connect most French cities with each other, and a number of the large cities with the rest of the world.

While the rates for domestic travel have been dropping, thanks to competition with the SNCF, Air France has not had much incentive to improve its international fares or service. You will find that traveling with Air France is generally one of the more expensive options. As in the United States, tickets can be purchased through travel agencies, at city ticketing offices, and at the airport. But as with train travel, tickets for Air France and Air Inter can also be reserved via the Minitel by dialing 3615 Air France.

Private Travel: The Open Road

Driving in France can be a real adventure, as anyone knows who has ever tried to navigate the place Charles-de-Gaulle, where twelve highly trafficked boulevards converge on the Arc de Triomphe. The French love to drive and more often than not seem to imagine themselves in some kind of Grand Prix as they speed along the *autoroutes* (highways) and even through small towns.

DRIVER'S LICENSE

If your stay in France will be short (less than one year), you may continue to use your American driver's license although you are advised to carry an International Driving Permit (issued by the AAA in the United States) or attach a French translation.

If you plan to drive in France for more than one year, you should begin thinking about getting a *permis de conduire*. In France, this is known to be a difficult and costly process. You must be at least eighteen. To begin the process, you must apply at the *préfecture de police* of your *département* to take the written and driving portions of the French license exam after one year of residence, although many people apply directly through a driving school *(auto-école)*. A list of some driving schools with English-speaking staff appears at the end of the chapter. A quick glance in the Yellow Pages under *"Auto-écoles"* will supply you with the numbers of schools closest to you. No matter how experienced a driver you may be, it is most likely in your best interest to attend an *auto-école* as both portions of the test are known to be difficult. The written test is dreaded because it is full of traps and tricks and the driving exam because examiners expect all maneuvers to be done according to French standards.

For a few lucky Americans, obtaining a French *permis de conduire* is a nonissue. Six American states—Illinois, New Hampshire, Kansas,

Michigan, South Carolina, and Kentucky—have signed agreements with France whereby persons with valid driver's licenses from these states can directly exchange their state license for a *permis*. To initiate the exchange, you must also go to your local *préfecture*.

ROAD ETIQUETTE

Because of the Grand Prix mentality, it is best to have some idea of the rules of the road before setting off on a journey or your daily commute. First of all, there are several main categories of roads. *Autoroutes* are France's superhighways. They are usually the fastest way to reach your destination but because they are run by private companies, they also charge hefty tolls. Blue signs with white letters indicate *autoroutes* along with the letter *A* followed by a number (for example, A1 or A72). In recent years, as European integration has progressed, some of the *autoroutes* have been identified by an *E* followed by a number (for example, E19). In any case, on most maps, the *autoroutes* are the highways drawn with the widest and usually multicolored lines. The theoretical speed limit on *autoroutes* is 130 kilometers per hour and you should keep to the right and reserve the left lane for passing cars.

Routes nationales (RN) are smaller state-run highways that cross the country. Traffic moves more slowly on the RN but they have more exits than the *autoroutes* and generally do not charge tolls. Signs for the RN are white with blue letters and the highways are identified by the letter *N* followed by a number (for example, N21 or N88). The RN tend to be more heavily congested than the *autoroutes* but often more pleasant as well. The posted speed limit is 90 kph.

The last major category of roads is the *routes départementales*, which are local, smaller roads connecting towns in the various *départements* of France. They can be identified by the letter *D* followed by a number (for example, D988 or D112) on a yellow background. The signs are also white with blue letters and these roads are generally the best way to see the French countryside. The speed limit on these roads is also 90 kph unless you are driving through towns or more residential areas where you are expected not to drive faster than 50 kph.

When driving, you should remember a few basic rules:

+ Seat belts are mandatory.
+ The car on the right always has the right of way in an intersection.

* Never pass on the right.
* The flashing of headlights from behind is a signal for you to move out of the way.
* Traffic in a rotary has the right of way (excluding of course place Charles-de-Gaulle in Paris, where driving is a free-for-all).

If you find that you would like more information on rules of the road, you should purchase the *Code de la Route*, which explains all the driving rules in France and is available in most bookstores.

Parking

Finding that ever-elusive parking space has become more and more of a challenge in Paris and other French cities. Though not quite as willing to flout the law as their Italian neighbors to the south, the French too are quite creative. In the cities, street parking is generally available in some areas and is often metered. To park in a metered spot, you purchase a ticket for a predetermined amount of time at a yellow (or gray) meter box (generally spread out every several hundred meters), which you then must display in your windshield. Parking in most cities is free from 7 P.M. until 9 A.M. and on Sundays.

You should always avoid parking on crosswalks or if you see signs stating *stationnement interdit* or *gênant* (parking forbidden or disturbing), or *livraisons* (deliveries). You risk a hefty fine or, worse still, being towed to a *fourrière* (tow yard), a very unpleasant experience.

If you join the club of the unfortunate and receive a parking ticket, you should pay it within one month to avoid regular increases in the fine—unless a presidential election is coming up soon, as an amnesty law traditionally passed after each presidential election cancels all outstanding parking tickets.

Buying a Car

If you are planning to live in France for less than one year, you can benefit from a French customs regulation that permits you to purchase a car duty-free, saving yourself the value-added tax. Such a purchase must be documented by the French Customs Office both before and after the sale. You will receive special license plates that will expire after one year and are not renewable. At this point, you will have to choose either to sell the car to another nonresident or to pay the value-added tax.

If, instead, you think you will need to have your own transportation on a long-term basis, you must not only pay duty but also follow all the standard steps for purchasing a car in France. The purchase (or sale) of any car must be registered with the local *préfecture*. If you buy a car from a dealer, they will handle the registration for you. The dealer will apply for permanent license plates and a *carte grise* (registration papers) for you. You will be asked to provide a copy of your *carte de séjour* and proof of residence. If, instead, you purchase a used car from an individual, the seller must hand over his *carte grise*, filling in your name instead of his, and supply you with a *certificat de vente* (proof of sale). You will have to register the car on your own by going to the *préfecture* and presenting the *carte grise, certificat de vente, carte de séjour*, and proof of residence, as well as an inspection certificate if the car is more than five years old. The *préfecture* will then issue you a new *carte grise* in your own name. In France, license plates move with the car unless they were issued in a different *département*. If you have moved the car from one *département* to another, you can have new plates made (with your new registration number) at almost any gas station.

Once you have purchased an automobile, you are also required to pay an annual circulation tax called *la vignette*. This tax, which is calculated according to the *puissance fiscale* (essentially the taxable horsepower of your car's engine) and indicated on your *carte grise*, can range from several hundred to several thousand francs. To pay this tax, you must go to any tobacconist *(tabac)* during the month of November (or to your Centre des Impôts all year long) and purchase the appropriate round sticker *(la vignette)*, which must be displayed at all times on the right-hand bottom corner of your windshield, much like American inspection stickers.

INSURANCE

French law requires that all automobiles must be covered by an unlimited third-party liability insurance policy and you must carry this *certificat d'assurance* (proof of insurance) with you in the car at all times and display it in your windshield near the *vignette*.

There are several documents that you must always keep in your

The TGV and advanced technology have made houses like this one, built for the person who was responsible for the crossing, obsolete. The SNCF has sold off most of these houses.

car: your driver's license, your *carte grise*, your *certificat d'assurance*, your *vignette*, and an accident form *(constat amiable d'accident)*, which your insurance company should provide you and which can be had in English. If you do have an accident in which no one has been hurt, you should not call the police but rather exchange with the other car or cars involved all the information required on the accident form. All the drivers involved should then send a copy of the form to their insurance company within twenty-four hours. The *constat amiable d'accident* is supposed to represent a "friendly" way to establish the dynamics and the liability in an accident but it is also binding. Be sure that you agree with all that is written before signing.

Car insurance is much more expensive in France than in the United States. Be sure to shop around and check on premiums before you buy a car, as prices vary widely depending on the make and model you choose. A good driving record will help reduce your rates. You receive a 5 percent discount for each consecutive claim-free year you've had, up to 50 percent. Ask your previous insurers for documentation to show to the French insurer.

Useful Addresses

SOME DRIVING SCHOOLS IN PARIS

Auto-école Bonne Conduite
4, place de la Pte-de-Bagnolet
75020 Paris
Tel. (01) 40 30 10 66
Auto-école Duroc
2, rue St-Jean-Baptiste-de-la-Salle
75006 Paris
Tel. (01) 45 66 77 70
Auto-Moto École
15, rue du Mont-Doré
75017 Paris
Tel. (01) 43 87 88 26
C.E.S.R.
25, rue Descombes
75017 Paris
Tel (01) 43 80 17 00
E.C.F. Levallois
103, rue Aristide-Briand
92300 Levallois
Tel: (01) 47 37 90 88
Fehrenbach Driving School
53, boulevard Henri-Sellier
92150 Suresnes
Tel. (01) 45 06 31 17
(for English-speakers only)
International Permis
62, boulevard Voltaire
75011 Paris
Tel. (01) 47 00 54 90
International Permis
63, Saint-Germain, 6th
75020 Paris
Tel. (01) 43 26 52 49

NATIONAL INSURANCE PROVIDERS
FOR AUTOMOBILES AND
MOTORCYCLES

Advantage Insurance Associates
17, rue de Châteaudun
75009 Paris

Tel. (01) 53 20 03 33
Fax. (01) 44 63 00 97
Eurofil
3, rue Eugène et Armand Peugeot
B.P. 200
92500 Rueil-Malmaison
Tel (01) 47 14 59 00
GAN
2, rue Pillet-Will
75448 Paris Cedex 09
Tel: (01) 42 47 50 00
Lloyd Continental
104, rue de Richelieu
75002 Paris
Tel: (01) 40 20 65 65
M.A.A.F.
10, boulevard Beaumarchais
75003 Paris
Tel. (08) 03 80 32 00
Fax. (01) 43 14 46 00
Xxarr Assurances
42, avenue Ste-Foy
92200 Neuilly-sur-Seine
Tel: (01) 46 43 88 00

PUBLIC TRANSPORTATION

SNCF
General train information·
Tel: (08) 36 67 68 69
Reservations.
Tel. (08) 36 35 35 35
(English-speaking operators available
upon request)
Web site. http.//www.sncf.fr
RATP Travel Assistance
For travel advice 24 hours a day.
Tel: (08) 36 68 77 14
Multilingual information.
Tel. (08) 36 68 41 14

Renoir, Rimbaud, et Côtes-du-Rhône: *Making the Most of French Cultural and Sports-Related Offerings*

If you've made it this far, you've moved to France, found a place to live, and settled in. Perhaps you've found a job or perhaps you've started studying. But you have been looking around for some ways to take advantage of your new home during your free time. Well, it is time to start making the most of French cultural and sports-related offerings.

Chances are that part of what inspired you to come to France was related to an interest in some aspect of French culture, whether it was art, architecture, or fine dining. Now that you are living in France, taking a continuing education course is a great way to gain a better understanding of what you love about France and a great way to get to make new acquaintances and expand your network of friends. The same holds true for participating in some of the athletic opportunities available in France, both in cities and in the countryside.

For opportunities with French organizations, it is best to contact your *mairie* or the institution directly to see whether courses in your area of interest are available. To find out what opportunities are available in English, check the English-language publications and bulletin boards in English or the American churches, bookshops, and other stores and ask around. An extensive listing of opportunities we have discovered can be found at the end of the chapter.

The Eiffel Tower

Art

France has some of the largest and most famous museums in the world. Visiting them should be a priority during the time you live there. Beyond visiting museums, opportunities abound to benefit from your proximity to great works of art and vibrant artistic communities. In Paris, the École du Louvre offers a variety of programs in art history, including a three-year degree course in Art History and Archaeology and a series of introductory art history lectures. Classes at the Louvre start in the fall and run through the spring. Museums in provincial cities like Avignon, Reims, Lyon, and Aix offer lecture and film series as well.

Numerous cultural organizations and institutes offer courses in disciplines ranging from bookbinding to trompe l'oeil painting and photography. The American Parsons School of Design offers a variety of courses in both applied and fine arts. Courses can be taken toward a Bachelor of Fine Arts degree in conjunction with Parsons School of Design in New York. Evening continuing education classes are also offered.

Music and Dance

Music lovers will find numerous occasions to satisfy their musical appetites in France. Each year Paris hosts the Fête de la Musique, which brings together musicians of all genres from around the country and around the world. In the late 1980s, Paris built the Cité de la Musique. The Cité, an enormous all-white complex, holds a concert hall, a library, studios, and a museum and was built to promote the study and development of music.

The French love music and generally find unusual ways to celebrate with music. Beyond the obvious classical and modern concerts and shows in theaters, opera houses, concert halls, and stadiums, music in France has thrived in unusual venues. Keep your eyes peeled for posters announcing chamber music or choral concerts in the local church or cathedral.

Most of the larger cities have a conservatory for students of music. Some offer evening classes to the public. They are often good resources for finding music teachers. For those who love to sing, many of the English-language churches have choirs.

Dance is popular in France, too. Even the smallest towns have schools to teach classical and modern dance to children and adults. One national school of dance is located in Montpellier. The Centre Chorégraphique National de Montpellier is housed in an ancient convent. Instructors offer courses for advanced and professional dancers five days a week.

On a lighter note, in my own experience, I've learned that the French love to dance at parties, as well. They specifically love to dance *le Rock*, a combination of swing and rock and roll, which adapts itself to nearly every type of music, from blues to rock to hip-hop to rap. In Lyon, the Swing Dance Club offers introductory, intermediate, and advanced dancing classes and also organizes social events each week.

Wine Appreciation and Cooking Courses

If your love of French wine and cuisine inspired your move to France, then you should avail yourself of the numerous opportunities to learn more about both. Many American churches and cultural organizations arrange wine tastings and excursions to vineyards in Bordeaux and Burgundy. If you don't happen upon an organized tour, it is worth it to amble off to see the rolling vineyards in the different French wine countries on your own. Even the smallest vineyard will generally offer a tasting if you just ring the bell, although it is considered more polite to call ahead if you are going to descend on the vineyard with a large group. Tastings are generally free of charge although it is appropriate to purchase several bottles of wine, more if you liked the wine of course.

Paris is home not only to some of the world's finest restaurants but also to some of the most famous cooking schools. The most famous of these is Le Cordon Bleu, which has a menu of courses ranging from daily demonstrations to the nine-month *grand cycle*. The cooking school at the Ritz Escoffier specializes in French classical and contemporary cuisine. The school offers diploma programs for serious students, and workshops, demonstrations, and wine tastings for visitors.

Sports

Even though the fashion of fitness is beginning to take hold in France, the French are not as athletic as Americans. As a culture, they don't like to be seen working too hard at anything, let alone working out. They still look askance at Americans who insist on jogging in the city, and bicycles have not taken off as a mode of transportation. There are some sports that have taken off, including skiing, tennis, and swimming (especially among women), and the whole concept of going to the gym is becoming more and more acceptable.

To find out what athletic opportunities are available in your city, you should check with your local *mairie*. The city hall generally manages a

Watching the opening ceremonies for the 1998 World Cup at place de la Concorde in Paris

swimming pool and municipal tennis courts and organizes lessons and classes for adults and children in the area.

Most sports also have a national *fédération*, divided into regional leagues. You can contact the *fédération* for the sport you are interested in to get information about teams, competitions, and other opportunities.

As the French become more and more accustomed to working out in a gym, health clubs are springing up at top speed. To begin searching for a gym, look in the local Yellow Pages under *"Clubs de Remise en Forme."* If you would like a full listing of health clubs, contact the Fédération Française d'Education Physique et de Gymnastique Volontaire. Some of the larger chains, including Gymnase Club and Vitatop, can be found around the country.

France also has a unique program for young people interested in learning and practicing sports. UCPA—which stands for Union des Centres de Plein Air (Union of Fresh Air Centers)—offers hundreds of reasonably priced courses all around the world in a range of sports. For more information, contact them and ask for their catalog. The address can be found at the end of the chapter.

Useful Addresses

While many of the listings below are for Paris, the programs may be able to supply information about offerings in other cities.

ARTS

École du Louvre
34, quai du Louvre
75001 Paris
Tel. (01) 55 35 18 35
Centre des Arts du Livre et de l'Estampe
63, rue de Monceau
75008 Paris
Tel: (01) 45 63 54 10
(courses in bookbinding and framing)
Cours Renaissance
286, rue de Noisy-le-Sec
93170 Bagnolet
Tel: (01) 48 97 00 85
(extensive courses in trompe l'oeil and decorative painting)
École Lesage
13, rue de la Grange-Batelière
75009 Paris
Tel. (01) 48 24 14 20
(school of embroidery)
École Nationale Supérieure des Beaux-Arts
17, quai Malaquais
75005 Paris
Tel: (01) 42 34 97 00
École Nationale Supérieure des Arts Décoratifs
31, rue d'Ulm
75006 Paris
Tel: (01) 43 29 97 00
(courses in decorative arts)
IESA (Institut des Études Supérieures des Arts)
5, avenue de l'Opéra
75001 Paris
Tel: (01) 42 86 57 01
(courses in antique and art gallery businesses)

PSF (Photography Studies in France)
8, rue Jules-Vallès
75011 Paris
Tel: (01) 40 09 18 58
Parsons School of Design—Paris
14, rue Letellier
75015 Paris
Tel: (01) 45 77 39 66
Paris Fashion Institute
Tel: (617) 268-0026
(month-long course in fashion and merchandising)
Paris American Academy
9, rue des Ursulines
75005 Paris
Tel: (01) 44 41 99 20
(courses in interior design, fine arts, and fashion)

MUSIC, DRAMA, AND DANCE

Conservatoire National Supérieur de Musique et de Danse de Paris
209, avenue Jean-Jaurès
75019 Paris
Tel: (01) 40 40 45 45
Acting International/Actors Studios
55, rue des Alouettes
75019 Paris
Tel: (01) 42 00 06 79
Académie du Gospel
Tel: (01) 48 87 12 14
(courses in gospel music)
Centre Chorégraphique National de Montpellier
Les Ursulines
boulevard Louis-Blanc
34000 Montpellier
Tel: (04) 67 60 06 70
Lyon Swing Dance Club
42, rue Professeur-Patel

69009 Lyon
Tel: (04) 78 36 65 97

COOKING AND WINE APPRECIATION

CIDD (Centre Information
Documentation et Dégustation)
30, rue de la Sablière
75014 Paris
Tel: (01) 45 45 44 20
Le Cordon Bleu
8, rue Léon-Delhomme
75015 Paris
Tel: (01) 53 68 22 50
Ritz Escoffier Cooking School
39, rue Cambon
75001 Paris
Tel: (01) 43 16 30 50
La Varenne
Château du Fey
89300 Villecien
Tel: (03) 86 63 18 34
(located in Burgundy)
Paris American Academy
9, rue des Ursulines
75005 Paris
Tel: (01) 44 41 99 20
(offers cooking classes in collaboration
with the École Supérieure de Cuisine
Française)

SPORTS

UCPA (Union National des Centres
Sportifs de Plein Air)
62, rue de la Glacière
75013 Paris
Tel: (01) 45 87 45 87
BASEBALL:
Baseball Club de France
29, rue de La Quintinie
75015 Paris
BASKETBALL.
Fédération Française de Basketball
117, rue Château des Rentiers
75013 Paris
Tel: (01) 53 94 25 00

CYCLING:
Fédération Française de Cyclisme
5, rue de Rome
92561 Roisny-sous-Bois
Tel: (01) 49 35 69 00
AMERICAN FOOTBALL:
Fédération Française de Football
Américain
13 bis, avenue de Général-Galliéni
92000 Nanterre
Tel: (01) 47 29 22 03
HORSEBACK RIDING.
Fédération Française d'Equitation
30, avenue d'Iéna
75116 Paris
Tel. (01) 53 67 43 43
SAILING.
Fédération Française de Voile
55, avenue Kléber
75116 Paris
Tel: (01) 44 05 81 00
SOCCER:
Fédération Française de Football
60 bis, avenue d'Iéna
75116 Paris
Tel. (01) 44 31 73 00
SWIMMING:
Fédération Française de Natation
148, avenue Gambetta
75020 Paris
Tel: (01) 40 31 17 70
(additionally, most towns and cities have
municipal pools)
TENNIS:
Fédération Française de Tennis
Stade Roland-Garros
2, avenue Gordon-Bennett
75016 Paris
Tel. (01) 47 43 48 00

La Vie Virtuelle: *Navigating French Cyberspace*

France has a long history of innovation and leadership in high technology. Although the country initially resisted the Internet and World Wide Web, today there is a thriving Internet sector in France with thousands of technology companies vying to be the French version of an Amazon.com, MSN, or Netscape. Like Silicon Valley in northern California, and New York City's "Silicon Alley," France has sometimes claimed the title of "Silicon Riviera," with its high concentration of technology companies in and around Nice, Marseille, and along the Côte d'Azur.

Today French is the second language of the Internet and there are tens of thousands of Web sites dedicated to providing information and services targeted toward France. It is becoming just as common to see Web addresses advertised on television and other media in France as it is in the United States, and many of the country's businesses and media have begun to publish information and sell goods and services over the Web. Once skeptical of the Internet and its development as a "new form of American colonialism" (as one French minister said in 1997), France has clearly cast its doubts aside and has taken steps to embrace the information superhighway on a national level. Signaling the end of its government-led ignorance and avoidance, France celebrated, for the first time, its "Fête de l'Internet," a two-day national celebration of the Internet, in March 1998. Since then, the French government has dedicated billions of francs to help fund more than five hundred local and national initiatives to promote the advancement of the Internet in France, help schools get on-line, and educate the population.

The Internet has also opened up a whole world of information that had been previously inaccessible or difficult to find. Most of France's government agencies have established in-depth Web sites, and there are thousands of publicly searchable databases available on-line, providing everything from educational resources to information about regional weather patterns. Just about anything you can find in English on the Web, you can also find in French, and vice versa. This goes for French government Web sites also: most pages can be navigated in either French or English.

In order to provide you with the most up-to-date information about the French Internet, we've created a Web site. At **www.liveinfrance.com** you can find regularly updated links to many of the organizations we list here.

France's Information Legacy, the Minitel

France has had its own internal information network, in the form of the ubiquitous Minitel, since the early 1980s. The Minitel is a simple videotext terminal that sits next to telephones in residences and businesses across France with which people can access thousands of fee-based information services. Because the Minitel was distributed by France Télécom, the country's national telephone company, as a complement to standard telephone service for a small additional charge, the Minitel found its way into more than seven million French households. Today, more than 80 percent of the country's businesses and more than 20 percent of its households have a Minitel. Although the Minitel terminal is slow, does not support graphics, and is very limited in its functionality, its ubiquity made its services the default "Internet" of France. The Minitel quickly became a wildly successful business. Minitel addresses (many of which begin with "3615," denoting a fee-based service) are advertised in France with the same enthusiasm as toll-free 800 numbers are in the United States. The Minitel was the world's first—and still the world's only—example of a successful mass-market network venture. While many of the most "successful" Web sites (such as Amazon.com) in the United States had yet to turn a profit by the end of 1998, the Minitel and its services have been a source of revenue in France for more than a decade.

Connecting to the Internet in France

There are about as many ways to connect to the Internet in France as there are in the United States. How you connect should depend on a number of factors including what types of services you will need and how long you're planning on living in France. The most important thing to consider is your Internet service provider (ISP), called a *fournisseur d'accès*. If you've got an account in the United States with one of the major on-line services like America Online or CompuServe, you can access your account in France via a local dial-up access number. If not, you will want to open an account with one of the many local French service providers. Most *fournisseurs d'accès* offer basic Internet access for about FF100 per month, which usually includes some amount of space on their servers for a personal Web site, your own E-mail address, and local access numbers in Paris and the major cities. Many U.S. ISPs will offer E-mail forwarding for a small fee, so if you have an E-mail address established in the United States, you can switch over gradually to your French one or continue to maintain both. Web-based E-mail services, offered for free by Yahoo!, Microsoft's Hotmail, and others, are also a good way to maintain a consistent E-mail address, and allow you to access your E-mail from any computer in the world that has an Internet connection and a Web browser. It is usually possible to configure a Web-based E-mail account to check mail for you if you have one or more other E-mail addresses, so you can read all your E-mail from one site. The list at the end of this chapter provides a short list of French ISPs, and you can sign up for Web-based E-mail from any computer with a Web browser.

The following sections outline a wide variety of resources and services offered on the Web for those interested in France. Please keep in mind that this chapter serves as an overview of Web sites at the time of publication. Because the Web is constantly changing, and new sites, new technologies, and new possibilities are popping up on an almost daily basis, this chapter serves merely as a snapshot of France-based resources at a specific time. Check with your favorite sites often, as they will certainly be changing and expanding to include new information and services as the Web matures. One more item of note: The national extension for Web sites based in France is ".fr" but many French sites also use the American system of ".com." Just because the Web address ends in ".com" does not mean that the server is based in the United States or is administered by an American company.

French Government and Official Sites: Making Daily Life Easier

The French government, which once looked at the Internet as a major threat to French language and culture, has become one of the most wired governments in Europe and the world. Every level of French government has embraced the Web, from the president of the Republic and the prime minister down to the smallest villages and communes. The Ministry of Culture and Communications in France maintains a drab, yet detailed Web site that provides links to hundreds of local and regional Web sites throughout France, as well as to all of the other government sites. More than fifty of France's largest cities have official Web sites, and there are descriptions of more than thirty-six thousand communities throughout France. The official city of Paris Web site, for example, has information about health and social operations, employment and training, the environment, culture and education, planning and housing policy, city government offices, and farmers' markets. The Ministry of Culture site is, in fact, one of the most interesting sites available, with information about everything from archaeology to law, to television and theater. It provides dozens of publicly searchable databases that contain information about millions of works of art and monuments, book and film library collections, images, and documents. The Ministry of Culture site provides links to all of the country's major museums and cultural institutions, including:

* The Louvre (www.louvre.fr). The Louvre site provides a way to buy tickets on-line and includes a virtual tour, in which you can view thousands of images from the museum's vast collections.
* The Musée d'Orsay (www.musee-orsay.fr). Includes detailed

information about many of the works of art in the museum's collection, as well as information about expositions, concerts, film festivals, and conferences.

* The Musée Rodin (www.musee-rodin.fr). Includes information and images about the museum's collections, a virtual tour of the gardens, and a history of the artist whom the museum celebrates.
* The Centre Georges Pompidou (www.cnac-gp.fr). Has an online multimedia revue called Tr@verses, as well as information about the modern art museum's collections, libraries, and visiting exhibits.
* The Château de Versailles (www.chateauversailles.fr). Offers panoramic images (using Quicktime VR technology) of the château and its grounds, as well as detailed information about the history, art, and architecture of the château.

Commercial and Individual Web Sites

There are tens of thousands of commercial Web sites offered in and about France. Unlike many of the government and official sites, most commercial sites are published only in French, although if you have a basic understanding of the language and brush up on a few useful terms associated with the Web, you'll be able to navigate through a wealth of information and services easily. Most Web sites have *actualités* (news) sections, one or more *bases de données* (databases), and information on weather *(météo)*. They may offer a subscription *(abonnement)*.

LES PAGES ZOOM (WWW.PAGESZOOM.COM)

The Pages Zoom Web site, sponsored by France Télécom, is an incredibly useful and interesting site, with on-line yellow and white pages for all of France, information on tourism, and links to other popular sites. The most interesting feature of Les Pages Zoom is its virtual walking tour of the entire city of Paris. You can navigate through an interactive database of more than 350,000 photographs of streets and buildings throughout the city. You type in a specific address and see a picture of the building located there, or plop yourself down somewhere on the city map and "wander" through the photos of the city.

Paris Anglophone (www.paris-anglo.com)

The Paris Anglophone is sponsored by the publisher of the book with the same name, a very complete and useful cultural and practical guide for Anglophones living in Paris. The site includes information on housing in France, links to the *Paris Free Voice* and other English-language publications (including *Frank*, the highly respected international literary journal published by the same company that publishes *Paris Anglophone*), and a directory to English-speaking Paris that so far includes more than 4,200 listings of services, businesses, and useful contacts for the expatriate community.

Paris France Guide (www.parisfranceguide.com)

Through a partnership between Europe Online and France Télécom, this site provides a wealth of cultural and practical information about Paris, including sections on living in France, studying in France, what's on in France, museums, waterways, and interviews.

Tennessee Bob's Famous French Links

This site (www.utm.edu/departments/french/french.html) may not be the most beautiful site in the world, but it includes more than seven thousand links to useful and popular French Web sites. The links are divided into the following categories: new Francophone sites; books and literature; art, music, film, and culture; history of France and the French-speaking world; virtual Francophone tourism; the French language; press, radio/TV, and telephone; education in French schools; and French in everyday life.

Search Engines

Most of the well-known U.S.-based search engines have extended their services in French with an eye to French sites. As in the United States, one of the most visited sites is the Yahoo! France portal site, which works just as the American Yahoo! site does. Through co-branding and partnership arrangements, much of the information that you'd find on a specific French news site can also be found on the various portal sites like Yahoo!, Lycos, Excite, and Infoseek. All of these sites provide similar services, although search results generally differ slightly from search engine to search engine. There are also a few French search engines that provide similar services to the U.S.-sponsored ones. Some

of the more popular French search engines include écila (www.ecila.
fr), Nomade (www.nomade.fr), and Lokace (www.lokace.fr).

News and Politics

There are many sources for news and political information on the Web.
All the major French media outlets have Web sites that provide extensive information about news and current events, politics, culture, and
society. Most major newspapers are available to read on-line, including
Libération (www.liberation.fr), *Le Monde* (www.lemonde.fr), *Le Figaro*
(www.lefigaro.fr), and even *Le Canard Enchaîné* (www.multimania.com/
lecanard). Some of them also have searchable archives and links to cultural sites of interest. In addition, many of the regional newspapers and
other media have Web sites as well. A quick search on one of the main
French search engines will return a complete list of French journalistic
enterprises on the Web. The main French radio and television stations
all have complementary Web sites as well.

Web 'Zines

As in the United States, there are thousands of independent Web 'zines
that exist in France, some of which provide interesting information and
entertainment. The (Virtual) Baguette (www.baguette.com) has regular
columns and sections on music, television, science fiction, games, car-
toons, and links to other interesting sites. Les Grenouilles Câblée ("the
wired frogs"; www.frogs.com) is an all-French site produced in San
Jose, California, in the heart of Silicon Valley, that is a virtual community for French people and Francophones in the United States and in
France. Nirvanet (www.nirvanet.fr) calls itself a "global network for
local nomads." It includes artistic and informational pages in English,
French, Spanish, and Japanese. You can access hip games, music, and
short video clips.

Wine and Food

Fromages.com, the cheese site (www.fromages.com), is a celebration of
France's cheese. The site includes a library of cheese, arranged by type
of milk, detailed instruction on the proper cutting of cheese, and interesting facts and information about all kinds of French cheese. Epicuria

(www.epicuria.fr) has tremendous amounts of information on French wine and food. You can order regional specialties, consult recipes, and read about seasonal products and local initiatives. Web-dinner (www.web-dinner.com) has a database of hundreds of restaurants in France that offer home delivery.

Transportation and Travel

Both the RATP (the agency that runs Paris's *Métro* system) and the SNCF (the French national railway system) have useful Web sites. The RATP site provides constantly updated information about *Métro* service in the city, delays, construction, and information about the new automated *météor* line. The SNCF site allows you to research and purchase rail tickets on the SNCF and to destinations outside France.

If you're looking for information on budget travel, there are literally hundreds of Web sites that can help you. Traveloco (www.traveloco.com) maintains a database of hundreds of hostels around the world, and has information on and can book you in more than 190 in France alone. It also provides maps, currency converters, weather information, and travel advisories for backpackers and budget travelers.

Finding General Information

The European Union maintains a Web site that includes sections on traveling, living, studying, and working in the EU. You can find links to each of these sections at www.cec.org.uk/pubs/facts/fact9701/. The site contains information about visa and residence requirements, schools and universities, finances, educational programs, retirement, voting, cars and transportation, and much more. The main European Union site can be found at www.europa.eu.int.

There is also a wide variety of Europe-wide search engines and Web resources. Some of the more notable ones include Euroseek (www.euroseek.net), which allows you to search the Web in more than forty languages, and limit the region where you would like to search. Euroferret (www.euroferret.com) indexes more than 30 million European Web pages and allows you to search them in one of five languages and limit the search to one of more than forty countries. YellowWeb (www.yweb.com) is another European search engine of note.

Useful Addresses

For the most current information about living, studying, and working in France, visit the Web site complement to this book at **www.liveinfrance.com.**

AMERICAN INTERNET SERVICES ACCESSIBLE IN FRANCE

America Online
Tel: (01) 69 19 94 50
Web site: http://www.aol.fr
CompuServe
Tel: (01) 21 13 49 49
Web site: http://www.go.compuserve.fr

MAJOR FRENCH INTERNET SERVICE PROVIDERS AND WEB HOSTING SERVICES

@ccès Internet
26, quai Claude-Bernard
69007 Lyon
Tel: (04) 78 58 99 19
Web site. http://www.accesinternet.com
Activnet
95867 Cergy-Pontoise Cedex
Tel: (01) 34 46 70 50
Fax: (01) 34 46 70 51
E-mail: info@activnet.fr
Web site: http://www.activnet.fr
AlmaNet
8, rue Dupont-des-Loges
75007 Paris
Tel: (01) 44 18 70 70
Fax: (01) 44 18 70 87
E-mail. info@alma-net.net
Web site: http.//www.alma-net.net
PSINet France/CalvaCom
8-10, rue Nieuport
78140 Vélizy
Tel: (01) 34 63 19 19
Fax: (01) 34 63 19 48
Web site: http://www.calvacom.fr
ClaraNET
68, rue du Faubourg-St-Honoré
75008 Paris

Tel: (01) 70 91 21 40
Fax: (01) 70 91 21 01
Web site: http://www.claranet.fr
Club-Internet
Grolier Interactive Europe / Online Groupe
11, rue de Cambrai
75927 Paris Cedex 19
Tel: 08 01 80 09 00
Web site: http://www.club-internet.fr
Cyber Café
Tel: (01) 39 64 16 73
E-mail: cyber@cyber.fr
Web site: http://www.cyber.fr
Direct Provider
23, rue du Départ
75014 Paris
E-mail: sales@directprovider.net
Web site: http://www.DirectProvider.net
EasyNet
23, rue du Renard
75004 Paris
Tel: (01) 44 54 53 33
Fax: (01) 44 54 53 39
Web site: http://www.easynet.fr
EUNet
1, rond-point Victor-Hugo
92137 Issy-Les-Moulineaux Cedex
Tel: (01) 41 09 60 60
Fax: (01) 40 95 16 10
E-mail: contact@EUnet.fr
Web site. http://www.France.eu.net
France Explorer
Tel: (04) 72 83 10 00
Web site: http://www.France-explorer.com
France Télécom/Transpac
(10 locations throughout France)
Agence Île-de-France
8, place du Maréchal-Juin
92136 Issy-Les-Moulineaux Cedex
Tel: (01) 41 23 92 19
Fax: (01) 41 23 92 20

Web site:
http://www.transpac.francetelecom.fr
Hor@Net
8, rue René-Coty
85007 La Roche-sur-Yon
Tel: (02) 51 62 68 14
Fax: (02) 51 62 68 21
Web site: http://www.horanet.fr
ICOR
228, rue Paul Gidon–Z. I. Bissy
73000 Chambéry
Tel: (04) 79 25 19 19
Fax: (04) 79 25 17 25
Web site: http://www.icor.fr
Imaginet
21, rue de la Fontaine-au-Roi
75011 Paris
Tel: (01) 53 36 66 00
Fax: (01) 43 38 42 62
Web site: http://www.imaginet.fr
Imp@ctNet
C.D. 158
78930 Guerville
Tel: (01) 30 42 64 00
Fax: (01) 30 93 92 34
E-mail: info@impact-net.com
Web site: http://www.impact-net.com
Infonie/Rega
Tour Kupka B
92906 Nanterre
Tel: (08) 03 07 50 66
Fax: (01) 41 02 80 01
Web site: http://www.rega.net
Internet Solutions
52, rue Étienne-Marcel
75002 Paris
Tel: (01) 55 34 97 97
Fax: (01) 55 34 97 98
Web site: http://www.starnet.fr

Magic OnLine
45, rue de la Procession
75015 Paris
Tel: (01) 53 69 54 59
Fax: (01) 53 69 54 56
Web site: http://www.magic.fr
Micronet
28, rue Desaix
75015 Paris
Tel: (01) 43 92 12 12
Fax: (01) 43 92 12 13
E-mail: bienvenue@micronet.fr
Web site: http://www.MicroNet.fr
Oleane/France Télécom
(Many locations throughout France)
Les Collines de l'Arche
Immeuble Opéra C
92057 Paris–La Défense Cedex
Tel: (01) 47 67 77 77
Web site: http://www.oleane.fr
Planete.net
5-7, rue Raspail
93100 Montreuil
Tel: (01) 49 88 65 00
Fax: (01) 49 88 75 15
Web site: http://www.planete.net
UUNet/MCI WorldCom
Le Clemenceau 2
215, avenue Georges-Clemenceau
92000 Nanterre
Tel: (01) 56 38 22 00
Fax. (01) 56 38 22 01
E-mail: info@fr.uu.net
Web site: http://www.fr.uu.net
Wanadoo/France Télécom
Tel: (08) 01 10 51 05
Web site: http://www.wanadoo.fr

Studying

CHAPTER TWELVE

Student Life

Studying abroad in France can be an incredibly rewarding experience. In fact, other than working, there is probably no better way to really get to know France—its people, its culture, and its language. Many European universities have a very international flavor. When I studied abroad during my junior year in college, I met students from all over Europe and all over the world. Because of France's colonial history, the French universities have a particularly diverse student body. Each year, France welcomes some 120,000 foreign students, which puts it in third place worldwide, behind the United States and Great Britain. With the exception of some restricted faculties (e.g., medicine), most programs in France have at least 10 percent international students.

While studying abroad, you will have the chance to learn French, and in many cases to take classes in a foreign language. You will make new friends and view the world from a new perspective and your eyes will open to the fact that the American college experience is unique in many ways. University life in France is very different from life on an American college campus.

Despite these many differences, or perhaps because of them, each year several thousand American college students spend time abroad at a French university. If you have decided that you would like to join them, you have a number of decisions to make. You will need to do some research as to where you would like to go, what kind of housing is best for your needs, and how to deal with stress abroad.

Deciding Where to Go

The decision of where to go will be based in large part on whether you decide to attend one of the many programs in France sponsored and recognized by American universities or opt to matriculate directly into one of the French universities. Most French cities have a university and Paris has nearly several dozen institutions of higher learning. The city you choose will depend on where in France you would most like to live as well as your own academic needs. Although most American students matriculate in one of the Parisian faculties or in historic Aix-en-Provence, the options are endless. The next few chapters address the advantages and disadvantages of both types of experiences and provide practical information on how to apply and enroll.

Where to Live

Finding a place to live while studying abroad in France is not necessarily as straightforward as it would be to set up house at an American college or university.

DORMITORIES

Traditionally, many French university students live at home while they complete their studies. Students prefer this both for the economic advantages living with their parents offers as well as the emotional support. For this reason, it is not standard policy for the university to provide students with housing on campuses in dormitories, as we know them. In fact, most French universities do not even have an American-style campus. While some universities have some residence facilities, they are often reserved for grant recipients. A number of the larger universities have arrangements to provide accommodation for international students who have matriculated in the traditional way, as well as international students who are spending a year abroad. One example in Paris is the Fondation des États-Unis, which provides lodging and cultural facilities to American graduate students, professors, and researchers. It is located in the Cité Internationale Universitaire de Paris and has 270 single rooms.

Often, even if the university itself does not own housing or dormitories, it may still have a housing office to help students, both national and international, find places to live. To better understand all of the available housing options, you should check with the university and the specific faculty you are planning to attend.

LIVING WITH A FRENCH FAMILY

Many American study abroad programs arrange for their students to find housing in the homes of French families. Living with a French family can be one of the best ways to immerse yourself in French culture and learn the language. If you live in a dorm for international students or on your own, you will not have the same opportunities to improve your language skills and see what life in a French family is like. Often the family will provide you with a bed and one or more meals a day. While experiences vary greatly, many American students report forming lasting bonds with their host families who take them in as one of their own, inviting them on trips and showing them the best of French life.

While this closeness can be culturally enriching, many American students who are used to having their independence on the college campus also find the host family experience a bit suffocating.

Before agreeing to live with a host family, it is important to understand the coordinating organization's procedures for changing families if you are unhappy. You should not feel that you have to stay in a situation that is not working out. Most organizations are extremely accommodating and understanding of the fact that the first match may not always be the best for both sides.

RENTING AN APARTMENT AND LIVING WITH OTHER STUDENTS

There are a number of resources for students who are looking to rent apartments or live with other students. If you are studying at or affiliated with a French university, the first of these is, of course, the student housing office. University housing offices generally keep lists of people who want to rent rooms or small apartments to students as well as lists of other students who are seeking roommates. Housing seekers can also turn to the classified ads both in French newspapers and in the English-language publications mentioned in Chapter 17.

Finally, another resource for students seeking housing are bulletin boards located in university cafeterias, libraries, and other common spaces, as well as in churches and bookstores.

In choosing whether to live with other American or English-speaking classmates or French students you will have to take a number of factors into consideration. If learning French is your priority, then you should think very seriously about living with French students. Even though it can be comforting to live with people who understand you effortlessly, the language benefits will differ dramatically between the two different arrangements.

Because of the potential for cultural differences and misunderstandings, if you choose to live with French students, it is even more important than it would be in the United States to be extremely clear about expectations and house rules.

Making the Most of Your Time Abroad

As a student living overseas, you are in an incredibly fortunate position. You have far more discretion over how you spend your time than an American working in France. You will have free blocks of time during the day with which to explore your new home. You will have long vacations, especially if you stay for an entire academic year, in which to travel. And you will have the opportunity to get to know and socialize with a large number of French young people outside of the constraints that govern professional behavior.

WHAT TO DO WITH THAT FREE TIME

Once you have settled into an academic routine, you may find that you have some free time during the day. Back home on your American campus, you would have been involved in a sport or a student group. Or perhaps you would have had an internship. Well, there is no reason you cannot do any of these things as a student abroad. For more information on activities and how to get involved, see Chapter 10, "Making the Most of French Cultural and Sports-Related Offerings," and Chapter 24, "Internships and Volunteering." As a student, you have a unique visa status and are legally allowed to work part-time as an intern.

You also have a unique opportunity to improve your language skills. You may want to sign up for an additional language course. Whenever

Students gathered on the steps of the Opéra

possible, seek out the company of French speakers. And you should do your best to read a daily paper, go to the cinema, and watch French television.

TRAVEL

Because of the different exam schedules, American students at European universities often find themselves with a lot of free time on their hands. Many of them see the long "studying" vacations as the perfect block of time to take off on a French or European holiday. People spend years discovering the beauty of France, and Amsterdam, London, Geneva, and Milan are all within four hours by train.

Travel does not have to be expensive, either. There are all sorts of advantageous rates offered by Air France, SNCF, and the other European railways. Air France offers special youth rates on airfare. The French railway SNCF also has discounted rates for young people who want to travel within France and Europe by train. Youth hostels are inexpensive and filled with young people from around the world.

Socializing

Living among students is one of the best ways to get to know French people up close. French students are very welcoming of their foreign counterparts and interaction is not governed by the rules and etiquette that surround professional relationships. French students know how to enjoy life and in most towns and cities there are numerous opportunities to socialize. Different student groups tend to frequent different cafés and bars during the day and at night. Once you have found a group of friends, you may find that you, too, have become a regular.

How to Deal with Stress Abroad

If your study abroad experience is the first time you have lived abroad alone, you may find it to be a rather stressful experience at times. You have to handle all the details of daily life in another language—buying groceries, paying the rent, signing up for classes. Everything that you take for granted at home is something to be struggled for in France. I remember when I was studying abroad, and I cracked when I found myself outside the pharmacy translating my request for aspirin before I even walked into the store.

On top of language and cultural difficulties, it is not easy to be so far away from home. Homesickness may set in. The time difference between France and the United States may make it difficult to call home. Letters take longer to arrive. And although the advent of E-mail has made real-time communication a lot more feasible, the Internet does not always compensate for loved ones far away.

If you are under twenty-one, you may be bowled over by the fact that France does not have an enforced drinking age and that many young French people smoke. If you don't drink or smoke, you may be bothered by some of your compatriots' behavior. Or you, too, may be drinking and smoking more than you are used to. These kinds of changes in consumption can also increase the levels of stress your body has to deal with.

None of these kinds of stress is unusual. The important thing is that you don't feel that you have to handle everything on your own. If you are feeling overwhelmed, be sure to take a moment to speak to a program director, or another trusted adult. The U.S. Embassy also publishes a listing of English-speaking counselors.

American Universities

France has been a major destination for college students for generations, and today the study abroad options are no longer limited to
students of French language and culture. There are programs and curricula for students of business, law, the sciences, and many other disciplines in addition to the more traditional language and arts programs.
Studying in France can provide you with an experience unavailable in
the United States or anywhere else. You will likely come away from the
experience with a deeper understanding of your own culture as well
as that of France. And, as many employers today understand the value
of experience abroad, you will also likely increase your professional
options.

The vast majority of American students in France participate in one
of the more than 160 American study abroad programs that are offered
throughout the country. Most American universities offer the opportunity for students to study in France, either independently or in collaboration with another college or university in the United States or in
France. If you're a student at an American college or university, the
best place to find out how to study in France is at your school's study
abroad office. There, you will be able to find out exactly what programs
are available to you, where in France they're located, and how much
they cost.

As most study abroad programs are offered as an option above and beyond the scope of standard degree requirements, they can be quite expensive—especially when sponsored by a private college or university. To offset these costs, you can sometimes arrange a student work permit or housing with a French family. Refer to Chapter 22, "Freelance, Part-Time, and Temporary Work," for more information on the work-study program sponsored by the Council on International Educational Exchange (CIEE), and check with your campus study abroad office to see if any other work-study programs are offered through your school.

In addition to standard study abroad programs, there are a number of American and international universities based entirely in France that offer full degree programs. These schools follow the organizational model, credit system, curricula, and teaching methods of American universities. The American University of Paris is a private, four-year undergraduate institution that offers more than 250 courses leading to B.A. and B.S. degrees, with instruction in English. New York's Parsons School of Design has a full Paris campus, and is the only school in France that offers a full four-year American Bachelor of Fine Arts (B.F.A.) curriculum. Parsons students can specialize in one of five majors: communication design, fashion design, fine arts, illustration, or photography. A four-year Bachelor of Business Administration in Design Marketing is also available. Schiller International University has campuses in Paris and Strasbourg and offers degrees in business administration, commercial art, economics, engineering management, languages, preengineering, premedicine, psychology, public administration, hotel management, and computer systems management. Contact information is offered in the address section at the end of this chapter.

Choosing a Study Abroad Program

There is a wide variety of study abroad programs available to American students wishing to study in France. Some programs are based entirely on coursework, while others offer opportunities for field trips, hands-on experience at an archaeological site, or other forms of cultural immersion. Usually, study abroad programs last a semester, a summer, or a full academic year, and are open to junior- and senior-level students who meet varying minimum requirements. If you're already enrolled in an American college or university, the credit you earn studying in France can usually count toward your degree program. If your school does not offer a program that suits you, it is often possible to enroll in a program offered by another college or university, and then transfer the credit. You should check with the study abroad office at your school to find out how to arrange this. Most of the study abroad programs listed at the end of this chapter are open to applicants from any school, not just the sponsoring institution.

COURSES OFFERED

Most study abroad programs offer a variety of courses that focus on art, history, culture, and language. Some programs are taught in both English and French, depending on the subject matter, and others give classes only in French. Sometimes American universities offer programs in conjunction with a French university, and students are expected to take a number of courses entirely in French, along with French students. For example, Boston University's Language and Liberal Arts Program in Grenoble is taught in conjunction with the Université de Grenoble, and all courses are taught in French with French faculty. Tufts University offers a program in ancient Roman art and archaeology that combines classroom instruction with field trips and fieldwork. The program begins with two weeks of intensive classroom study, followed by four weeks excavating Roman ruins. New York University offers a program where students majoring in French, international relations, art history, languages, literature, social sciences, politics, or humanities can take courses taught by French professors in one of Paris's universities. In addition, some of the more popular programs are sponsored by the State University of New York, the University of California, Scripps College, Temple University, Cornell University, and Brown University. This is by no means a comprehensive list; review the contact information at the end of this chapter and do your homework. There are dozens of programs that you might find interesting or pertinent to your field of study.

GRADUATE PROGRAMS

Study abroad programs are not limited to undergraduates. There is a wide variety of graduate programs to choose from in France, some of which are sponsored by U.S.-based educational institutions and others that exist at American universities based in France. If you're a working professional living in France, Paris's Saint Xavier University offers an M.B.A. program through part-time evening and weekend courses, or as a full-time curriculum. New York University's Paris program offers master's degrees in French language and civilization, or French literature. The American Graduate School of International Relations and Diplomacy is a relatively new school, located in Paris's posh sixteenth arrondissement, that offers both a master's degree and Ph.D. program in international relations and diplomacy.

There are also many study abroad programs offered in France that can enhance traditional vocational or professional studies. Students with at least one year of law school experience can apply to Hofstra University's International Law summer program in Nice, offered in cooperation with the Faculté de Droit de l'Université de Nice. Classes are taught in English by Hofstra University School of Law faculty and other American law professors from universities including Fordham and Yale. Also for law students, the University of San Diego's Institute on International and Comparative Law offers a program that provides an introduction to foreign law and institutions through visits to courts and other legal institutions. For business students, Bentley College's Business Programs Abroad is offered in cooperation with Paris's American Business School, a division of France's top-rated Institut de Gestion Sociale.

Paying for Study Abroad

Studying in France can be an expensive undertaking, so it is important to thoroughly research the costs involved and the financing options before you enroll in a specific program. Many American colleges and universities will allow you to apply financial aid that you would normally receive for study on campus to a study abroad program. In addition, if you're receiving aid in the form of work-study, some schools will allow you to convert this into a Stafford or Perkins loan that you can use to fund studying abroad. When you're applying for a study abroad program at your school, you should ask about program-specific grants and other low-interest loans that might be available. Another option is to approach a faculty member at your school to ask about doing research for him or her as a paid research assistant in France. Most universities have programs like these, and it will often pay to investigate all your options.

There are also dozens of scholarships available to American students wishing to study in France. The International Study and Travel Center at the University of Minnesota offers a searchable on-line database that lists more than thirty scholarships available to American students heading to France; its Web address is listed at the end of this chapter. There are grants available from the U.S. government, Fulbright grants, minority grants, arts scholarships, and many others. Fulbright grants, handed out by the Institute of International Education (IIE) since 1946, are highly competitive year-long grants intended to increase mutual understanding between Americans and people of other countries. Generally, Fulbright grants are made to individuals pursuing university and other types of teaching positions, advanced research, or graduate study. For the 1999–2000 academic year, there were a total of fifty-six Fulbright grants available for qualified applicants.

Useful Addresses

STUDY ABROAD RESOURCES
Council on International Educational Exchange (CIEE)
International Headquarters
205 East 42nd Street
New York, NY 10017-5706
Tel: (212) 822-2600
Fax: (212) 822-2699
E-mail. Info@ciee.org
Web site: http://www.ciee.org
Institute of International Education (Fulbright Grants)
U.S. Student Programs Division
809 United Nations Plaza
New York, NY 10017
Web site: http://www.iie.org
International Study and Travel Center
University of Minnesota
48 Coffman Union
300 Washington Avenue, SE
Minneapolis, MN 55455

Tel: (612) 626-ISTC
Fax: (612) 626-0979
E-mail: istc@tc.umn.edu
Web site: http://www.istc.umn.edu

AMERICAN AND INTERNATIONAL
UNIVERSITIES IN FRANCE
American University of Paris
31, avenue Bosquet
75007 Paris
Tel: (01) 40 62 07 20
Fax: (01) 47 05 34 32
Web site: http://www.aup.fr
Boston University
15, rue Pondichéry
75015 Paris
Tel: (01) 45 66 59 49
New York University in France
56, rue de Passy
75016 Paris
Tel: (01) 53 92 50 80

Saint Xavier College
Graham School of Management
20, rue de Saint-Pétersbourg
75010 Paris
Tel: (01) 42 93 13 87
Fax: (01) 45 22 12 65
Schiller International University
32, boulevard de Vaugirard
75015 Paris
Tel: (01) 45 38 56 01
Fax: (01) 45 38 54 30
Scripps in France (Claremont College)
78, rue du Cherche-Midi
75006 Paris
Tel: (01) 45 48 77 50
Fax. (01) 45 48 77 54
Temple University
School of Business and Management
107, rue de Marseille
69007 Lyon
Tel: (04) 72 73 47 83
Fax: (04) 72 72 93 57
Cornell University
Avenue Bernard-Hirsch
B.P. 105
95021 Cergy-Pontoise Cedex
Tel: (01) 34 43 30 00
Fax: (01) 34 43 17 01
Paris Photographic Institute
8, rue Jules-Vallès
75011 Paris
Tel: (01) 40 09 18 58 or (800) 258-8492
Fax: (01) 40 09 84 97
E-mail: pymahe@speos.fr
Web site. http://www.speos.fr
Paris American Academy
The Secrets of Paris Fashion
9, rue des Ursulines
75005 Paris
Tel: (01) 44 41 99 20
Fax. (01) 44 41 99 29

AMERICAN ORGANIZATIONS AND
UNIVERSITIES WITH PROGRAMS IN
FRANCE
PARIS:
Nicholls State University
Program in France
P.O. Box 2080
Thibodaux, LA 70310
Tel: (504) 448-4440
Fax: (504) 449-7028
Educational Programs Abroad
2815 Sarles Drive
Yorktown Heights, NY 10598
University of Rochester
Internships in Europe
Lattimore 206
Rochester, NY 14627-0408
Tel: (716) 275-7532
Fax: (716) 461-5131
Miami-Dade Community College
Office of International Education
Summer Program in France
11011 SW 104th Street
Miami, FL 33176-3393
Tel: (305) 237-2535
Fax: (305) 237-2949
E-mail: ccis@intr.net
Web site: http://www.studyabroad.com/
ccis/ccishome.html
Columbia University
Reid Hall Programs in Paris
2970 Broadway, Mail Code 4115
New York, NY 10027
Tel: (212) 854-2559
Fax. (212) 854-5861
E-mail: reidhall@columbia.edu
Web site: http://www.columbia.edu/
cu/ssp/reidhall/
DePaul University
Foreign Study Program—SAC 530
2320 North Kenmore Avenue
Chicago, IL 60614-3298
Tel: (312) 325-7450
E-mail: wrldinfo@wppost.depaul.edu
Parsons School of Design
66 Fifth Avenue
New York, NY 10011

Tel: (800) 252-0852 or (212) 229-8910
Fax: (212) 229-8975
E-mail: parsadm@newschool.edu
Web site: http://www.parsons.edu
University of Minnesota
Design in Europe
Department of Design, Housing and
Apparel
240 McNeal Hall
St. Paul, MN 55108
Tel: (612) 626-1257
E-mail: dguerin@ch2.che.umn.edu
University of San Diego
School of Law—Summer Law Study
Institute on International and
Comparative Law
5998 Alcala Park
San Diego, CA 92110-2492
Tel: (619) 260-4597
Fax: (619) 260-2230
E-mail: cking@usdlaw.acusd.edu or
cking@acusd.edu
Web site. http://www.acusd.edu/usdlaw
**PTPI Collegiate and Professional
Studies Program**
501 East Armour Boulevard
Kansas City, MO 64109-2200
Tel: (816) 561-7502
E-mail: ptpi@vax1.umkc.edu
Bentley College
Business Program Abroad: Paris
175 Forest Street, AGC 160
Waltham, MA 02154-4705
Tel. (781) 891-3474
Fax: (781) 891-2819
Web site: http://www.bentley.edu/
resource/international/studyabroad
IES/IAS
IES Programs in France
223 West Ohio Street
Chicago, IL 60610
Tel: (800) 995-2300
Fax: (312) 944-1448
E-mail: recruit@iesias.org
Web site: http://www.iesias.org/
europe/paris.html

Boston University
Paris Internship Program
Division of International Programs
232 Bay State Road, 5th Floor
Boston, MA 02215
Tel: (617) 353-9888
Fax: (617) 353-5402
E-mail. abroad@bu.edu
Web site: http://web.bu.edu/abroad
**Kentucky Institute for International
Studies**
Summer Program in France
P.O. Box 9
Murray, KY 42071-0009
Tel: (502) 762-3091
Fax: (502) 762-3434
Mankato State University
Summer Study in France
Department of Modern Languages
P.O. Box 8400, MSU Box 87
Mankato, MN 56002-8400
Tel: (507) 389-1817 or (507) 389-2116
Fax: (507) 389-5887
New York University
Center for International Study
NYU in France
269 Mercer Street, Room 812
New York, NY 10003-6687
Graduate School of Arts and Science
Office of Enrollment Services
P.O. Box 907
New York, NY 10276-0907
Tel: (212) 998-8175
E-mail: nyufrance@nyu.edu
Web site: http://www.nyu.edu/
studyabroad/
American Institute for Foreign Study
University of Paris (Sorbonne)
102 Greenwich Avenue
Greenwich, CT 06830
Web site: http://www.aifs.org
Louisiana State University
Academic Programs Abroad
365 Pleasant Hall
Louisiana State University
Baton Rouge, LA 70803-1522
Tel: (504) 388-6801

STUDYING

The University of Kansas
Office of Study Abroad
203 Lippincott Hall
Lawrence, KS 66045-1731
Tel: (913) 864-3742
Fax. (913) 864-5040
E-mail: osa@falcon.cc.ukans.edu
ACCENT
Summer in Paris
870 Market Street, Suite 1026
San Francisco, CA 94102
Tel: (800) 869-9291
Fax: (415) 835-3749
E-mail: sfaccent@aol.com
Web site: http://www.accentintl.com
State University of New York at New Paltz
Summer Study in Paris
Office of International Education
HAB 33
New Paltz, NY 12561
Tel. (914) 257-3125
Fax. (914) 257-3129
American University
Washington, DC 20016-8083
Tel: (202) 895-4900 or (800) 424-2600
Fax: (202) 895-4960
E-mail: washsem@american.edu
Tufts in Paris
Tufts University European Center
108 Packard Avenue
Medford, MA 02155
Tel. (617) 627-3152
Fax: (617) 627-3457
Web site: http.//www.tufts.edu/as/tuec
Rutgers, The State University of New Jersey
Study Abroad Office
102 College Avenue
New Brunswick, NJ 08901
Tel: (908) 932-7787
Fax: (908) 932-8659
E-mail. ru_abroad@email.rutgers.edu
Web site: http://www.rutgers.edu/
Academics/Study_Abroad
Alma College
Program in Paris, France

Director, International Office
614 West Superior Street
Alma, MI 48801-1599
Tel: (517) 463-7247
Web site: http://www.alma.edu/
academics/international
SUNY at Brockport
The Brockport Paris Program
Office of International Education
350 New Campus Drive
Brockport, NY 14420
Tel: (800) 298-SUNY
Fax: (716) 637-3218
E-mail: overseas@po.brockport.edu
Web site: http://www.studyabroad.com/
suny/brockport/paris.html
Georgia Institute of Technology
Atlanta, GA 30332-0155
Tel: (404) 894-2992
Fax: (404) 894-0572
E-mail: richard.dagenhart@arch.
gatech.edu
George Mason University
Center for Global Education
235 Johnson Center
4400 University Drive
Fairfax, VA 22030
Tel: (703) 993-2154
Fax: (703) 993-2153
E-mail: cge@gmu.edu
Web site: http://www.gmu.edu/
departments/edu
Middlebury College
Office of Off Campus Study
Middlebury, VT 05753
Tel: (802) 443-5527
Fax: (802) 443-2075
E-mail: anna_sun@flannet.
middlebury.edu
Web site: http://www.middlebury.edu/~ls
Missouri Western State College
Summer Study in Paris and Annecy,
France
Dept. of English, Foreign Languages and
Journalism
4525 Downs Drive
St. Joseph, MO 64507

Tel: (816) 271-5813
Fax: (816) 271-4543
E-mail: hennessy@griffon.mwsc.edu
Web site: http://www.mwsc.edu/
~engdept/abroad/france.html
Santa Rosa Junior College
International Studies Coordinator
Educational Programs and Services
1501 Mendocino Avenue
Santa Rosa, CA 95401
Tel: (707) 527-4441
Fax. (707) 522-2653
E-mail: steve_olson@garfield.
santarosa.edu
Universities Abroad
2400 Pearl Street
Austin, TX 78705
Tel: (512) 478-6011 or (888) 290-3884
Fax: (512) 478-2632
E-mail. go@uabroad.edu
Web site: http://www.uabroad.com
Skidmore College
Study Abroad in Paris
Department of Foreign Languages and
Literatures
Saratoga Springs, NY 12866-1632
Tel: (518) 581-7400, ext. 2639
Fax: (518) 584-7963
E-mail: janzalon@skidmore.edu
Sweet Briar College
Sweet Briar, VA 24595
Tel: (804) 381-6109
Fax. (804) 381-6283
Web site: http://www.sbc.edu
University of Delaware
Department of Foreign Languages and
Literatures
326 Smith Hall
Newark, DE 19716
Tel: (302) 831-6458
Fax: (302) 831-0597
E-mail: lisa.chieffo@mvs.udel.edu
Web site: http://www.udel.edu/
IntlProg/studyabroad
MONTPELLIER:
The College of William and Mary
Programs Abroad Office

P.O. Box 8795
Williamsburg, VA 23187-8795
Tel: (804) 221-3594
Fax: (804) 221-3597
E-mail. Ann@Reves.is.wm.edu
Web site: http://www.wm.edu/
academics/Reves/abroad.html
University of New Orleans
Division of International Education
UNO Box 569
New Orleans, LA 70148
Tel: (504) 280-7455
Fax. (504) 280-7317
E-mail: mekmc@uno.edu
Web site. http://www.uno.edu/
~inst/Welcome.html
University of Minnesota
The Global Campus
102 Nicholson Hall
Minneapolis, MN 55455-0138
Tel: (612) 626-9000
Fax: (612) 626-8009
E-mail: UMabroad@tc.umn edu
Web site: http://www.UMabroad.umn.
edu/tgc/montpellier.html
AVIGNON:
Northern Illinois University
French Language and Literature in
Avignon, France
Study Abroad Office
Williston Hall 417
DeKalb, IL 60115
Tel: (815) 753-0700
Miami-Dade Community College
Semester Program in France—Avignon
11011 SW 104th Street
Miami, FL 33176-3393
Tel: (305) 237-2533 or (305) 237-2535
Fax: (305) 237-2949
E-mail: ccis@intr.net
Web site: http://www.studyabroad.com/
ccis/ccishome.html
LILLE:
Arizona State University
Program in France
Student Program Coordinator
International Programs

Tel: (602) 965-5965
Fax: (602) 965-4026
North Carolina State University
Summer Intensive Language Program
2118 Pullen Hall
Box 7344
Raleigh, NC 27695-7103
Tel: (919) 515-2087
Fax: (919) 515-6021
E-mail: study_abroad@ncsu.edu
NICE:
Hofstra Law School
Hofstra International Law Summer
Program
Room 219
Hempstead, NY 11549
Tel: (516) 463-5771
Fax: (516) 463-6338
E-mail: lawszt@hofstra.edu or
www.hofstra.edu/law
Web site: http://www.hofstra.edu/law
University of Maryland
Study Abroad Office
3125 Mitchell Building
College Park, MD 20742
Tel: (301) 314-7746
Fax: (301) 314-9347
E-mail: studyabr@deans.umd.edu
Web site: http://www.inform.umd.edu/
INTL/studyabroad/nice
AIX-EN-PROVENCE:
Institute for American Universities
United States Office
1830 Sherman Avenue
P.O. Box 592
Evanston, IL 60204
Tel. (800) 221-2051
E-mail: iauadm@univ-aix.fr
Web site: http://www.iau-univ.org
Miami-Dade Community College
Semester Program in France—
Aix-en-Provence
11011 SW 104th Street
Miami, FL 33176-3393
Tel: (305) 237-2533 or (305) 237-2535
Fax: (305) 237-2949
E-mail: ccis@intr.net

Web site: http://www.studyabroad.com/
ccis/ccishome.html
Northern Illinois University
Studio Art at the Marchutz School in Aix-
en-Provence
Study Abroad Office
Williston Hall 417
DeKalb, IL 60115-2854
Tel: (815) 753-0420
Fax: (815) 753-0825
E-mail: ideromana@niu.edu
Web site: http://www.niu.edu/depts/
intl_prgms/intl.html
TOULOUSE:
Dickinson College
Office of Off-Campus Studies
P.O. Box 1773
Carlisle, PA 17013
Tel. (717) 245-1341
Fax: (717) 245-1688
E-mail: ocs@dickinson.edu
Web site: http://www.dickinson.edu/
GlobalCampus/toulouse.htm
School for International Training
P.O. Box 676, Kipling Road
Brattleboro, VT 05302
Tel: (800) 336-1616 (U.S. only)
Fax: (802) 258-3500
E-mail: csa@sit.edu
Web site: http://www.worldlearning.org/
csa/europe/france1.html
OTHER CITIES.
Pennsylvania State University
(Besançon)
225 Penn State Scanticon
University Park, PA 16802-7002
Tel: (814) 863-5170 or (800) 778-8632
Fax: (814) 863-5190
E-mail: lion@cde.psu.edu
Web site: http://www.cde.psu.edu/pssea/
Georgia Institute of Technology (Metz)
Atlanta, GA 30332-0250
Tel: (404) 894-0076
Fax: (404) 894-2997
E-mail: gtl-academic@gtl.gatech.edu
Web site: http://www.georgiatech-metz.fr

American Universities

Northwestern University (Arles)
2115 N. Campus Drive, Suite 162
Evanston, IL 60208
Tel: (800) FINDS NU or (847) 491-5250
Fax: (847) 491-3660
E-mail: summer@nwu.edu
Web site: http://nuinfo.nwu.edu/
summernu/
Carlson School of Management (Lyon)
Office of International Program
Development
Tel: (612) 625-9361
Fax: (612) 624-8248
E-mail. ip@csom.umn.edu
Web site: http//www.csom.umn.edu/
IntlProg/

Boston University (Grenoble)
Division of International Programs
232 Bay State Road, 5th Floor
Boston, MA 02215
Tel: (617) 353-9888
Fax: (617) 353-5402
E-mail: abroad@bu.edu
Web site: http://web.bu.edu/abroad
Syracuse University (Strasbourg)
119 Euclid Avenue
Syracuse, NY 13244-4170
Tel: (315) 443-3471
Fax: (315) 443-4593
E-mail: DIPA@suadmin.syr.edu
Web site: http://sumweb.syr.edu/dipa/

CHAPTER FOURTEEN

French Universities and Other Programs

The rich history and romanticism of the Sorbonne, established in 1253, is part of the allure of Paris, and universities were also established in Montpellier and Toulouse in the thirteenth century. The Latin Quarter of Paris was given its name due to the presence of the university and the large numbers of students there who conversed in the streets in Latin. Postrevolutionary French culture embraced the concepts of individual liberty and social equality, and these tenets were extended to the educational system. Unfortunately, the university system in France today is, in many ways, a complicated, unforgiving, challenging, and overcrowded mess. The system today suffers from tremendous competition, overcrowding, high dropout rates, poor facilities, and a perpetual shortage of funds.

It may be bad today, but it was much worse before the 1960s. The university system underwent a vast reorganization during the late 1960s, sparked by the infamous student uprisings of May 1968. Students took to the streets to protest overcrowding that had reached unheard-of levels, tremendously imbalanced student-faculty ratios, and the traditionally impersonal relations between staff and students that had been an unpleasant feature of the French academic system for centuries. Still today, the events of May 1968 conjure up mixed feelings in the French cultural psyche; the uprisings were as defining to the

French as Kent State and the assassinations of Robert Kennedy and Martin Luther King Jr. were to Americans.

Although the problems of France's university system today are complex, they can be ascribed in part to a dichotomy between two strong and competing traditions: egalitarianism and elitism. There are basically two types of universities in France: traditional universities and *les grandes écoles*. Entrance to one of the country's seventy-two traditional universities (thirteen of which are in Paris) is guaranteed to all students who pass the French *baccalauréat*, a loose equivalent to a U.S. high school diploma although considerably more advanced. About one million students attend these schools, representing about one-third of those who pass the *bac*. These schools are financed entirely by the government and do not charge tuition. There are virtually no programs to help students cope with the difficulties of the university, and large numbers of students fail to complete their programs and drop out each year. Others take their time and complete their education slowly: the average age for university graduates in France is twenty-nine, but these days having a degree is by no means a guarantee of securing a career. There are thousands of foreign students enrolled in French universities, mostly from former French colonies in Africa.

The 250 *grandes écoles* in France were founded by Napoléon and specialize in a range of professional vocations including engineering, research, political science and civil service, and agriculture. In contrast to the regular university system, the *grandes écoles* are lavish, well-financed institutions, largely because the country's Ministry of Education does not administer them; rather, they are funded and controlled by individual ministries that deal with their specific focus. Only about seventy thousand students attend these schools and entrance is far from guaranteed: applicants must complete a two-year preparatory program at a special school, then pass a rigorous exam. Foreigners are rarely accepted into these programs.

General Enrollment Procedures

It is much easier to apply for entrance to a French university through a program sponsored by an American university, and it is generally advisable to do as much preparation in the United States as possible before you arrive in France. An American high school diploma is

STUDYING

generally not an acceptable equivalent to the French *bac*; Americans will need to complete a French or international *baccalauréat* program or to finish at least a year or two of college before admission to a French university will be granted. Check with the study abroad office at a local college or university to find out if it has a program or advisers to help students enroll in French universities.

The French university system is administered on a national level by the Ministry of Education and the Centre National des Oeuvres Universitaires et Scolaires (CNOUS), which sets policy, distributes funds, and generally oversees the system. Foreign students are handled by the Centre Régional des Oeuvres Universitaires et Scolaires (CROUS). CROUS can provide you with information about the various university programs offered, where they are, and what documents you'll need to complete an application process. It's also a good idea to talk to other American students who have studied at French universities to help you decide where and how to apply, and what to study. You can also inquire at a French consulate or the French Embassy in Washington, D.C.

In general, you will be required to complete a *dossier de demande d'inscription préalable*, which is basically an academic résumé stating all the coursework you've completed, the schools you've attended, and your academic standing. You will also need to indicate three preferences of schools you wish to attend. The deadline for this application is usually February 1 for the fall semester that begins in October. Unless you can meet very strict residency requirements for the Île-de-France (Paris and its surroundings), you will probably not be allowed to choose a Paris-based university as a preference. Along with the *dossier de demande d'inscription préalable*, you will also have to provide a variety of supporting documents including transcripts, a birth certificate, your passport, and your student visa, all translated into French. Never send original documents unless they are specifically required; make photocopies and have them authenticated by university officials. After the dossier is received, you'll also have to pass a French language exam.

The application will probably take several weeks to a few months to process, and in all likelihood, you will be accepted by one of the schools on your list. If not, you can appeal your case to the Ministry of Education, but if you have completed the French *baccalauréat* or equivalent, you are guaranteed admission.

Costs

The French university system is government-funded and free for qualifying students. That said, there are many costs associated with studying in France, including housing, board, insurance, and registration fees. Generally speaking, registration fees are minimal—probably about F1,500 per academic year. University housing is in short supply and of notoriously poor quality, and foreign students are put at the bottom of the priority list. If you do manage to secure university accommodation, it will not cost you much when compared with renting an apartment. You can expect to pay between F1,500 and F5,000 per month for housing, depending on where your university is located. Larger cities cost more and Paris costs a lot more.

Health insurance is another complicated matter. The French *sécurité sociale étudiante* will reimburse you for about 80 percent of your medical bills if you have been paying into the social security system for the six-month period required to qualify. If you do qualify, you may want to consider purchasing additional coverage from a *mutuelle* that will pay for the remaining 20 percent. Otherwise, you will have to take out a full policy from a private insurance company. These companies offer policies that cover a range of issues, from health care to personal property and more.

Transferring Credits Back Home

If you're not out to get a degree or certificate from a French university, you will probably want to apply credit for French programs or courses at an American university. Because of the structural and academic differences between the French and the American university systems, however, you may encounter problems. The best way to avoid them is to have the program or course that you want to take in France approved by the American university you'll be attending before you leave for France. This can usually be done through individual academic departments at your university, or through a study abroad office. If you can't get French programs or courses approved, you will either have to enroll in a preapproved program sponsored by an American college at a French university or resign yourself to live without the credit for the course you take outside your American curriculum.

Understanding the French University System

The system of university education in France is considerably more complex than the American system, and can be a challenge for many outsiders to understand. There are three phases, or *cycles*, to higher education. The first two *cycles* are roughly equivalent to a bachelor's degree from an American university and the third *cycle* is similar in focus and depth to postgraduate work. As in the United States, students can take a variety of courses during the *premier cycle*, although they concentrate in a specific field of study. This phase lasts two years and ends with the student being awarded a *diplôme d'études universitaires générales* (DEUG). Alternatively, students can opt to study at an *institut universitaire de technologie* (IUT) where, after two years of intensive training, they are issued a *diplôme universitaire de technologie* (DUT), a professional, vocational degree offered in a variety of specializations. The DUT was introduced several years ago in an attempt to provide students with the focus and specialization necessary to enter the workforce more quickly.

The dropout rate is high, but if a student successfully completes the *premier cycle* and obtains a DEUG, he or she can continue to the *deuxième cycle*. During the *deuxième cycle*, there are two separate certificates that are granted. A *licence* is granted after the first year and a *maîtrise* after one additional year of more focused education. Before the end of the *maîtrise*, students must prepare and present a mini-thesis. If a student chooses to continue into the *troisième cycle*, he or she can be granted a *diplôme d'études approfondies* (DEA) after one year, or go on to receive a *doctorat d'État* (DE), which can take years to complete.

Programs for Foreign Students

France is very proud of its language and heritage, and the French university system has traditionally offered a variety of programs to educate foreign students in the language and culture of France. These programs are incredibly varied and flexible, and the beginning courses require only a basic knowledge of French. Many of these programs can be applied for and entered via an American university; in such cases, credit is usually granted in the United States. These programs are

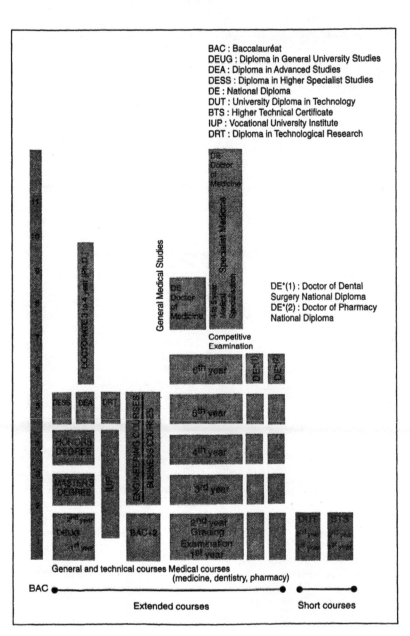

BAC : Baccalauréat
DEUG : Diploma in General University Studies
DEA : Diploma in Advanced Studies
DESS : Diploma in Higher Specialist Studies
DE : National Diploma
DUT : University Diploma in Technology
BTS : Higher Technical Certificate
IUP : Vocational University Institute
DRT : Diploma in Technological Research

DE*(1) : Doctor of Dental
Surgery National Diploma
DE*(2) : Doctor of Pharmacy
National Diploma

General Medical Studies

DOCTORATE 3 to 4 year (Ph.D.)

DESS   DEA   DRT

HONORS DEGREE

MASTER'S DEGREE

2nd year
DEUG
1st year

ENGINEERING COURSES
BUSINESS COURSES

IUP

BAC+2

DE Doctor of Medicine

4 to 5 year Medical Specialization

Specialist Medicine

DE Doctor of Medicine

Competitive Examination

6th year

5th year

4th year

3rd year

2nd year
Grading
Examination
1st year

DE*(1)   DE*(2)

DUT   BTS
1st year   1st year
2nd year   2nd year

General and technical courses   Medical courses
(medicine, dentistry, pharmacy)

BAC

Extended courses   Short courses

Degree Level and Other Higher Learning Programs

offered during holiday periods and summer vacations, and there are
semester- and year-long programs available as well. If you are interested in enrolling in a *cours de langue et civilisation française*, expect to
pay: programs such as these can cost more than $3,500 for an academic
year.

Useful Addresses

EDUCATIONAL RESOURCES

**Council on International Educational
Exchange (CIEE)**
1, place de l'Odéon
75006 Paris
Tel: (01) 44 41 74 74
**Service National d'Accueil aux
Étudiants Étrangers**
69, quai d'Orsay
75007 Paris
**Centre Régional des Oeuvres
Universitaires et Scolaires (CROUS)**
39, avenue Georges-Bernanos
75231 Paris Cedex 05
Tel: (01) 40 51 36 00
**Centre National des Oeuvres
Universitaires et Scolaires (CNOUS)**
69, quai d'Orsay
75007 Paris
Tel: (01) 44 18 53 00
Fax: (01) 45 55 48 49
E-mail: sdbeal@cnous.fr
Web site: http://www.cnous.fr
**Ministère de l'Education Nationale, de
la Recherche et de la Technologie**
173, boulevard St-Germain
75007 Paris
Tel: (01) 55 55 65 90
Fax: (01) 45 44 57 87
Web site: http://www.education.gouv.fr
**Office de Documentation et
d'Information sur l'Enseignement Privé**
(Private Education Documentation and
Information Office)
45, avenue Georges-Bernanos
75005 Paris
Tel: (01) 43 25 61 28

Fax: (01) 43 29 90 70
Ministère des Affaires Étrangères
Direction Générale des Relations
Culturelles, Scientifiques et Techniques
(Department of Cultural, Scientific and
Technical Relations)
244, boulevard St-Germain
75303 Paris Cedex 07
Tel: (01) 43 17 90 00
Fax: (01) 40 18 42 95
Web site: http://www.france.diplomatie.fr
**CIES (International Student and
Trainee Centre)**
28, rue de la Grange-aux-Belles
75010 Paris
Tel: (01) 40 40 58 58
Fax: (01) 42 00 70 08
E-mail: bertrand.sulpice@mail.cies.fr
Web site: http://www.cies.fr
**ADCUEFE (Association of University
Centres of French Studies for
Foreigners)**
Web site: http://
www.signserver.univlyon2.fr/adcuefe
Alliance Française
101, boulevard Raspail
75270 Paris Cedex 06
Tel: (01) 45 44 38 28
Fax: (01) 45 44 89 42
Web site:
http://www.Paris.alliancefrancaise.fr

PUBLIC FRENCH UNIVERSITIES

AIX-MARSEILLE:
Université de Provence: Aix-Marseille I
3, place Victor-Hugo
13331 Marseille Cedex 3

Tel: (04) 91 10 60 00
Fax: (04) 91 10 60 06
Université de la Méditerranée: Aix-Marseille II
Jardin du Pharo
58, boulevard Charles-Livon
13264 Marseille Cedex 07
Tel: (04) 91 39 65 00
Fax: (04) 91 31 31 36
Université de Droit, d'Économie et des Sciences: Aix-Marseille III
3, avenue Robert-Schuman
13628 Aix-en-Provence Cedex 01
Tel: (04) 42 17 27 18
Fax: (04) 42 64 03 96
Université d'Avignon et des Pays du Vaucluse
Site Universitaire Sainte-Marthe
74, rue Louis-Pasteur
F-84029 Avignon Cedex 01
Tel: (04) 90 16 25 00
Fax: (04) 90 16 25 10
Minitel: 3614 UNIVA84

AMIENS:
Université Picardie-Jules-Verne: Amiens
Chemin du Thil
80025 Amiens Cedex 1
Tel: (03) 22 82 72 72
Fax: (03) 22 82 75 00
Université de Technologie de Compiègne
Centre Benjamin-Franklin
Rue Roger-Couttolenc
B.P. 649
60206 Compiègne Cedex
Tel: (03) 44 23 44 23
Fax: (03) 44 23 43 00
BESANÇON:
Université de Franche-Comté: Besançon
1, rue Goudimel
25030 Besançon Cedex
Tel: (03) 81 66 66 66
Fax: (03) 81 66 50 25

BORDEAUX:
Université Bordeaux I
Sciences et technologies (Science and technology)
351, cours de la Libération
33405 Talence Cedex
Tel: (05) 56 84 60 00
Fax: (05) 56 80 08 37
Webmaster: mailto:
Webmaster@cribx1.u-bourdeaux.fr
Université "Victor Segalen": Bordeaux II
146, rue Léo-Saignat
33076 Bordeaux Cedex
Tel: (05) 57 57 10 10
Fax: (05) 56 99 03 80
Webmaster: mailto:leicht@
u-bordeaux2.fr
Université Michel de Montaigne: Bordeaux III
Esplanade Michel-de-Montaigne
33405 Talence Cedex
Tel: (05) 56 84 50 50
Fax: (05) 56 84 50 90
Webmaster: mailto:webers@
montaigne.u-bordeaux.fr
Université Montesquieu: Bordeaux IV
Droit, sciences sociales et politiques, sciences économiques et de gestion (Law, social science and politics, economics, and management)
Avenue Léon-Duguit
33608 Pessac Cedex
Tel: (05) 56 84 85 86
Fax: (05) 56 84 83 20 (or 56)
Webmaster: mailto:
webmaster@montesquieu.u-bordeaux.fr
Université de Pau et des Pays de l'Adour
Avenue de l'Université
B.P. 576
64012 Pau Cedex
Tel: (05) 59 92 30 00
Fax: (05) 59 80 83 80
Webmaster: mailto:webmaster@univ-pau.fr

CAEN:
Université de Caen
Esplanade de la Paix
14032 Caen Cedex
Tel: (02) 31 56 55 00
Fax: (02) 31 56 56 00

CLERMONT-FERRAND:
Université d'Auvergne: Clermont-Ferrand I
49, boulevard Gergovia
B.P. 32
63001 Clermont-Ferrand Cedex 1
Tel: (04) 73 34 77 77
Fax. (04) 73 35 55 18

Université Blaise Pascal: Clermont-Ferrand II
34, avenue Carnot
B.P. 185
63006 Clermont-Ferrand Cedex 1
Tel: (04) 73 40 63 63
Fax: (04) 73 40 64 31

DIJON:
Université de Bourgogne: Dijon
Campus Universitaire de Montmuzard
(Montmuzard Campus)
B.P. 138
21004 Dijon Cedex
Tel: (03) 80 39 50 00
Fax: (03) 80 39 50 69

GRENOBLE:
Université de Savoie: Chambéry
27, rue Marcoz
B.P. 1104
73011 Chambéry Cedex
Tel: (04) 69 75 95 85
Fax. (04) 79 75 85 55

Université Joseph-Fourier: Grenoble I
621, avenue Centrale
Domaine Universitaire de St-Martin-d'Hères/Gières (The Saint Martin d'Hères/Gières section)
B.P. 53 X
38041 Grenoble Cedex 9
Tel: (04) 76 51 46 00
Fax: (04) 76 51 48 48

Université Pierre Mendes-France: Grenoble II
(Sciences sociales)
151, rue des Universités
Domaine Universitaire de St-Martin-d'Hères (The Saint Martin d'Hères section)
B.P. 47
38040 Grenoble Cedex 9
Tel: (04) 76 82 54 00
Fax: (04) 76 82 56 54

Université Stendhal: Grenoble III
Domaine Universitaire de St-Martin-d'Hères (The Saint Martin d'Hères section)
B.P. 25
38040 Grenoble Cedex 9
Tel. (04) 76 82 43 00
Fax: (04) 76 82 43 84

Institut National Polytechnique de Grenoble
46, avenue Félix-Viallet
38031 Grenoble Cedex 1
Tel: (04) 76 57 45 00
Fax: (04) 76 57 45 01

LILLE:
Université d'Artois
(Arras, Béthune, Douai, Lens)
9, rue du Temple
B.P. 665
62030 Arras Cedex
Tel: (03) 21 60 37 00
Fax. (03) 21 60 37 37

Université des Sciences et Technologies de Lille: Lille I
59655 Villeneuve-d'Ascq Cedex
Tel: (03) 20 43 43 43
Fax: (03) 20 43 49 95

Université du Droit et de la Santé: Lille II
42, rue Paul-Duez
59800 Lille
Tel: (03) 20 96 43 43
Fax: (03) 20 88 24 32 (or 20)

Université Charles-de-Gaulle: Lille III
Domaine Universitaire Littéraire de Villeneuve-d'Ascq (The Villeneuve-d'Ascq literary section)
Pont-de-Bois
B.P. 149

59653 Villeneuve-d'Ascq Cedex
Tel: (03) 20 41 60 00
Fax: (03) 20 91 91 71
Université du Littoral
9, quai de la Citadelle
B.P. 1022
59375 Dunkerque Cedex 1
Tel: (03) 28 23 73 73
Fax: (03) 28 23 73 13
Université de Valenciennes et du Hainaut-Cambrésis
Le Mont-Houy
B.P. 311
59304 Valenciennes Cedex
Tel: (03) 27 14 12 34
Fax: (03) 27 14 11 00
LIMOGES:
Université de Limoges
Hôtel Burgy
13, rue de Genève
87065 Limoges Cedex
Tel: (05) 55 45 76 01
Fax: (05) 55 45 76 34
LYON:
Université Claude Bernard: Lyon I
43, boulevard du 11-novembre-1918
69622 Villeurbanne Cedex
"La Doua":
Tel: (04) 72 44 80 00
Fax: (04) 72 43 10 20
"Rockefeller":
Tel: (04) 78 77 70 00
Fax: (04) 78 77 71 58
Université Lumière: Lyon II
86, rue Pasteur
69365 Lyon Cedex 07
Tel: (04) 78 69 70 00
Fax: (04) 78 69 56 01
Université Jean Moulin: Lyon III
1, rue de l'Université
B.P. 0638
69239 Lyon Cedex 02
Tel: (04) 72 72 20 20
Fax: (04) 72 72 20 50
Université Jean Monnet: Saint-Étienne
34, rue Francis-Baulier
42023 Saint-Étienne Cedex 02

Tel: (04) 77 42 17 00
Fax: (04) 77 42 17 99
MONTPELLIER:
Université Montpellier I
5, boulevard Henri-IV
B.P. 1017
34006 Montpellier Cedex 1
Tel: (04) 67 41 20 90
Fax: (04) 67 41 74 56
Université Montpellier II
Place Eugène-Bataillon
34095 Montpellier Cedex 5
Tel: (04) 67 14 30 30
Fax: (04) 67 14 30 31
Université Paul Valéry: Montpellier III
Route de Mende
34199 Montpellier Cedex 5
Tel: (04) 67 14 20 00
Fax: (04) 67 14 20 52
Université de Perpignan
52, avenue de Villeneuve
66860 Perpignan Cedex
Tel: (04) 68 66 20 00
Fax: (04) 68 66 20 19
NANCY-METZ:
Université de Metz
Île du Saulcy
B.P. 794
57012 Metz Cedex 1
Tel: (03) 87 31 50 50
Fax: (03) 87 31 50 55
Pôle Universitaire Européenne de Nancy-Metz
34, cours Léopold
54052 Nancy Cedex
Tel: (03) 83 17 67 67
Fax: (03) 83 17 67 65
Maison du Pôle
2, rue Winston-Churchill
57000 Metz
Tel: (03) 87 65 81 40
Fax: (03) 87 65 81 41
Université Henri Poincaré: Nancy I
24-30, rue Lionnois
B.P. 3069
54013 Nancy Cedex
Tel: (03) 83 85 48 00

Fax: (03) 83 85 48 48
Université Nancy II
Rue Baron-Louis
B.P. 454
54001 Nancy Cedex
Tel: (03) 83 34 46 00
Fax: (03) 83 30 05 65
Institut National Polytechnique de Lorraine
2, avenue de la Forêt-de-Haye
B.P. 3
54501 Vandoeuvre-les-Nancy Cedex
Tel: (03) 83 59 59 59
Fax: (03) 83 59 59 55
NANTES:
Université d'Angers
30, rue des Arènes
B.P. 3532
49035 Angers Cedex 01
Tel: (02) 41 23 23 23
Fax: (02) 41 23 23 00
Université du Maine: Le Mans
Avenue Olivier-Messiaen
B.P. 535
72017 Le Mans Cedex
Tel: (02) 43 83 30 00
Fax: (02) 43 83 30 77
Université de Nantes
1, quai de Tourville
B.P. 1026
44035 Nantes Cedex 01
Tel. (02) 40 99 83 83 '
Fax: (02) 40 99 83 00
NICE:
Université de Nice Sophia-Antipolis
Parc Valrose
28, avenue de Valrose
06108 Nice Cedex 2
Tel: (04) 92 07 60 60
Fax: (04) 92 07 66 00
Université de Toulon et du Var
Avenue de l'Université
B.P. 132
83957 La Garde Cedex
Tel: (04) 94 14 20 00
Fax. (04) 94 14 21 57

ORLÉANS-TOURS:
Université d'Orléans
Château de la Source
B.P. 6749
45067 Orléans Cedex 2
Tel: (02) 38 41 71 71
Fax: (02) 38 41 70 69
Université François Rabelais: Tours
3, rue des Tanneurs
37041 Tours Cedex
Tel: (02) 47 36 66 00
Fax: (02) 47 36 64 10
PARIS AND ÎLE-DE-FRANCE REGION:
Université Panthéon-Sorbonne:
Paris I
12, place du Panthéon
75231 Paris Cedex 05
Tel: (01) 46 34 97 00
Fax: (01) 46 34 20 56
Université Panthéon-Assas: Paris II
Droit, économie, sciences sociales (law, economics, social sciences)
12, place du Panthéon
75231 Paris Cedex 05
Tel: (01) 44 41 57 00
Fax: (01) 44 41 55 13
Université de la Sorbonne Nouvelle:
Paris III
17, rue de la Sorbonne
75230 Paris Cedex 05
Tel: (01) 40 46 28 97/99 (accueil
Sorbonne—for information) or
(01) 45 87 40 00 (standard centre
Censier—main switchboard)
Fax: (01) 43 25 74 71
Université Paris-Sorbonne:
Paris IV
1, rue Victor-Cousin
75230 Paris Cedex 05
Tel: (01) 40 46 22 11
Fax: (01) 40 46 25 88
Université René Descartes: Paris V
12, rue de l'École-de-Médecine
75270 Paris Cedex 06
Tel: (01) 40 46 16 16
Fax. (01) 40 46 16 15

Université Pierre et Marie Curie:
Paris VI
4, place Jussieu
75252 Paris Cedex 05
Tel: (01) 44 27 44 27
Fax: (01) 44 27 38 29

Université Denis Diderot: Paris VII
2, place Jussieu
75251 Paris Cedex 05
Tel: (01) 44 27 44 27
Fax: (01) 44 27 69 64

Université Paris Dauphine: Paris IX
Place du Maréchal-de-Lattre-de-Tassigny
75775 Paris Cedex 16
Tel: (01) 44 05 44 05
Fax: (01) 44 05 41 41

Université de Marne-la-Vallée
5, boulevard Descartes
Champs-sur-Marne
77454 Marne-La-Vallée Cedex 2
Tel: (01) 60 95 75 00
Fax. (01) 60 95 75 75

Université Paris Vincennes: Paris VIII
2, rue de la Liberté
93526 Saint-Denis Cedex 02
Tel: (01) 49 40 67 89
Fax: (01) 48 21 04 46

Université Paris-Val-de-Marne:
Paris XII
61, avenue du Général-de-Gaulle
94010 Créteil Cedex
Tel: (01) 45 17 10 00
Fax: (01) 42 07 70 12

Université Paris-Nord: Paris XIII
Avenue Jean-Baptiste-Clément
93430 Villetaneuse
Tel. (01) 49 40 30 00
Fax: (01) 49 40 38 93

Université de Cergy-Pontoise
33, boulevard du Port
95011 Cergy-Pontoise Cedex
Tel: (01) 34 25 60 00
Fax: (01) 34 25 61 01

Université d'Évry-Val d'Essonne
Boulevard François-Mitterrand
91025 Évry Cedex
Tel: (01) 69 47 70 00

Fax: (01) 64 97 27 34

Université Nanterre: Paris X
200, avenue de la République
92001 Nanterre Cedex
Tel: (01) 40 97 72 00
Fax: (01) 40 97 75 71

Université Paris Sud: Paris XI
15, rue Georges-Clemenceau
91405 Orsay Cedex
Tel: (01) 69 15 67 50
Fax: (01) 69 15 61 35

Université de Versailles Saint-
Quentin-en-Yvelines
23, rue du Refuge
78035 Versailles Cedex
Tel: (01) 39 25 40 00
Fax: (01) 39 25 78 01

POITIERS:
Université de Poitiers
15, rue de l'Hôtel Dieu
86034 Poitiers Cedex
Tel. (05) 49 45 30 00
Fax: (05) 49 45 30 50

Université de la Rochelle
23, avenue Albert-Einstein
17071 La Rochelle Cedex 9
Tel. (05) 46 45 91 14
Fax: (05) 46 44 93 76

REIMS:
Université de Reims Champagne-
Ardenne
Villa Douce
9, boulevard de la Paix
51097 Reims Cedex
Tel. (03) 26 05 30 00
Fax: (03) 26 05 30 98

Université de Technologie de Troyes
12, rue Marie-Curie
B.P. 206
10010 Troyes
Tel: (03) 25 71 76 00
Fax: (03) 25 71 76 77

RENNES:
Université de Bretagne Occidentale:
Brest
Rue des Archives
B.P. 808

29285 Brest Cedex
Tel: (02) 98 01 60 00
Fax: (02) 98 01 60 01
Université de Bretagne Sud (Lorient-Vannes)
12, avenue St-Symphorien
56000 Vannes
Tel: (02) 97 68 16 20
Fax: (02) 97 68 16 39
Université Rennes I
2, rue du Thabor
35065 Rennes Cedex
Tel: (02) 99 25 36 36
Fax: (02) 99 25 36 00
Université de Haute Bretagne: Rennes II
6, avenue Gaston-Berger
35043 Rennes Cedex
Tel: (02) 99 14 10 00
Fax: (02) 99 14 10 15
ROUEN:
Université du Havre
25, rue Philippe-Lebon
B.P. 1123
76063 Le Havre Cedex
Tel: (02) 35 19 55 00
Fax: (02) 35 21 49 59
Université de Rouen
1, rue Thomas-Becket
76821 Mont-Saint-Aignan Cedex
Tel: (02) 35 14 60 00
Fax: (02) 35 14 63 48
STRASBOURG:
Université de Haute-Alsace: Mulhouse
2, rue des Frères-Lumière
68093 Mulhouse Cedex
Tel: (03) 89 33 63 00
Fax: (03) 89 33 63 19
Université Louis Pasteur: Strasbourg I
4, rue Blaise-Pascal
67070 Strasbourg Cedex

Tel: (03) 88 41 60 00
Fax: (03) 88 60 75 50
Université des Sciences Humaines: Strasbourg II
22, rue René-Descartes
67084 Strasbourg Cedex
Tel: (03) 88 41 73 00
Fax: (03) 88 41 73 54
Université Robert Schuman: Strasbourg III
1, place d'Athènes
B.P. 66
67045 Strasbourg Cedex
Tel: (03) 88 41 42 00
Fax: (03) 88 61 30 37
TOULOUSE:
Université des Sciences Sociales: Toulouse I
Place Anatole-France
31042 Toulouse Cedex
Tel: (05) 61 63 35 00
Fax: (05) 61 63 37 98
Université Toulouse–Le Mirail: Toulouse II
5, allées Antonio-Machado
31058 Toulouse Cedex 1
Tel: (05) 61 50 42 50
Fax: (05) 61 50 42 09
Université Paul Sabatier: Toulouse III
118, route de Narbonne
31062 Toulouse Cedex
Tel: (05) 61 55 66 11
Fax: (05) 61 55 64 70
Institut National Polytechnique de Toulouse
Place des Hauts-Murats
B.P. 354
31006 Toulouse Cedex
Tel: (05) 62 25 54 00
Fax: (05) 61 53 67 21

CHAPTER   FIFTEEN

Language Schools

Although its prevalence may be diminishing, French remains a global language. As a second language, French is the second most frequently taught language in the world after English. Most international organizations, including the United Nations, the International Monetary Fund, and the International Olympic Committee, make a policy of using both French and English as official languages. It is the main spoken language in thirty-three countries and is the only language other than English to be officially spoken on five continents. Most years, the United States does more business and trade with French-speaking countries than with either Japan or Spanish-speaking countries. French is also the second language of the Internet and the world of information technology.

Obviously, the ability to speak French is an important part of living, studying, and working in France. For many people, learning French is one of their main motivators for going to France in the first place. For others, spending time in France will provide an invaluable context for years of classroom or literary French education. Regardless of your motivations and background, the ability to make yourself understood will open doors and generally make your experience in France more pleasurable. In addition, many of the differences and quirks of French culture are more fully understood with an understanding of the language. Language and culture are inexorably linked, and the French take their language very seriously.

University Study Centers and Certificates and Language Diplomas

The government-run university system, consisting of seventy-two institutions throughout France, has for many years offered introductory and immersion courses for foreigners on French language and culture. If you're looking for something with more credence than an easily framed piece of paper, there are a number of programs that offer university credit, a full-fledged diploma, or both. The Institut Français de Langue et de Civilisation Françaises offers free courses on French civilization and a five-course language program that will grant you a diploma after the fourth and fifth level. The popular *cours de langue et civilisation françaises* at the Sorbonne can be taken for credit at undergraduate and graduate levels. This program is offered throughout the academic year and during the summer, and provides a foundation in French language, history, and culture. If you're still looking for something more serious, you may consider enrolling in a full-fledged French language degree program from one of France's many government-run universities. There are two degrees offered: the *diplôme élémentaire de langue française* (DELF) and the *diplôme advancé de langue française* (DALF). These programs are based on a modular series of in-depth college courses, and are well suited for foreigners serious about studying French culture, language, and literature. When completed, these degrees prepare students to function in French society and business with a high level of fluency.

Language Schools

There are literally hundreds of schools, cultural centers, social organizations, and companies offering language courses of varying size, focus, and cost all over the country. Some specialize in teaching children or young adults, others teach business and professional French to executives, and some are more intensive programs on literature, language, and culture. Some offer courses combined with an activity like a cultural or architectural tour, cooking, or art. Almost any language school you attend will grant you a certificate upon successful completion of your course. If you're thinking of enrolling in one of these programs, it is a good idea to do some research. The programs listed at the end of this chapter vary significantly as to the size of the classes, the specialty or focus, and the teaching methodology. Ask if you can audit a class or two before signing up, or if they have a refund policy should you find that the course is not for you. Different people learn languages very differently; it is important to find a course and teacher that you respond well to. And unless you're a language whiz, don't expect to be fluent overnight. Even students who have taken many years of French in the United States find their conversation skills lacking once they're immersed in French society. Give yourself time and you'll arrive.

One-on-One Private Instruction

If you're not the classroom type, many of the language schools listed at the end of this chapter also offer individual or small group courses. These courses are usually substantially more expensive than the group courses, and while there are significant benefits to working with a trained language teacher, there are many ways to get individualized attention for a lot less money. One thing to keep in mind is that wherever you happen to be, there are probably just as many people looking to improve their English skills as there are foreigners seeking assistance with French. Check the bulletin boards at places frequented by foreigners and expatriates, and you're likely to find a variety of requests for conversation exchange or "friendship" ads. While some of these friendship seekers might be looking for more, many are just wanting cheap and friendly ways to improve their language skills. If you mainly need to work on your conversational French or your accent, finding a conversation partner might be the best way to go, not to mention the least expensive.

In addition, there are also many social groups and expatriate organizations that put together events and gatherings that encourage cross-cultural exchange. Again, the bulletin boards are a good place to seek out these opportunities, as is the English-language press available in Paris and other urban centers. *France-USA Contacts,* one of Paris's popular English-language ad rags, usually has dozens of listings for these types of activities in addition to language schools, private instruction by individuals and companies, and university programs.

Finding More Information

The English-language press is one of the best places to find ads for language schools, university programs for foreigners, and classified ads for individuals offering language instruction or seeking conversation partners. From the United States, you can contact the nearest French consulate or the French Embassy for a current list of language programs. The Council on International Educational Exchange (CIEE) and its sister company, Council Travel, have lots of glossy brochures advertising the language and work abroad programs they sponsor, and they have offices on many American college campuses in addition to their New York headquarters. You can also find a tremendous amount of information on the Web, which might be your best bet for the most current offerings. See Chapter 11, *"La Vie Virtuelle:* Navigating French Cyberspace," for the best Web sites to surf.

Useful Addresses

PARIS AND THE ÎLE-DE-FRANCE

Accord—École de Langues
52, rue Montmartre
75002 Paris
Tel: (01) 42 21 17 44
Fax: (01) 42 21 17 91
ACTE—International
39, rue du Sahel
75012 Paris
Tel: (01) 43 42 48 84
Fax: (01) 43 41 51 17
E-mail: acte_int@mail.club-internet.fr
(places students in language schools or universities throughout France)
Alliance Française de Paris
101, boulevard Raspail
75270 Paris Cedex 06
Tel: (01) 45 44 38 28
Fax: (01) 45 44 89 42
E-mail: info@paris.alliancefrançaise.fr
American Dream Center
163, rue de Charenton
75012 Paris
Tel: (01) 43 42 26 00
Fax: (01) 43 42 12 00

Berlitz
38, avenue de l'Opéra
75002 Paris
Tel: (01) 44 94 50 00
Fax: (01) 44 94 50 05
Berlitz
23, avenue Victor-Hugo
75016 Paris
Tel: (01) 45 00 08 68
Fax: (01) 45 01 63 97
Berlitz
31, rue du Sommerard
75005 Paris
Tel: (01) 46 33 98 77
Fax: (01) 46 33 92 14
Berlitz
15, place de la Nation
75011 Paris
Tel: (01) 43 73 28 47
Fax: (01) 43 73 26 37
Berlitz
35, avenue Franklin-D.-Roosevelt
75008 Paris
Tel: (01) 40 74 00 17
Fax: (01) 45 61 49 79

Cap Monde
11, quai Conti
78430 Louveciennes
Tel: (01) 30 82 15 15
Fax: (01) 30 82 22 22
(specializes in providing school
groups with language, sporting, or
cultural trips)
CEI
104, rue de Vaugirard
75006 Paris
Tel: (01) 44 39 32 22
Fax: (01) 45 44 91 56
(organizes language courses for young
people around France)
Citylangues
Immeuble "Les Saisons"
4, place des Saisons
Paris–La Défense 6
92400 Courbevoie
Tel. (01) 47 89 38 05
Fax: (01) 49 05 40 47
E-mail: citylangues@wanadoo.fr
**Cours de Civilisation Française de la
Sorbonne**
47, rue des Écoles
75005 Paris
Tel: (01) 40 46 26 77
Fax: (C1) 40 46 32 29
Demos Langues
20, rue de l'Arcade
75008 Paris
Tel: (01) 44 94 16 32
Fax: (01) 44 94 16 35
E-mail: langues@demos.fr
**École de Langue Française pour
Étrangers (ELFE)**
8, villa Ballu
75009 Paris
Tel: (01) 48 78 73 00
Fax: (01) 40 82 91 92
École de la Tournelle
"Les Petites Roches"
B.P. 1
78790 Septeuil
Tel: (01) 30 93 41 83
Fax: (01) 30 93 84 78

**École Suisse Internationale de Français
Appliqué**
10, rue des Messageries
75010 Paris
Tel: (01) 47 70 20 66
Fax: (01) 42 46 34 57
EF
3, rue de Bassano
75116 Paris
Tel. (01) 47 20 18 02
Fax: (01) 47 20 18 80
L'Étoile
38, boulevard Raspail
75007 Paris
Tel: (01) 45 48 00 05
Fax: (01) 45 48 62 05
Eurocentre
13, passage Dauphine
75006 Paris
Tel: (01) 40 46 72 00
Fax: (01) 40 46 72 06
E-mail: 100632.133@compuserve.com
Euroskill
11, avenue du Hoggar
91953 Les Ulis Cedex
Tel: (01) 69 07 55 35
Executive Language Services (ELS)
20, rue Ste-Croix-de-la-Bretonnerie
75004 Paris
Tel: (01) 44 54 58 88
Fax: (01) 48 04 55 53
E-mail: els@club-internet.fr
Formalangues
87, rue La Boétie
75008 Paris
Tel: (01) 53 93 67 89
Fax: (01) 53 93 67 80
**Formation Postuniversitaire
Internationale**
11, rue Tiquetonne
75002 Paris
Tel: (01) 40 28 04 03
Fax: (01) 40 28 49 22
France Langue
14, rue Léonard-de-Vinci
75116 Paris
Tel: (01) 45 00 40 15

163

Fax: (01) 45 00 53 41
E-mail: frlang@club-internet.fr
Geste
4, boulevard Edgar-Quinet
75014 Paris
Tel: (01) 43 22 35 13
Fax: (01) 43 21 58 61
IELP
98, boulevard de Sébastopol
75002 Paris
Tel. (01) 42 33 35 84
Fax: (01) 42 21 04 66
Inlingua—Bastille
28, boulevard de La Bastille
75012 Paris
Tel: (01) 53 17 07 77
Fax. (01) 53 17 07 08
Inlingua—La Défense
CNIT
B.P. 451
92053 Paris–La Défense
Tel: (01) 46 92 25 70
Fax: (01) 46 92 25 68
Inlingua—Rive Gauche
109, rue de l'Université
75007 Paris
Tel: (01) 45 51 46 60
Fax: (01) 47 05 66 05
Institut Britannique de Paris
Dépt. d'Études Françaises
11, rue de Constantine
75340 Paris Cedex 07
Tel. (01) 44 11 73 73
Fax. (01) 45 50 31 55
E-mail: L.Mitchell@gmw.ac.uk
Institut de Langue et de Culture
Françaises
21, rue d'Assas
75270 Paris Cedex 06
Tel: (01) 44 39 52 68
Fax. (01) 44 39 52 09
E-mail: ilcf@icp.fr
Institut de Langue Française
3, avenue Bertie-Albrecht
75008 Paris
Tel: (01) 45 63 24 00
Fax: (01) 45 63 07 09

Institute of Applied Languages
41, rue de Turenne
75003 Paris
Tel: (01) 44 59 25 10
Fax: (01) 44 59 25 15
E-mail: ial@calva.net
Institut Européen de Langues
1, place de la République
75003 Paris
Tel: (01) 48 87 82 36
Fax: (01) 48 87 65 33
Institut International de Rambouillet
Le Vieux Moulin
48-50, rue Georges-Lenôtre
78120 Rambouillet
Tel: (01) 34 85 73 12
Fax: (01) 30 46 53 13
E-mail: iir@easynet.fr
Institut Parisien de Langue et de
Civilisation Françaises
87, boulevard de Grenelle
75015 Paris
Tel: (01) 40 56 09 53
Fax: (01) 43 06 46 30
International Language Centres
Group
20, passage Dauphine
75006 Paris
Tel: (01) 44 41 80 20
Fax: (01) 44 41 80 21
E-mail: 106310.1071@compuserve.com
Language Plus Services
33, quai de Grenelle
75738 Paris Cedex 15
Tel: (01) 40 59 30 82
Fax: (01) 40 59 31 04
Language Studies International
350, rue St-Honoré
75001 Paris
Tel: (01) 42 60 53 70
Fax: (01) 42 61 41 36
E-mail: Isifrance@wanadoo.fr
Langues Onze
15, rue Gambey
75011 Paris
Tel: (01) 43 38 22 87
Fax: (01) 43 38 36 01

Langues Plus / Sprachcaffe
15, rue d'Hauteville
75010 Paris
Tel: (01) 48 00 06 93
Fax: (01) 42 46 92 62
Linguarama Paris—Champs-Élysées
6, rue de Berri
75008 Paris
Tel: (01) 40 76 07 07
Fax: (01) 40 76 07 76
E-mail: paris@linguarama.com
Linguarama Paris—La Défense
Tour Eve, 7 Étage
Paris–La Défense
92806 Puteaux Cedex
Tel: (01) 47 73 00 95
Fax: (01) 47 73 86 04
E-mail: defense@linguarama.com
Paris Langues
30, rue Cabanis
75014 Paris
Tel: (01) 45 65 05 28
Fax: (01) 45 81 26 28
PERL (Paris École des Roches Langues)
6-8, rue Spinoza
75011 Paris
Tel: (01) 47 00 99 98
Fax: (01) 43 57 14 46
Regency Langues
1, rue Ferdinand-Duval
75004 Paris
Tel: (01) 48 04 99 97
Fax: (01) 48 04 34 96
Regent International
33, rue Claude Bernard
75005 Paris
Tel: (01) 43 31 48 78
Fax: (01) 43 31 48 74
E-mail: regent@club-internet.fr
Télélangue Boulogne
Bureau du Pont de Sèvres
Tour Amboise
92100 Boulogne
Tel: (01) 46 09 20 80
Fax: (01) 46 09 98 03
Treizième sans Frontières
16 bis, rue Ernest et Henri-Rousselle

75013 Paris
Tel: (01) 45 89 52 00
Fax: (01) 45 88 69 32
Union Nationale des Organisations de Séjours Linguistiques
15-19, rue des Mathurins
75009 Paris
Tel: (01) 49 24 03 61
Fax: (01) 42 65 39 38
(represents 40 schools around France)
Université de la Sorbonne Nouvelle: Paris III
13, rue Santeuil
75231 Paris Cedex
Tel: (01) 45 87 40 81
Fax: (01) 43 29 70 13
Université Paris III
46, rue St-Jacques
75230 Paris Cedex 05
Tel: (01) 45 87 40 77
Fax: (01) 40 46 29 29

THE NORTH AND NORTHEAST

AMIENS:
Université de Picardie-Jules-Verne
Chemin du Thil
80025 Amiens Cedex 1
Tel: (03) 22 82 72 51
Fax: (03) 22 82 75 00
LILLE:
Université Catholique de Lille
Centre de Langues, Relations
Internationales et Formation
(CLARIFE)
27, rue d'Armentières
59800 Lille
Tel: (03) 20 57 92 19
Fax: (03) 20 15 29 30
E-mail: 101625.3230@compuserve.com
REIMS:
Université de Reims
SUEE-CIEF
17, rue du Jard
51100 Reims
Tel: (03) 26 47 04 11
Fax: (03) 26 47 05 40

OTHER NORTH AND NORTHEAST:
Centre International Linguistique et Sportif
1, route de Paris
B.P. 36
51700 Troissy
Tel: (03) 26 52 73 08
Fax: (03) 26 52 72 07
E-mail: CILS.FLE@wanadoo.fr
Université Charles-de-Gaulle: Lille III
Dépt. des Étudiants Étrangers
B.P. 149
59653 Villeneuve-d'Ascq Cedex
Tel: (03) 20 41 63 81
Fax: (03) 20 47 23 62
Université d'Été de Boulogne/Mer
B.P. 149
59653 Villeneuve-d'Ascq Cedex
Tel: (03) 20 91 97 66
Fax: (03) 20 47 23 62

EAST TO THE ALPS

ANNECY:
Institut Français d'Annecy (IFALPES)
52, rue des Marquisats
74000 Annecy
Tel: (04) 50 45 38 37
Fax: (04) 50 45 86 72
E-mail: ifalp74@icor.fr
GRENOBLE:
Demos Langues
4, place Robert-Schuman
Europole
38000 Grenoble
Tel: (04) 76 49 96 19
Fax: (04) 76 49 94 71
E-mail: langues@demos.fr
Logos Language Studies
2, chemin des Marronniers
38100 Grenoble
Tel: (04) 76 49 68 16
Fax: (04) 76 70 03 24
E-mail: logos@isworld.com
Université de Stendhal: Grenoble III
Centre Universitaire d'Études
Françaises

B.P. 25
38040 Grenoble Cedex 9
Tel: (04) 76 82 43 27
Fax: (04) 76 82 41 15
NANCY:
Université de Nancy II
Cours d'Été pour Étudiants Étrangers
23, boulevard Albert-1er
B.P. 3397
54015 Nancy Cedex
Tel: (03) 83 96 43 92
Fax: (03) 83 96 70 19
E-mail: taveneau@clsh.u-nancy.fr
Université de Nancy II (SUEE)
23, boulevard Albert-1er
54015 Nancy Cedex
Tel: (03) 83 96 70 05
Fax: (03) 83 96 70 19
E-mail: carton@clsh.u-nancy.fr
STRASBOURG:
Association Internationale Langues et Cultures
1a, place des Orphelins
67000 Strasbourg
Tel: (03) 88 24 18 92
Fax: (03) 88 37 97 25
CIEL de Strasbourg
Immeuble "Le Concorde"
4, quai Kléber
67000 Strasbourg
Tel: (03) 88 22 02 13
Fax: (03) 88 75 73 70
Université des Sciences Humaines de Strasbourg
Institut International d'Études
Françaises
Palais Universitaire
9, place de l'Université
67000 Strasbourg Cedex
Tel: (03) 88 35 53 22
Fax: (03) 88 25 08 63
E-mail: ief@ushs.u-strasbg.fr
OTHER EAST AND THE ALPS:
Université de Franche-Comté
Centre de Linguistique Appliquée
6, rue Gabriel-Plançon
25030 Besançon Cedex

Tel: (03) 81 66 52 00
Fax: (03) 81 66 52 25
E-mail: cla@univ.fcomte.fr
**INSTED (Institute of Foreign
Education)**
B.P. 131
74404 Chamonix-Mont-Blanc
Tel: (05) 46 41 21 39
E-mail: info@insted.se
Institut Français de Chambéry
371, rue de la République
73000 Chambéry
Tel: (04) 79 85 83 16
Fax: (04) 79 85 13 56
E-mail: ifalp73@icor.fr
Linguarama Grenoble
Mini Parc Alpes Congrès
6, rue Roland-Garros
38320 Eybens
Tel: (04) 76 62 00 18
Fax: (04) 76 25 89 60
E-mail: grenoble@linguarama.com
Université de Savoie
ISEFE
Campus de Jacob Bellecombette
B.P. 1104
73011 Chambéry Cedex
Tel: (04) 79 75 84 14
Fax: (04) 79 75 84 16
E-mail: isefe@univ-savoie.fr

THE SOUTH AND SOUTHEAST

AIX-EN-PROVENCE:
Forma Plus Méditerranée
3, place Martin-Luther-King
13090 Aix-en-Provence
Tel: (04) 42 64 02 13
Fax: (04) 42 95 02 73
IS Aix-en-Provence
9, cours des Arts et Métiers
13100 Aix-en-Provence
Tel: (04) 42 93 47 90
Fax: (04) 42 26 31 80
E-mail: 100662.1761@compuserve.com
Université d'Aix Marseille III
Institut d'Études Françaises pour
Étudiants Étrangers

23, rue Gaston-de-Saporta
13625 Aix-en-Provence
Tel: (04) 42 21 70 90
Fax: (04) 42 23 02 64
Université de Provence
Service Commun d'Enseignement du
Français aux Étudiants Étrangers
29, avenue Robert-Schuman
13621 Aix-en-Provence Cedex 1
Tel: (04) 42 20 48 80
Fax: (04) 42 95 36 32
AVIGNON:
**Association de Langue Française
d'Avignon (ALFA)**
4, impasse Romagnoli
84000 Avignon
Tel: (04) 90 85 86 24
Fax: (04) 90 85 86 24
E-mail: alfavignon@avignon.pacwan.net
**Centre d'Études Linguistiques
d'Avignon (CELA)**
16, rue Ste-Catherine
84000 Avignon
Tel: (04) 90 86 04 33
Fax. (04) 90 85 92 01
E-mail: acomi@avignon-et-
provence.com
**Université d'Avignon et des Pays de
Vaucluse**
Centre de Cours Internationaux
d'Avignon
1, avenue St-Jean
84000 Avignon
Tel. (04) 90 86 61 35
Fax. (04) 90 85 08 08
CANNES.
College International de Cannes
1, avenue du Docteur-Alexandre-Pascal
06400 Cannes
Tel· (04) 93 47 39 29
Fax. (04) 93 47 51 97
E-mail: cic@imaginet.fr
Languazur
22, boulevard de la République
06400 Cannes
Tel: (04) 93 39 02 90
Fax: (04) 93 99 44 02

MARSEILLE:
Alliance Française
55, rue Paradis
13006 Marseille
Tel: (04) 91 33 28 19
Fax: (04) 91 33 70 30
MONACO:
Regency School of English & French
7, avenue Prince-Pierre
98000 Monaco
Tel: (377) 92 05 21 21
Fax: (377) 92 05 27 29
MONTPELLIER:
ABM
6, rue des Loriots
Les Aubes
34000 Montpellier
Tel: (04) 67 02 75 00
Fax: (04) 67 02 76 00
Alliance Française
6, rue Boussairolles
34000 Montpellier
Tel: (04) 67 58 92 74
Fax: (04) 67 92 90 83
APRE—Institut Culturel Français
B.P. 5032
34032 Montpellier Cedex
Tel: (04) 67 72 22 77
Fax: (04) 67 79 15 28
Centre de Français Langue Étrangère
3191, route de Mende
B.P. 5056
34033 Montpellier Cedex 1
Tel: (04) 67 04 60 02
Fax: (04) 67 54 25 27
E-mail: peral@iamm.fr
École Méditerranéenne
31, rue de l'Argenterie
34000 Montpellier
Tel: (04) 67 66 14 51
Fax: (04) 67 66 12 01
E-mail: Ecolemed@wanadoo.fr
EUROFAEC (Association Européenne
d'Education et de Culture)
Montpellier-Facultés
B.P. 4113
34091 Montpellier Cedex 5

Tel: (04) 67 68 20 15
Fax: (04) 67 50 60 90
Eurolingua Institute
Havre Saint-Pierre
265, allée du Nouveau Monde
34000 Montpellier
Tel: (04) 67 15 04 73
Fax: (04) 67 15 04 73
E-mail: enquiry@eurolingua.com
ILP
3, rue Auguste-Comte
34000 Montpellier
Tel: (04) 67 92 05 55
Fax: (04) 67 92 30 10
IMEF
Espace Universitaire Albert Camus
21, avenue du Professeur-Grasset
34093 Montpellier
Tel: (04) 67 91 70 00
Fax: (04) 67 91 70 01
E-mail: imef@fle.fr
Institut Montarry
École de Langues en Oc
210, avenue du Val-de-Montferrand
34090 Montpellier
Tel: (04) 67 52 57 79
Fax: (04) 67 52 31 26
E-mail: elo@westminsternet.co.uk
Novalangue
43, rue de l'Université
34000 Montpellier
Tel or Fax: (04) 67 60 92 09
E-mail: novalangue@hotmail.com
Sud-Langue
8, place de la Comédie
34000 Montpellier
Tel: (04) 67 66 30 11
Fax: (04) 67 66 30 11
Université Paul Valéry:
Montpellier III
IEE et CFP
Service des Relations Internationales
Route de Mende
B.P. 5043
34032 Montpellier Cedex 1
Tel: (04) 67 14 21 01
Fax: (04) 67 14 23 94

Language Schools

NICE:
Actilangue École Privée de Langue Française
2, rue Alexis-Mossa
06000 Nice
Tel: (04) 93 96 33 84
Fax: (04) 93 44 37 16
E-mail: actilangue@imaginet.fr
Alliance Française
2, rue de Paris
06000 Nice
Tel: (04) 93 62 67 66
Fax: (04) 93 85 28 06
Alpha-B Institut Linguistique
7, boulevard Prince-de-Galles
06000 Nice
Tel: (04) 93 53 11 10
Fax: (04) 93 53 11 20
E-mail: alpha.b@webstore.fr
Azurlingua
25, boulevard Raimbaldi
06000 Nice
Tel: (04) 93 62 01 11
Fax: (04) 93 62 22 56
Info@azurlingua.com
Web site: http://www.azurlingua.com
Interactive magazine:
www.bonjourdefrance.com
Côte d'Azur Langues
9, quai des Deux-Emmanuel
06300 Nice
Tel: (04) 92 00 00 92
Fax: (04) 92 00 00 93
EF
21, rue Meyerbeer
06000 Nice
Tel: (04) 93 88 84 85
Fax: (04) 93 88 10 21
France Langue Schools of Paris and Nice / Riviera
Web site: http://www.france-langue.fr
14, rue Léonard-de-Vinci
75116 Paris
Tel: (01) 45 00 40 15
Fax: (01) 45 00 53 41
E-mail: frlang_p@club-internet.fr

Address in Nice:
22, avenue Notre-Dame
06000 Nice
Tel: (04) 93 13 78 88
Fax: (04) 93 13 78 89
E-mail: frlang_n@club-internet.fr
International House Centre de Langues Riviera
62, rue Gioffredo
06000 Nice
Tel: (04) 93 62 60 62
Fax: (04) 93 80 53 09
E-mail: info@ih-nice.com
Langueurop
30, rue de France
06000 Nice
Tel: (04) 93 88 51 47
Fax: (04) 93 88 11 62
Pluriel Langues, Nice
213, promenade des Anglais
06200 Nice
Tel: (04) 93 97 16 73
Fax: (04) 93 96 84 85
E-mail: 106441.241@compuserve.com
Université de Nice Sophia-Antipolis
Études Françaises pour l'Étranger
98, boulevard E. Herriot
06204 Nice Cedex 3
Tel: (04) 93 37 53 89
Fax: (04) 93 37 54 98
Université de Nice Sophia-Antipolis
Université Internationale d'Été
Faculté des Lettres
98, boulevard E. Herriot
06200 Nice
Tel: (04) 93 37 53 94
Fax: (04) 93 37 54 66
PERPIGNAN:
Université de Perpignan
52, avenue de Villeneuve
66860 Perpignan Cedex
Tel: (04) 68 66 60 50
Fax: (04) 68 66 03 76
E-mail: ue@univ-perp.fr
TOULOUSE:
Alliance Française Toulouse
9, place du Capitole

31000 Toulouse
Tel: (05) 34 45 26 10
Fax: (05) 34 45 26 11
OTHER SOUTH AND SOUTHEAST:
Association Interlangue
14, impasse de la Source
34200 Sète
Tel: (04) 67 51 31 00
Fax: (04) 67 43 03 82
Campus International
B.P. 133
83957 La Garde Cedex
Tel: (04) 94 08 94 08
Fax: (04) 94 21 43 41
Centre International d'Accueil et de Formation
Château de Deomas
07104 Annonay Cedex
Tel: (04) 75 69 26 00
Fax. (04) 75 69 26 19
E-mail: ciaf@mail.mairie-annonay.fr
Centre International d'Antibes
28, avenue du Château
06600 Antibes
Tel: (04) 93 74 47 76
Fax: (04) 93 74 57 11
Centre International des Langues
166, avenue Majoral-Arnaud
04100 Manosque
Tel: (04) 92 72 46 19
Fax: (04) 92 87 82 81
E-mail: cil@lac.gulliver.fr
Web site: http://www.chez.com/artlingua
Centre Méditerranéen
Chemin des Oliviers
06320 Cap d'Ail
Tel. (04) 93 78 21 59
Fax: (04) 93 41 83 96
E-mail: centremed@monte-carlo.mc
Crealangues
Le Monastère de Ségriès
Parc Régional du Verdon
04360 Moustiers-Sainte-Marie
Tel: (04) 92 77 74 58
Fax. (04) 92 77 75 18
E-mail: CREA.Langues@wanadoo.fr

ELFCA
(Institut International d'Enseignement de la Langue Française sur la Côte d'Azur)
66, avenue de Toulon
83400 Hyères
Tel: (04) 94 65 03 31
Fax: (04) 94 65 81 22
E-mail: elfca@elfca.com
Web site: http.//www.elfca.com
Equivalence Langues et Communication
Place Sophie-Laffitte
P.B. 127
06903 Sophia-Antipolis
Tel: (04) 92 96 57 05
Fax. (04) 92 96 57 01
E-mail: equiset@riviera-isp.com
France Langue et Culture
Le Vallis Curans B
Avenue de Valescure
83700 Saint-Raphaël
Tel: (04) 92 09 54 50
Fax: (04) 92 09 54 50
E-mail: france.langue@swipnet.se
French-American Center of Provence
10, montée de la Tour
30400 Villeneuve-les-Avignon
Tel: (04) 90 25 93 23
Fax: (04) 90 25 93 24
Institut de Français
23, avenue Général-Leclerc
06230 Villefranche-sur-Mer
Tel: (04) 93 01 88 44
Fax: (04) 93 76 92 17
E-mail: insfran@aol.com
The Marzio School
5-7, rue des Baumes
13800 Istres
Tel: (04) 42 55 01 25
Fax: (04) 42 55 10 83
E-mail: marzio.school@aix.pacwan.net
Le Monastère de Ségriès
Parc Régional du Verdon
04360 Moustiers-Sainte-Marie
Tel: (04) 92 77 74 58
Fax. (04) 92 77 75 18

E-mail: crea.langues.be@ibm.net
(info and booking)
E-mail: CREA.Langues@wanadoo.fr
(school and management)
Web site: http://perso.wanadoo.fr/
crea-langues/
Université d'Été/ Office de Tourisme de Menton
B.P. 239
1, avenue St-Jacques
06500 Menton
Tel: (04) 93 35 83 33
Fax: (04) 93 28 35 99

CENTRAL FRANCE

CLERMONT:
Université Blaise Pascal
Service Universitaire des Étudiants
Étrangers
34, avenue Carnot
63006 Clermont-Ferrand Cedex 1
Tel: (04) 73 40 64 97
Fax: (04) 73 40 62 83

DIJON:
Alliance Française de Bourgogne
ESC
29, rue Sambin
21000 Dijon Cedex
Tel: (03) 80 72 59 81
Fax: (03) 80 72 58 71
Linguarama Dijon
Amphypolis
10, rue Paul-Verlaine
Rond Point de l'Europe
21000 Dijon
Tel: (03) 80 78 77 30
Fax: (03) 80 78 77 35
E-mail: dijon@linguarama.com
Université de Bourgogne
Centre International d'Études
Françaises
Esplanade Erasme
B.P. 28
21001 Dijon Cedex
Tel: (03) 80 39 35 60
Fax: (03) 80 39 35 61
E-mail: cief@u-bourgogne.fr

LYON:
Alliance Française
11, rue Pierre-Bourdan
69003 Lyon
Tel: (04) 78 95 24 72
Fax: (04) 78 60 77 28
Demos Langues
33, cours de la Liberté
69003 Lyon
Tel: (04) 78 60 15 60
Fax: (04) 78 62 25 18
E-mail: langues@demos.fr
Discours et Méthode
23, quai Claude-Bernard
69007 Lyon
Tel: (04) 78 69 39 75
Fax: (04) 78 69 39 75
E-mail: dismet@compuserve.com
Info Langues
52, avenue Barthélemy-Buyer
69009 Lyon
Tel: (04) 78 36 11 11
Fax: (04) 78 25 32 19
Institut Lyonnais pour la Diffusion de la Langue et de la Culture Françaises
40, rue de Gerland
69007 Lyon
Tel: (04) 78 69 25 04
Fax: (04) 78 69 14 30
Université Catholique de Lyon
Institut de Langue et de Culture
Françaises
25, rue du Plat
69288 Lyon Cedex 02
Tel: (04) 72 32 50 53
Fax: (04) 72 32 51 82
Université Lumière: Lyon II
Centre International d'Études Françaises
16, quai Claude-Bernard
69365 Lyon Cedex 07
Tel: (04) 78 69 71 35/36
Fax: (04) 78 69 70 93
E-mail: jeannez@diogene.univ-lyon2.fr

ORLÉANS:
Université d'Orléans
Programmes Internationaux
Château de la Source

B.P. 6749
45067 Orléans Cedex 2
Tel. (02) 38 41 71 88
Fax: (02) 38 41 70 69
TOURS:
Association Contacts
3, rue du Maréchal-Foch
37000 Tours
Tel: (02) 47 20 20 57
Fax. (02) 47 20 68 92
(organizes linguistic and cultural
programs around France)
CLE (Centre Linquistique pour
Étrangers)
7-9, place du Châteauneuf
37000 Tours
Tel: (02) 47 64 06 19
Fax: (02) 47 05 84 61
E-mail: cle@lenet.fr
Institut de Touraine
place du 14-Juillet
B.P. 2047
37020 Tours Cedex
Tel: (02) 47 05 76 83
Fax: (02) 47 20 48 98
E-mail: Institut.Touraine@wanadoo.fr
Université de Tours
CLCFEE
3, rue des Tanneurs
37041 Tours Cedex
Tel: (02) 47 36 66 34
OTHER CENTRAL FRANCE:
Alliance Française Vendôme
21, place St-Martin
41100 Vendôme
Tel: (02) 54 73 13 20
Fax: (02) 54 73 23 20
INSA—Lyon Service de Français
20, avenue Albert-Einstein
69621 Villeurbanne Cedex
Tel: (04) 72 43 83 66
Fax: (04) 72 43 88 95
E-mail: servfran@insa-lyon.fr
Centre International d'Études
Françaises de Touraine
Château du Bois Minhy
41700 Contres

Tel: (02) 54 79 51 01
Fax: (02) 54 79 06 26
Université Jean-Monnet
Centre International de Langue et
Civilisation
30, rue Ferdinand-Gambon
Site Gambon A
42100 Saint-Étienne
Tel: (04) 77 46 32 00
Fax: (04) 77 46 32 09
Eurocentres
9, mail St-Thomas
B.P. 214
37402 Amboise Cedex
Tel: (02) 47 23 10 60
Fax: (02) 47 30 54 99
E-mail. 101510.2352@compuserve.com
Saint Denis European School
19, avenue du Général-de-Gaulle
B.P. 146
37601 Loches Cedex
Tel: (02) 47 59 04 26
Fax: (02) 47 94 04 50
E-mail: saint-denis@touraine.com

THE WEST AND NORTHWEST
ANGERS:
Centre International d'Études
Françaises
3, place André-Leroy
B.P. 808
49008 Angers Cedex 1
Tel. (02) 41 88 30 15
Fax. (02) 41 87 71 67
E-mail: iplv@uco.fr
Université d'Angers
Services des Relations Internationales
30, rue des Arènes
B.P. 3532
49035 Angers Cedex
Tel: (02) 41 23 23 23
Fax: (02) 41 23 23 00
BORDEAUX:
BLS
1, cours Georges-Clemenceau
33000 Bordeaux
Tel: (05) 56 51 00 76

Fax: (05) 56 51 76 15
E-mail: bls@imaginet.fr
LA ROCHELLE:
CUFLE (Centre Universitaire de Français Langue Étrangère)
Université de la Rochelle
Faculté des Langues, Arts et Sciences Humaines
Parvis Fernand Braudel
17071 La Rochelle Cedex 9
Tel: (05) 46 45 68 00
Fax. (05) 46 50 59 95
E-mail: pgrange@flash.univ-lr.fr
Eurocentres
Avenue Marillac
17024 La Rochelle
Tel: (05) 46 50 57 33
Fax: (05) 46 44 24 77
E-mail: 106307.217@compuserve.com
Institut d'Études Françaises de la Rochelle
(Université de Poitiers)
102, rue de Coureilles
Les Minimes
17024 La Rochelle Cedex 1
Tel: (05) 46 51 77 50
Fax: (05) 46 51 77 53
E-mail: ief@ief-la-rochelle.fr
RENNES:
CIREFE (Centre International Rennais d'Études du Français pour Étrangers)
Université Rennes II—Haute Bretagne
6, avenue Gaston-Berger
35043 Rennes Cedex
Tel: (02) 99 14 13 01
Fax: (02) 99 14 13 10
E-mail: Cirefe@uhb.fr
Web site: http://www.uhb.fr/cirefe
Langue et Communication
16, rue de Penhoët
35065 Rennes Cedex
Tel: (02) 99 78 15 62
Fax: (02) 99 79 33 91
Maison des Langues
1, place du Maréchal-Juin
35000 Rennes
Tel: (02) 99 30 25 15

Fax: (02) 99 30 34 54
Université de Rennes II
Cours Universitaire d'Été de St. Malo
6, avenue Gaston-Berger
35043 Rennes Cedex
Tel: (02) 99 54 66 44
Fax: (02) 99 59 50 20
E-mail: jean-françois.bouillard@uhb.fr
ROUEN:
Alliance Française
79, quai du Havre
76000 Rouen
Tel: (02) 35 98 55 99
Fax: (02) 38 89 98 58
OTHER WEST AND NORTHWEST:
CEFA Normandie / Centre d'Études de Lisieux
10–14, boulevard Carnot
B.P. 176
14104 Lisieux Cedex
Tel: (02) 31 31 22 01
Fax: (02) 31 31 22 21
Centre d'Études des Langues de St. Malo
Le Moulin du Domaine
B.P. 6
35430 Saint-Jouan-des-Guérets
Tel: (02) 99 19 15 46
Fax: (02) 99 81 48 78
Centre International des Langues et Cultures
2, rue Mélusine
85240 Foussais-Payre
Tel: (02) 51 51 45 34
Fax: (02) 51 51 45 58
Centre International pour Enfants
Château de Bellevue
49781 Le Bourg-d'Iré
Tel: (02) 38 88 21 16
Fax: (02) 41 61 56 18
Château de la Baudonnière
Les Chambres
50320 La Haye-Pesnel
Tel: (02) 33 60 46 95
Fax: (02) 33 60 50 23
(courses in Normandy for school groups only)

CIEL
B.P. 35
29480 Le Relecq-Kerhuon
Tel: (02) 98 30 57 57
Fax: (02) 98 28 26 95
E-mail: gueguen@ciel.fr
École des Roches
B.P. 710
Avenue Edmond-Desmolins
27137 Verneuil-sur-Avre
Tel. (02) 32 23 40 00
Fax: (02) 32 60 11 44
En Famille in Brittany
354, rue Kerdanet
22420 Plouaret
Tel: (02) 96 38 80 63
La Ferme—Centre Linguistique
Résidentiel
La Petite Éguille
17600 Saujon
Tel: (05) 46 22 84 31
Fax. (05) 46 22 91 38
E-mail: fer@filnet.fr
Institut Français des Alpes
B.P. 15
35660 Cournonterral
Tel: (04) 67 78 36 42
Fax: (04) 67 78 36 47
(HQ address only; courses in Megève in
Mont-Blanc area)
Institut Français des Alpes et
Méditerranée
B.P. 15
35660 Cournonterral
Tel: (04) 67 78 36 42
Fax: (04) 67 78 36 47
(HQ address; courses in Sète)
La Maison Bilingue
La Ville Ès Goutés

22650 Ploubalay
Tel: (02) 96 27 34 29
Fax: (02) 96 27 22 08
Université de Caen
Cours Internationaux d'Été
Vissol, avenue de Bruxelles
B.P. 5186
14032 Caen Cedex
Tel: (02) 31 56 55 38
Fax: (02) 31 93 69 19
E-mail. ceuie@setter.cgi.unicaen.fr
Université de Caen
Centre d'Enseignement Universitaire
International pour Étrangers
Vissol, avenue de Bruxelles
B.P. 5186
14032 Caen Cedex
Tel. (02) 31 56 55 38
Fax: (02) 31 93 69 19
E-mail: ceuie@setter.cgi.unicaen.fr
Université de Nantes
Centre d'Enseignement du Français
Langue Étrangère
Chemin de la Sensive-du-Tertre
B.P. 1025
44036 Nantes Cedex 1
Tel: (02) 40 14 10 10
Fax: (02) 40 14 13 10
Université de Poitiers
Centre de Français Langue Étrangère
95, avenue Recteur-Pineau
86022 Poitiers
Tel: (05) 49 45 32 94
Fax: (05) 49 45 32 95
E-mail: Centre.FLE@cri.univ-poitiers.fr
Université de Rouen
1, rue Thomas-Becket
76130 Mont Saint Aignan
Tel: (02) 35 14 63 41

Primary and Secondary Schools

For many families moving abroad, a major concern is what to do with school-aged children. The experience of moving to a foreign country can be very different for children than it is for adults. Uprooting a family and moving into an entirely different culture can be a stressful experience, especially for children who have developed ties with people, places, and things around the home they are used to. How well a child adapts to a major relocation is dependent on his or her age and particular personality, and on how the move is approached by the family. Generally speaking, younger children tend to do better than older kids and teenagers. The youngest children—infants and toddlers for whom virtually everything is new—usually have the easiest time. Young children have an immense capacity for soaking up language and social nuance, and you might find that they can adapt more quickly and easily than you. This is particularly apparent when it comes to language, and children under about ten years of age generally pick up language much more easily and quickly than older children and adults. You might be embarrassed to find that your son or daughter, after only a short time in France, is coming home from school speaking French better than you ever will. For older children, especially teenagers, moving away from home and leaving friends and familiar places can be a very stressful experience. Teenagers and adolescents typically have a more difficult time since they're at an age when friends and environment are particularly important. Of course this is not always the case; you might find that your child or teenager adapts very easily to life abroad and relishes the experience of living in a new culture and discovering a new way of life.

Regardless of the age of your child or teenager, finding the right school for him or her is certainly of the utmost importance. Your child's options will vary depending on where in France you'll be living, how much you can afford to spend on a school, and what type of curriculum you wish your child to follow. Many Americans moving to France send their children to a private school or a special school for expatriate children, rather than an ordinary public school. The curriculum at such schools is similar to those of U.S. schools, so children are less likely to fall behind their Stateside peers. Most companies will help their workers find an appropriate school, and some will pay all or part of the tuition. There are many differences between the French school system and the American one that you should understand regardless of where your child goes to school. When deciding where to send your child or teenager to school, you should also take into consideration how long you intend to live in France, or travel elsewhere, before returning home. Many families are more likely to put younger children into a French school, while older children or teenagers might find an international or American school less disruptive unless they intend to complete the entire French curriculum.

In addition, American high school students are increasingly electing to spend a semester or longer in France or another foreign country, and parents often find that this can be a very rewarding experience for their children. While it is a much more common activity for college-aged students, there are many programs that will place teenagers in French families and enroll them in a French school for a semester or longer in exchange for your family or another American household accepting a foreign child. If you're a high schooler or parent of a high schooler going abroad for school, there are many choices when it comes to education in France. The Council on Standards for International Educational Travel (CSIET) publishes an annual directory of exchange programs; refer to the address at the end of this chapter for contact information.

The French School System

In France, most children start school when they're between two and three years of age, at a *jardin d'enfants* or *école maternelle*, and are obliged to attend school until the age of sixteen. Unlike the university system in France, which is wildly overcrowded and lacking in resources, French primary and secondary schools are quite good and provide children with a high level of education, generally considered to be better than the American equivalent. Between the ages of six and ten or eleven, children attend an *école primaire*, and then continue to a *collège* and then a lycée. Once they've completed the lycée, at about the age of eighteen or nineteen, and passed the challenging *baccalauréat* exam, French students have more or less the educational equivalent of an American associate's degree, or about two years of a four-year American university. Many French schools do not hold classes on Wednesdays, but require that students attend a half-day on Saturday. Children who are enrolled in the French school system generally must attend the school closest to their home, but you can often request that your child attend a different school through a special arrangement with the *mairie* of your village or town.

While the French school system is generally considered to be very good, it has also been criticized for being too strict and impersonal, providing little time for extracurricular activities, and not encouraging creativity. Even in French private schools, art is not a standard subject, and it is rare to find a colorful classroom with students' art plastered all over the walls, while this type of environment is commonplace, even expected, in the United States. This apparent lack of creativity is more evident in the *collèges* and lycées than in schools for younger children, but there are subtle, yet unmistakable, differences that appear throughout the French educational system. If you do find that your child's school lacks programs for sports or other extracurricular activities, there are usually dozens of local programs and clubs for children that make up for the in-school deficiency. That said, it is important to shop around, and find a school in which your child will feel comfortable.

Very Young Children

If you've got a toddler or preschool-aged child, the French school system may be a good option. Even if you're planning on being in France for only a relatively short time, young children can come away with a native fluency in French and a fluidity in French culture that they will never lose. The French system of nursery schools, or *écoles maternelles*, is completely subsidized by the government, and tuition is free. Like American nursery schools, the *écoles maternelles* are designed to teach children basic coordination and social skills and provide the foundation for reading and writing. Once you get to France, information about *écoles maternelles* can be found at your local *mairie*, or city hall. French parents generally start a child in *école maternelle* after he or she is properly toilet trained—sometime between the ages of two and four. Before that, working parents can send their toddler to a *jardin d'enfants* or a *crèche*, or nursery, for day care until the child is ready to enter a regular nursery school. Most *écoles maternelles* hold flexible hours and school is optional for children until they are six.

Primary School

French children start primary school at the age of about six and continue until they're about eleven. *École primaire* is generally comparable to first through fifth grade in the United States, although the "grade" system is more or less reversed. Students begin *école primaire* in the *onzième* and will finish the *septième* before moving on to the first stage of secondary school, a *collège*. There is no exam at the end of the French primary school curriculum, but a student's transcripts are forwarded to his or her *collège*. Primary schools can be public or private, and may offer a variety of different curricula.

Secondary School

When children are about eleven years old, they enter the French secondary school program at a *collège*. The secondary school system is divided into the first cycle *(premier cycle)*, which goes from the *sixième* through *troisième*, which a child completes at about fifteen. Then students continue with the second cycle at a lycée, which covers three additional years of more specialized education. The three years of lycée are sequentially called *"seconde," "première,"* and *"terminale."*

Other Schools

There are schools that adhere to a more or less American, British, or other foreign curriculum, and others that adhere to the French system but are bilingual or multicultural in orientation. Most of these specialized schools are private and located in Paris, although there is at least one international school that can be found in each of several of the country's larger cities including Cannes, Lille, Grenoble, Lyon, Bordeaux, Strasbourg, and Nice. In addition, there are private Montessori and Rudolph Steiner (Waldorf) schools that adhere to nontraditional curricula. Some of these schools also offer preparation for the International Baccalaureate (IB) exams, a series of standardized tests that was designed to address the diversity of European educational systems. The IB curriculum is rigorous and difficult, but is accepted as sufficient university preparation almost universally, both in the United States and abroad. Many students who successfully complete the IB curriculum can be granted a year's worth of credit at an American university.

National and International Schools

Most "national" schools, or schools that are fully accredited by a country other than France and follow that country's curriculum, are private and located in Paris. The American School of Paris offers classes taught entirely in English, preparation for the U.S. College Board exams such as the SAT, and an American diploma upon graduation. The Marymount School, located just outside Paris in the well-to-do suburb of Neuilly-sur-Seine, is an American Catholic K–8 school. The International School of Paris offers either an American diploma or preparation for the International Baccalaureate (IB) or the British A-level exams. There are also national schools in Paris that adhere to the British, Japanese, German, and Italian school systems. For American and international schools located outside of Paris, refer to the address section that follows this chapter.

Bilingual Schools

The French school system includes a variety of schools that teach classes in both French and English and prepare students for continuing

179

education outside of France. While many of these schools are considered to be private, some are subsidized by the government and are less expensive than the fully private national and international schools. In addition, some public French *collèges* and lycées offer special sections for foreign students. If your child already speaks some French and won't mind a more substantial immersion into French language and culture, bilingual schools can offer an affordable and attractive educational option. These schools and programs vary immensely, so you should thoroughly research the curriculum and understand exactly what classes are taught, and in what languages, before enrolling your child. The address section at the end of this chapter includes a variety of schools that offer bilingual curricula.

Useful Addresses: American, International, and Bilingual Schools in France

FOR A DIRECTORY OF EXCHANGE
PROGRAMS

CSIET (Council on Standards for International Educational Travel)
212 South Henry Street
Alexandria, VA 22314
Tel: (703) 739-9050
Fax: (703) 739-9035
E-mail: exchanges@aol.com

PRIMARY AND SECONDARY SCHOOLS
PARIS:
The American School of Paris
41, rue Pasteur
92210 Saint-Cloud
Tel: (01) 41 12 82 82
Fax: (01) 46 02 23 90
Marymount International
72, boulevard de la Saussaye
92200 Neuilly-sur-Seine
Tel: (01) 46 24 10 51
Fax: (01) 46 37 07 50
International School of Paris
6, rue Beethoven
75006 Paris
Tel: (01) 42 24 09 54
Fax: (01) 45 27 15 93

British School in Paris
38, quai de l'Écluse
78290 Croissy-sur-Seine
Tel: (01) 34 80 45 94
École Active Bilingue
Five locations:
16, rue Marguerite
75017 Paris
Tel. (01) 46 22 40 20
6, avenue Van Dyck
75008 Paris
Tel. (01) 46 22 14 24
117, boulevard Malesherbes
75008 Paris
Tel: (01) 45 63 47 00
24 bis, rue de Berri
75008 Paris
Tel: (01) 47 63 30 73
123, rue de la Pompe
75016 Paris
Tel: (01) 45 53 89 36
École Active Bilingue Jeannine Manuel
Two locations:
70, rue du Théâtre
75015 Paris
Tel: (01) 44 37 00 08
15, rue Edgar-Faure

75015 Paris
Tel: (01) 47 34 27 72
The Bilingual Montessori School
Two locations:
65, quai d'Orsay
75007 Paris
Tel: (01) 45 55 13 27
23, avenue George-V
75008 Paris
Tel. (01) 47 20 28 10
Eurecole
5, rue de Lübeck
75016 Paris
Tel: (01) 40 70 12 81
Institut de la Tour
86, rue de la Tour
75116 Paris
Tel: (01) 45 04 73 35
OUTSIDE PARIS.
Lycée Internationale Stendhal
1, rue Raoul-Blanchard
38000 Grenoble
Tel: (04) 76 54 83 83
Fax: (04) 76 54 62 45
Cité Scolaire Internationale de Lyon
2, place de Montréal
69006 Lyon Cedex
Tel: (04) 78 69 60 06
Fax: (04) 78 69 60 36
École Active Bilingue Jeannine Manuel
418 bis, rue Albert-Bailly
59700 Marcq-en-Baroeul
Tel: (03) 20 65 90 50
Fax: (03) 20 98 06 41
Lycée-Collège International des Pontonniers
1, rue des Pontonniers
67081 Strasbourg Cedex
Tel: (03) 88 37 15 25
Fax. (03) 88 37 98 94

KINDERGARTEN AND NURSERY SCHOOLS
United Nations Nursery School
40, rue Pierre-Guérin
75016 Paris
Tel: (01) 45 27 20 24
Fondation Croix Saint-Simon
3, rue Oudinot
75007 Paris
Tel: (01) 43 06 11 16
Fax: (01) 47 34 43 88
The American Kindergarten
3 bis, rue Émile-Duclaux
Mailing address.
35, avenue de Ségur
75007 Paris
Tel: (01) 42 19 02 14
La Petite École Bilingue
Two locations:
17, rue Cardinet
75017 Paris
Tel: (01) 43 80 25 34
9, rue Verniquet
75017 Paris
Tel: (01) 43 80 25 34
Rencontres et Échanges
84, rue de la Folie-Méricourt
75011 Paris
Tel: (01) 53 36 81 10
Les Petits Dragons
Tel: (01) 42 28 56 17
Three locations.
2, rue Jacquemont
75017 Paris
Saint-George's Church
7, rue Auguste-Vacquerie
75116 Paris
17, rue Bayard
75008 Paris
The Lennen Bilingual School
65, quai d'Orsay
75007 Paris
Tel: (01) 47 05 66 55

CHAPTER SEVENTEEN

Bookstores, Libraries, and Research

When I moved to France to work as a journalist, it was after having lived and worked in several other European countries. My overseas research experience had not been positive. While doing research in France is not as straightforward a process as it is in the United States, I was delighted to discover all the resources available to international scholars and book lovers alike.

The first thing to know about finding books in France is that in France a bookstore is called a *librairie* and a library is called a *bibliothèque*. So to be sure we understand each other, I could say "tracking down texts and other documents in French *bibliothèques* and *archives* can be a chore but a plethora of *librairies* (French and English) made up for the hassle."

English-Language Bookstores

All the major cities and large towns in France have at least one foreign-language bookstore. Paris and some of the larger cities have far more. If you happen to live in a more rural part of the country, check in some of the French-language bookstores for English-language reading material, as they often have sections dedicated to English literature.

As the capital, Paris has an overwhelming selection of bookstores that run the range from the huge international chain W. H. Smith to smaller more intimate shops like Tea and Tattered Pages. For an extensive list of bookshops in Paris, see the list at the end of this chapter. While some stores have a large selection of books, almost all are willing to work with you and order books that might not be in stock. Along with the many bookstores dedicated exclusively to English-language texts and periodicals, there are also several enormous multimedia chains in Paris. Both the Virgin Mégastore and FNAC, two media department stores, have fairly large English-language sections and carry a great selection of American music and often original language videocassettes. FNAC department stores are found all over France.

The English-language bookstores in Paris are great for networking, too. Many of them post small ads and announcements for events in the English-speaking community. They also all serve as distribution points for the various free English-language newspapers and magazines, like *FUSAC*, *Paris Free Voice*, and *The Eyes* (a magazine for Irish citizens living in Paris). Many also publish quarterly newsletters and invite authors to speak.

If you are frustrated with the selection or high prices at the English-language bookstores, you can always order your books by telephone directly from the publisher or over the Internet and have them shipped to you, if the company is willing to ship overseas. In addition, a new type of service has sprung up in France as of late: companies that will order books for you from the United States and arrange for them to be shipped.

English-Language Libraries

There is a host of English-language reference and lending libraries in France, with a heavy concentration in Paris. The shining star among these is the American Library in Paris, located just behind the Eiffel Tower. Founded in 1920, the ALP has a collection of more than 100,000 volumes, including more than eight thousand books and tapes for children and young adults. The ALP also has a full range of modern research facilities including CD-ROM indexes, a collection of more than 450 periodicals some going back as far as the nineteenth century, and a computerized card catalog. Members can also access the research facilities of the American University Library, in the building adjacent to the ALP. The library is also a social and networking hub for Americans in Paris. The library sponsors story hours and other special events for children, courses, gala dinners, and a now-famous series of evenings with authors.

The wall behind the current periodicals section is plastered with handwritten classified ads and announcements by various organizations of ongoing events and happenings and is a great place to network. The library is a nonprofit organization and membership is open to everyone. The library offers a range of membership options as well as the possibility to purchase a one-time entrance for consultation of the library. For those who do not live in Paris, the library also has branches in Angers, Montpellier, Nancy, and Toulouse.

There are a number of other English-language reference and lending libraries in Paris including the British Council Library, an English library with books, records, and videotapes mainly concerned with British culture; WICE, an American nonprofit educational and cultural association with reference and lending libraries; the English Language Library for the Blind, which provides audio-books to English-speaking blind and visually handicapped subscribers outside the English-speaking world; and the American Tax Institute in Europe, SA, which has an extensive library of U.S. tax documentation.

French Archives and Research Institutes

If you've come to France to perform serious primary source research you will want to head to one or more of the many archives and research institutes. Even if you know where the archives you are interested in are located (which is already half the battle), you then have to secure access. The primary source of official French records and documents are the *Archives nationales*. While much of the documentation contained in the *Archives nationales* can be found in Paris, for certain subject areas, the material has been distributed to different archival research centers. For primary source research at the regional and departmental level, you will have to turn to the *Archives départementales*.

Anyone can gain access to the National Archives by presenting himself at the *bureau d'inscriptions* at any of the National Archives with a photo ID. It is possible to choose between a temporary and an annual membership. Temporary membership, valid for fifteen days, costs half the price of an annual membership and is renewable only once. Individuals bearing a membership card from any one of the National Archive Research Centers can access any of the others.

Most documents related to the domestic activities of the federal government are housed in the main Parisian *Archives nationales*. Research relating to the *"outre-mer"* and former French colonies is housed in the CAOM, the Centre des Archives d'Outre-Mer, in Aix-en-Provence. The Foreign Ministry has two sets of its own archives which are divided between the Centre Parisien des Archives Diplomatiques and the Deuxième Centre des Archives Diplomatiques in Nantes. Documentation relating to business, the economy, and the world of work is housed in the Centre des Archives du Monde du Travail (CAMT) in Roubaix. Finally, the documents related to the activities of the most recent administrations are located in Fontainebleau, just outside Paris at the Centre des Archives Contemporaines.

Obtaining texts and documentation from any of these libraries is a fairly complicated process. Once you have acquired a library card, you can begin to study the library's inventory to discover the code of the precise document you are looking for. You must then request the document, several hours and at times several days before you can actually even see it. Once you have been given access to the document, it is then reserved for your private consultation in the library facilities for the following seven days. To make this process a bit easier, if you have a library card, you can also consult some of the inventory and request documents using Minitel and dialing 3616 CARAN. Most of the archives are open from nine to five Monday through Friday and closed on national holidays. Some of the research centers have limited hours on Saturday. Like much else in France, the archives tend to close for the month of August. So be sure and plan any research expeditions around that inconvenience.

French Libraries

The Bibliothèque Nationale in Paris, which like our Library of Congress contains a copy of every book published in France, is only open to graduate students and researchers. To do research here, you have to bring references from a professor and a description of your work.

In addition to the National Library, most French cities and towns also have what are known as *bibliothèques municipales*. Outside of cities, these *bibliothèques* are often quite poorly supplied and open only sporadically. However, in Paris and in some of the larger towns and cities, these can be quite a treat. The Pompidou Center library in Paris is one that springs to mind. With a wonderful view of the city and a fairly large collection, especially relating to the arts and cinema, this is one library that begins to resemble American standards. Many of the fifty-five municipal libraries in Paris and some in larger cities will also likely have a section of English-language books. You can find out more information about these libraries and their opening hours at your local town hall.

University libraries are another good source of information. Depending on the library, you may or may not have to be enrolled to be permitted to consult texts. If you know that a university library or a library belonging to a museum or a private collection has material that you need, try to arrange access before coming to France. At the very least, it is wise to bring along an open letter from a professor.

Most of the large French newspapers keep back issues and if you have a valid request and are willing to pay the price of photocopies and to wait several days, they are often quite helpful. Just contact the newspaper in question and ask for their archives.

Doing Genealogical Research in France

If you have French ancestors and are interested in tracing your roots, you would be best off to gather as much information as possible ahead of time, especially relating to the residences of those relatives, as each city maintains its own archives. There are several places to begin looking. If you know the exact name of the town, you can head to the *mairie* (the town hall) and apply to the *bureau de l'État civil* to obtain copies of birth certificates *(extraits de naissance)*, death certificates *(actes de décès)*, and marriage certificates *(extraits d'acte de mariage)*. In Paris, some of these records are housed on microfilm in the National Archives. If you want information on records relating to former Parisian residents, you must direct your request to the Archives de Paris. There is no charge for copies of any of these documents.

Another option is to enlist the help of one of France's many professional *généalogistes*. A partial list of Parisian *généalogistes* can be found

The Jardin de Luxembourg in Paris is the perfect place to sit with a book.

at the end of this chapter. To find a genealogist in your area, look in the professional Yellow Pages under *"Généalogistes."*

Useful Addresses

ENGLISH-LANGUAGE BOOKSTORES

Abbey Bookshop
29, rue de la Parcheminerie
75005 Paris
Tel: (01) 46 33 16 24
Albion
13, rue Charles-V
75004 Paris
Tel: (01) 42 72 50 71

Attica Bookshop
64, rue de la Folie-Méricourt
75011 Paris
Tel: (01) 49 29 27 27
Australian Bookshop
23, rue Monge
75005 Paris
Tel. (01) 43 29 08 65

Book Seller
23, rue Jean-de-Beauvais
75005 Paris
Tel: (01) 46 34 62 03
Brentano's
37, avenue de l'Opéra
75002 Paris
Tel: (01) 42 61 52 50
FNAC Librairie Internationale
71, boulevard St-Germain
75006 Paris
Tel: (01) 44 41 31 50
Galignani
224, rue de Rivoli
75001 Paris
Tel: (01) 42 60 76 07
Golden Books
3, rue de Larochelle
74014 Paris
Tel. (01) 43 22 38 56
Librairie Flammarion 4
La Maison Rustique
26, rue Jacob
75006 Paris
Tel: (01) 43 25 67 00
Nouveau Quartier Latin
78, boulevard St-Michel
75006 Paris
Tel: (01) 43 26 42 70
San Francisco Book Co.
17, rue Monsieur-le-Prince
75006 Paris
Tel: (01) 43 29 15 70
Shakespeare & Company
37, rue de la Bûcherie
75005 Paris
Tel: (01) 43 26 96 50
Tea and Tattered Pages
24, rue Mayet
75006 Paris
Tel: (01) 40 65 94 35
Village Voice Bookshop
6, rue Princesse
75006 Paris
Tel: (01) 46 33 36 47
Virgin Mégastore
52, avenue des Champs-Élysées
75008 Paris
Tel: (01) 49 43 50 00

W. H. Smith
248, rue de Rivoli
75001 Paris
Tel: (01) 44 77 88 89

Books by Mail Order
Book Master
Tel: (01) 47 14 04 24
US to You
36, rue des États-Généraux
78000 Versailles
Tel: (01) 39 07 01 01
Fax: (01) 39 07 00 77

English-Language Libraries
American Library in Paris
10, rue du Général-Camou
75007 Paris
Tel. (01) 53 59 12 60
Fax: (01) 45 50 25 83
American Library in Paris
Angers Branch
60, rue Boisnet
49100 Angers
Tel: (02) 41 24 97 07
American Library in Paris
Montpellier Branch
4, rue St-Louis
34000 Montpellier
Tel: (04) 69 92 30 66
Fax. (04) 67 58 98 20
American Library in Paris
Nancy Branch
34, cours Léopold
54000 Nancy
Tel: (03) 83 17 67 58
Fax: (03) 83 17 67 65
American Library in Paris
Toulouse Branch
56, rue du Taur
31000 Toulouse
Tel: (05) 61 22 58 19
American Tax Institute in Europe S.A.
184, rue du Faubourg-St-Honoré
75008 Paris
Tel: (01) 42 89 49 50
Fax: (01) 42 56 00 45
British Council Library
9-11, rue de Constantine

75007 Paris
Tel: (01) 49 55 73 00
Centre Georges Pompidou
18, rue Beaubourg
75004 Les Halles
English Language Library for the Blind
35, rue Lemercier
75017 Paris
Tel and fax: (01) 42 93 47 57
WICE
20, boulevard du Montparnasse
75015 Paris
Tel: (01) 45 66 75 60
Fax. (01) 40 65 96 53

FRENCH ARCHIVES, RESEARCH
INSTITUTES, AND LIBRARIES

Centre d'Accueil et de Recherche des Archives Nationales (CARAN)
11, rue des Quatre-Fils
75003 Paris
Tel: (01) 40 27 64 19
Minitél: 3616 CARAN
Centre des Archives d'Outre-Mer (CAOM)
29, chemin de Moulin-de-Testa
13090 Aix-en-Provence
Tel: (04) 42 93 38 50
Fax. (04) 42 93 39 89
Centre des Archives Diplomatiques I
37, quai d'Orsay
75007 Paris
Tel. (01) 43 17 42 42
Fax: (01) 43 17 52 84
Centre des Archives Diplomatiques II
17, rue du Casterneau
44000 Nantes
Tel: (02) 51 77 25 25
Fax: (02) 51 77 24 60
Centre des Archives Contemporaines
2, rue des Archives
77300 Fontainebleau

Tel: (01) 64 31 73 00
Fax: (01) 64 31 73 96
Centre des Archives du Monde du Travail (CAMT)
78, boulevard du Général-Leclerc
B.P. 405
59057 Roubaix Cedex 1
Tel: (03) 20 65 38 00
Fax: (03) 20 65 38 01
Archives de Paris
18, boulevard Sérurier
75019 Paris
Tel: (01) 53 72 41 23
Bibliothèque Nationale
11, quai François-Mauriac
75013 Paris
Tel: (01) 53 79 59 59
Fax: (01) 53 79 43 70

INFORMATION, ASSISTANCE, AND
LODGING FOR AMERICAN
GRADUATE STUDENTS,
PROFESSORS, AND SCHOLARS

Fondation des États-Unis
15, boulevard Jourdan
75690 Paris Cedex 14
Tel: (01) 53 80 68 80

GENEALOGISTS

Archives Généalogiques Andriveau
18, rue du Cherche Midi
75006 Paris
Tel: (01) 49 54 75 75
Fax: (01) 49 54 75 76
Étude Généalogique Coutot-Roehrig
Département Étranger
21, boulevard St-Germain
75005 Paris
Tel: (01) 44 41 80 80

Working

Job Hunting

You're an expatriate. You've lost touch with the soil. You get
precious. Fake European standards have ruined you. You
drink yourself to death. You become obsessed by sex. You
spend all your time talking, not working. You are an expatri-
ate, see? You hang around cafés.

—ERNEST HEMINGWAY, *The Sun Also Rises*, 1926

Hemingway was not alone in his view of expatriate life in France during the Roaring Twenties and he would not be alone today. Yet while at
first the idea of lounging in cafés, beret in hand, might seem to meet
your ideal of continental bliss, unless you are independently wealthy,
the day will come when you will need to find a job. Better still, at the
end of a successful job search, you will find yourself employed and all
the more able to enjoy café life as a paying customer.

Employment Prospects

THE FRENCH ECONOMY

France is a prosperous nation and its people have a high standard
of living, making the country all the more appealing to foreigners of
all origins. This prosperity resulted largely from sweeping economic
changes that have been made since the 1940s. Before World War II, the
French economy was based primarily on small farms and family-owned
businesses. After the war, the French government worked to modern-
ize the economy through a series of initiatives designed to foster
national recovery and increase governmental direction of the economy.
Included in the so-called Monnet plans was the principle of nation-
alization of certain industries, notably railroad and air transportation

systems, major banks, and coal mines. The government, in addition, became a major shareholder in the automotive, electronics, and aircraft industries, as well as the primary investor in the development of both oil and natural-gas reserves. Partly as a result of such plans and programs, the national product of France increased by nearly 50 percent between 1949 and 1954, by 46 percent between 1956 and 1964, and at an average annual rate of 3.8 percent during the 1970s. At the end of 1997, France's gross domestic product per capita had reached $24,847, affirming the country's position as one of the wealthiest nations in the world.

Like most other European countries, France has been wading through a severe recession and at the end of 1998, unemployment was running at about 12 percent. More discouraging still, unemployment among those under age twenty-five is double the national average. These dramatic numbers have led to some rather innovative approaches to the job search especially among the younger generation. At the end of 1995, a thousand men and women under twenty-five got a boost when their résumés were printed on a million wine bottles in southern France. The hope was that future employers would eat, drink, and hire them as the wine was distributed to a thousand supermarkets, wine cellars, and restaurants around the country. While such creative strategies have had their effect on the micro level, unemployment remains high. At the end of 1996, more than three million people were seeking jobs. Unemployment is also very costly to the French government thanks to very generous unemployment benefits and expensive retraining programs that have long been institutionalized in the socialist country. The welfare system has an accumulated debt of over $60 billion, which has to be reduced if France ever hopes to meet the Maastricht criteria for a common European currency.

A Foreigner's Chances

Fortunately, finding a job in France isn't always as difficult as the employment figures may suggest, particularly in Paris and other large cities, depending of course on your qualifications and French language ability.

As a foreigner, you face many of the obstacles that lie in the way of French job seekers and some other more intimidating ones, yet you are operating on a different playing field. You have skills and traits that native French people cannot hope to have by the simple nature of their background.

Since July 1974, there has been a virtual freeze on the employment of nationals of all countries other than member countries of the European Common Market. Thus as an EU national, you would be as eligible for positions as your French counterparts, provided you had the qualifications for the job and could demonstrate competency in the language. As a non-EU national, you may find that you have less difficulty landing a job in France than obtaining the necessary *carte de séjour*, the French long-term residency visa and work permit that the hiring company must request on your behalf. Before the Ministry of Labor will issue a *carte de séjour*, the company must demonstrate that there is no one else *en règle*—with his or her working status already established—who could perform the job you are seeking. Americans, except for those in privileged situations (e.g., married to a French national), must obtain the long-stay visa, as a worker, before entering France. If you disregard the visa requirement and apply in France for a work permit upon finding a position, you will be required to leave the country to obtain the appropriate visa at a French consular office in the United States.

That said, facing the job market as a foreigner gives you a unique perspective. Depending on your background, you may have skills and training that no one else has. A friend, John Meier, for example, had earned a Ph.D. in a field of electrical engineering that was being exclusively developed and studied by a professor at a prestigious American university. John dreamed of working in France and obtained a French minor as an undergraduate. When he presented himself to a major French defense contractor, he had little trouble convincing them that he was qualified in a very unique way. While not everyone will have John's qualifications, each person has something unique to offer simply by virtue of his or her non-French background. Both English language skills and knowledge of American business practices and protocols can turn you, an American, into a hot commodity. French companies that do business with American firms and American businesses operating in France often have space and need for people who can function fluently in English and operate across cultural lines to facilitate communication and avoid misunderstandings. Also, as an American, you have access to certain kinds of contacts simply because you are from the United

States. The American network, in Paris especially but in France in general, is rather close-knit and you can expect to find that you may travel across social confines more freely than you would at home and, more importantly, more freely than your French counterparts.

When considering how to approach your job search, one of the first decisions you must make is whether to start the hunt before leaving the United States or to seek a position directly in France. If you are able to find a job while you are still at home, it dramatically simplifies the problem of legalizing your work status. Of course, before you are offered a job, you must usually have an interview. And having an interview with a company across the ocean in its French headquarters could be a bit complicated if you are not able to leave the United States. If the company you are interested in has an office in the United States, one possibility may be to try to organize an interview there. So while seeking a job in France from the United States may be the smoothest way bureaucratically, it can be a bit logistically complicated.

Another equally effective but less obvious and perhaps less direct option would be to seek employment at the American offices of a French firm or an American business that operates in France and to request a transfer after a certain amount of time has elapsed. At the very least, preparing your job search from the United States should enable you to arrive in France with a well-researched list of companies, organizations, and perhaps even individuals that you plan to contact.

Preparations for Job Hunting

To prepare for your job search, there are a number of preparatory assignments you must complete. It is important to be well prepared and organized. Completing the following tasks will make your candidacy that much stronger.

HOMEWORK

Before taking on the task of job hunting in France, it is critically important that you evaluate your motivations and your objectives. If living in France appeals to you because Hemingway's description of life as an expatriate in *The Sun Also Rises* sounds like the ideal way to pass time, you might want to consider an extended vacation in France. Likewise if you really love French cheese, wine, and haute cuisine, and the idea of gastronomic bliss composes the foundation of your motivation to find a job in France, you could consider a cooking course. All of these are valid reasons for loving the country but they are not going to serve as particularly convincing professional motivations to a future employer.

As you plan your job search, you should carefully examine your qualifications and credentials. You should ask yourself what you realistically hope to do in France and what you feel you can offer to a potential employer. Will your professional qualifications and credentials be recognized in France? If you have a particular trade, what are the requirements for practicing that trade in France? You can find out more about the recognition of degrees and certifications by contacting the French consulate or chamber of commerce closest to you. You should also ask yourself if there are job possibilities in the region of France where you wish to live. Answering all of these questions is a difficult process and may take time but it is better to ask them before you leave rather than after you have arrived in France.

PARLEZ-VOUS FRANÇAIS?

How good is your French? This may be another difficult question to answer but realistically speaking it is the most important one to answer honestly. Very few French companies will be willing even to consider a candidate who does not have at least a working knowledge of French. Most will interview only those foreign candidates who profess a high level of skill in French both spoken and written. Therefore it is truly naive and unwise to expect to find employment in France without having done at least a recent intensive language course. It is also important not to lie or overstate your language abilities. If you write on your résumé that you are fluent or even very comfortable with the language, you can expect the interview to be conducted in French. If you have lied or exaggerated, you will most likely end up trying to extract yourself from an embarrassing situation and excusing yourself for having wasted the interviewer's time.

If you haven't studied French before or if you studied it in high school and can't remember much more than *bonjour*, you have several options. You can look into taking an intensive course at your local university or community college or through the Académie Française if you are lucky enough to have one nearby. The Académie Française has offices to promote the French culture and language in major U.S. cities including New York, Washington, and Boston. If you have the financial resources, you could consider the possibility of moving to France and

197

enrolling in one of the many intensive language courses held in Paris, Provence, and throughout the rest of the country. For more information on language programs, see Chapter 15.

CURRICULUM VITAE

Ah, the curriculum vitae or the CV, as it is more commonly referred to in France. This listing of your life's experiences has some very notable differences from the résumé as we know it. It may seem like a chore but if you are at all serious about finding a job in France, be sure to translate your résumé into French.

On the next pages you will see some examples of original French CVs and an example of an American who translated her CV into French.

As you will see, the first CV was prepared by a translator with some experience. The second CV belongs to an American banker looking for another job in France. The third CV was prepared by a journalist who has reached a fairly high point in her career and is looking for a change.

Though presentation can vary from the very simple to the more elaborate, every CV must include several key elements. As in the American résumé, you must include your name, address, and phone number as well as information about your current position, your former jobs, your education, and your language and computer skills. However, in addition to this elementary information, the French CV calls for some personal information that Americans and other foreigners may find invasive and sexist. First among these is your date of birth or age. If this information is not listed on your CV it will certainly be among the first questions asked if you reach an interview. Second on the list is your nationality, and third and perhaps most personal is your civil status. You must indicate whether you are single (célibataire) or married (marié or mariée) as well as the number of children you have and their ages. If you are a newly married woman without any children, do not be surprised if an interviewer asks if you plan to become a mother any time in the near future. Companies may tend to ask this question as maternity benefits and leave are extremely costly in France and many firms would prefer to avoid the expense with a new employee. While this may seem sexist, it is considered standard practice in France. For their part, men are expected to note whether or not they have completed their military service, if it is required of them in their home country.

CV 1

Catherine Leblanc   Tél. pers.: 01.45.39.01.11
10, avenue Foch   Née le 3 octobre 1967 à Paris
75016 Paris   Célibataire

EXPERIENCE PROFESSIONNELLE

Juillet 1997	**Relectrice - Société de Software** Grande-Bretagne • Test, relecture et adaptation d'un jeu vidéo
Janvier 1996– Juillet 1997	Rédactrice-lexicographe au sein du Département langues de Vario Éditions Paris • Dictionnaire français-allemand : contrôle des travaux rédactionnels, coordination avec les traducteurs extérieurs, gestion de la documentation éditoriale • Dictionnaire de poche : supervision et contrôle des travaux rédactionnels, gestion des bases de données (fichiers SGML)
Février 1993– Janvier 1996	Traductrice-terminologue à la Direction Cantonale Berne, Suisse • Traduction de textes normatifs et juridictionnels, rapports, interventions parlementaires, correspondance, notamment dans les domaines de la justice, de l'adoption des enfants, de l'aménagement du territoire, des assurances sociales et de l'informatique • Alimentation de LINGUA, banque de données terminologiques du canton de Berne

ÉTUDES ET FORMATION

1992	Diplôme de traductrice-terminologue de l'ISIT (Institut Supérieur d'Interprétation et de Traduction), Paris Combinaison linguistique : français, allemand, anglais
1991	Diplôme de la Chambre de commerce franco-britannique, Paris
1990	Diplôme de la Chambre de commerce franco-allemande, Paris
1989	D.E.U.G. d'allemand à la Sorbonne, Paris IV
1986–1988	Classe préparatoire littéraire, Lycée Jules Ferry, Paris
1986	Baccalauréat A2, Lycée Charles de Gaulle, Chartres

DIVERS

Informatique: Windows 95, Winword 7.0, Access, langage SGML, dBASE
Centres d'intérêt et loisirs: voyages, cinéma, voile, ski, natation

WORKING

CV 2
Mark SMITH
9, Avenue des Guignols
75008 Paris
Tél: (01) 44 43 69 11

Né le 20 mars 1970; Célibataire
Nationalité américaine
(permis de travail en France).

FORMATION

1989–1993 — **GEORGETOWN UNIVERSITY** (Washington, D.C., USA)
École de Commerce et des Affaires Étrangères
Bachelor of Science, mention Très Bien
- Dominante : Commerce et Finance International
- Cursus: marketing; analyse financière; marchés de capitaux; finance d'entreprise; comptabilité

09/95–11/95 — **ESSEC** (Cergy-Pontoise)
- Cours de finance et marketing

Été 91 — **Goethe Institut** (Berlin, Allemagne)
- Études d'allemand: obtention du "Mittelstufe II Diplom"

Été 90 — **Instituto de Lenguas** (San José, Costa Rica)
- Études des relations entre les États-Unis et l'Amérique Latine

EXPÉRIENCE

11/95–03/96 — **BANQUE FRANÇAISE** (Paris)
Assistant de Marketing—Front Office Actions et Dérivés
- Analyse des produits concurrents.
- Réalisation de supports de ventes pour les commerciaux.
- Participation à l'élaboration de nouveaux produits financiers.

09/94–09/95 — **BANQUE AMÉRICAINE** (Paris)
Analyste financier
- Analyse des résultats financiers de grandes entreprises des secteurs pétroliers et automobiles.
- Identification des risques avec recommandations pour l'attribution de crédits.
- Modélisation financière sur micro-ordinateur.

01/94–05/94 — **SOCIÉTÉ DE VÊTEMENTS** (Miami)
Assistant de Marketing
- Mise en place d'un programme de marketing direct.
- Organisation de salons professionnels et du programme de Relations Publiques.

DIVERS

Langues : anglais—langue maternelle; bon niveau—allemand, espagnol, français
Informatique : Maîtrise de Word, Windows, Excel, Power Point, et Lotus 1-2-3
Voyages effectués dans 45 pays sur cinq continents

200

CV 3

Jeanne MICHEL
107, rue Saint Cloud, 75018 Paris
Tél : 01 43 76 43 18 (domicile) .
01 53 76 45 44 (bureau)
Fax: 01 44 44 21 78
E-mail: *michel@francenet.fr*

née le 24/03/68
française
célibataire

EXPÉRIENCE PROFESSIONNELLE

Depuis 1995   Rédactrice-en-chef adjointe, RÉSEAU DE PRESSE
Réseau international de presse en Europe, Asie et Afrique
—Coordination des suppléments thématiques bi-annuels
—Coordination de l'agence de presse du Réseau
—Conception et suivi du site Internet du Réseau

1994–1995   Rédactrice, JOURNAL
—Rédactrice au desk du service international
—Articles, reportages pour les services "France" et "Culture"

1994   Rédactrice-pigiste, REVUE
—Rédactrice-pigiste au service "société, culture et politique"

1993–1994   Chargée d'études, CHAÎNE DE TÉLÉVISION
—Chargée d'études au service des Études et de la
Programmation

FORMATION

1993   **DIPLÔME DE L'IEP (SCIENCES PO PARIS)**
Institut d'Études Politiques de Paris (Section Communication et
Ressources Humaines).

1991   **LICENCE DE DROIT**
Université de Paris V

1991   **DIPLÔME DE POLONAIS**
INALCO (Langues Orientales)

1987   **LETTRES SUPÉRIEURES HYPOKHÂGNE MODERNE**

COMPÉTENCES LINGUISTIQUES / COMPÉTENCES BUREAUTIQUES

Anglais : bilingue   Maîtrise des logiciels Word 5, Excel, File Maker Pro
Polonais : bilingue
Allemand : bonnes notions
Espagnol : notions

For more information on how to translate your résumé into an exemplary CV, you should refer to the *Handbook of Commercial French*, published by Routledge. Lastly, the French are real sticklers for grammar so at the very least have a native speaker reread your CV for grammatical errors if you choose not to have it professionally translated.

LA LETTRE DE CANDIDATURE

The cover letter in France, as in the United States, is key to a successful candidacy. On the following pages, you will find several examples of cover letters in French. As in English, cover letters can fall into two main categories: letters that respond to an advertisement or a job opening and letters that generally propose your candidacy without responding to a particular opening. Letter one is an example of the first category, a *lettre de réponse à une annonce*. Letter two is an example of the second category and is a *lettre de candidature spontanée*.

In both letters you would want to indicate the subject of your letter or the *objet* and begin the letter by introducing yourself. In the *lettre de réponse*, you should make explicit reference to the advertisement in question and then proceed to elaborate your qualifications for the position described. It is also not unheard of to indicate the salary you would expect, if you have an idea of the approximate remuneration. Remember to indicate whether that figure is net or gross. In the *lettre de candidature spontanée*, you should describe your current position or status and the contribution you expect to make to the company.

In France the cover letter is generally handwritten. This practice, which may seem cumbersome and outdated to us, is in fact a fundamental part of the French recruiting process. The handwritten cover letter is seen as more polite and considerate but more importantly it generally provides a writing sample for the in-house graphologist. Based on psychology, graphology or handwriting analysis deduces personality from handwriting characteristics such as size, pressure, and whether letters are joined. Graphology is a well-steeped tradition for many French companies. Estimates vary but it is generally believed that somewhere from 80 to 90 percent of French companies rely on handwriting analysis, even if only 40 percent admit it. In fact a major French building materials group, Saint-Gobain, sparked a national debate when it announced at the end of 1997 that it would be giving up handwriting analysis as an aid to recruitment. Though controversial, the practice remains and—for the foreseeable future—the handwritten cover letter seems destined to remain a fixture of the French job search. As a foreigner, you can try to sidestep handwriting the cover letter but chances are you will be asked to provide a writing sample at some point in the recruitment process.

Despite the more personal effect of handwriting a cover letter, French business letters in general and cover letters specifically are very formally composed. The French have created a vast repertoire of courteous formulae that are used particularly in the opening and closing sentences of a letter. Examples of the most important of these can be found in the sample cover letters on the following pages.

A letter must open with a direct salutation. *Messieurs, Monsieur, Mesdames,* or *Madame* are all acceptable. In professional correspondence, you would include neither an equivalent of "Dear" nor the addressee's name in the salutation.

A standard formula to describe your interest in being considered as a candidate is: *je me permets de vous proposer ma candidature en tant que. . . .*

If you are responding to an ad, you would precede that formula with *À la suite de votre annonce, parue le 10 février dernier dans* le Monde, . . .

Whereas if you are writing an open letter, you could begin with *Sans connaître vos besoins réels. . . .*

As important as the salutation is the way in which you conclude your letter. Both of the sample letters have good examples for the next to last sentence, which thanks the potential employer for his time and consideration. Both

> J'espère avoir retenu votre attention et vous remercie de la suite
> que vous voudrez bien donner à mon offre de candidature.

and

> Je reste à votre entière disposition pour tout renseignement
> complémentaire et pour un éventuel entretien au cours duquel
> je pourrais vous donner de plus amples informations.

work well.

The closing sentence is always a formula that courteously reflects your salutation. The examples used in the sample letters are almost always appropriate.

Je vous prie de croire, Messieurs, à l'expression de mes
sentiments respectueux.
Veuillez agréer, Monsieur, mes salutations distinguées.

Both of these sentences repeat the opening address, *Messieurs* or
Monsieur.

Again, for more specific information about different kinds of professional correspondence, seek out *Handbook of Commercial French*,
published by Routledge, or *Le Français de la Communication Professionnelle* (C.L.E. International, Paris).

Lettre de réponse à une annonce

Michel Chirac
4, rue Vineuse
75016 Paris
Tél: 45.91.87.56

Paris, le 20 mars 1997

Objet : proposition de candidature

Monsieur, À la suite de votre annonce, parue le 10 mars dernier
dans le Monde, je me permets de vous proposer ma candidature
à un poste d'assistant export en bureautique.

À la lecture de mon curriculum vitae, vous pourrez constater que je viens de terminer des études de commerce international au Centre Trudaine du Commerce de Paris. J'ai acquis,
grâce à cette formation, les bases indispensables à l'administration internationale des ventes.

Par ailleurs, je possède des connaissances techniques en
bureautique qui me permettent de prétendre au poste actuellement vacant au sein de votre entreprise.

Mes prétentions sont de 7000 francs net par mois.

J'espère avoir retenu votre attention et vous remercie de la
suite que vous voudrez bien donner à mon offre de candidature.

Veuillez agréer, Monsieur, mes salutations distinguées.

Michel Chirac

Lettre de candidature spontanée

Julie Chatraîne
34, Boulevard Raspail
75007 Paris

Paris, le 24 janvier 1997

Objet : proposition de candidature

Messieurs, Sans connaître vos besoins réels, je me permets de vous proposer ma candidature en tant qu'assistante en Commerce International. En effet, je cherche actuellement un emploi qui serait susceptible de développer mes capacités.

Le poste que j'occupe aujourd'hui, au sein du service exportation de la Minarelli, ne m'offre plus la perspective d'une évolution intéressante. Il m'a pourtant offert la chance d'acquérir un expérience certaine dans un domaine passionnant, celui des échanges internationaux.

Très active, dynamique, je suis à même d'assurer avec efficacité les responsabilités rattachées au poste envisagé.

Par ailleurs, comme vous le constaterez à la lecture de mon curriculum vitae, dans les tâches diverses que j'ai effectuées auprès du directeur du service exportation, j'ai pris de nombreuses initiatives et responsabilités, aussi bien au niveau de la traduction, la rédaction du courrier, que du suivi de dossiers sur le plan international.

En conséquence, je suis prête à étudier toutes propositions qui me permettraient d'une part, d'utiliser mes compétences et, d'autre part, d'épanouir d'autres aptitudes.

Je reste à votre entière disposition pour tout renseignement complémentaire et pour un éventuel entretien au cours duquel je pourrais vous donner de plus amples informations.

Je vous prie de croire, Messieurs, à l'expression de mes sentiments respectueux.

Julie Chatraîne

The Interview

The work you have done up until now will hopefully lead you to an interview, the opportunity for you to showcase your skills and talents. This is the moment that counts. While interviewing for a job in France is not much different than in the United States, you should be very prepared to explain the unique ways in which you can help the company in question as well as your motives for wanting to work in France. As with all interviews, you should know the company. Read the available literature and brochures and consult annual reports. You should know the points you would like to make about yourself and your personal history and be prepared to answer the standard questions about your strengths and weaknesses. It is also always wise to have prepared one or two questions you wish to ask the interviewer.

If the interview is to be in French, it is also a wise idea to prepare answers in French to some general questions you may be asked. This will give you the time and the opportunity to look up some tricky vocabulary words that could leave you stumbling in an actual interview. If your language ability is a weak point, be sure to insert a comment on how you are currently working on improving your French and your plans to continue doing so in the future. This shows initiative and determination and may help compensate for a lack of facility with the language.

The Offer

After the interview, you should continue your job search. It is not wise to put all your eggs in one basket and, as the hiring process takes much longer in France than in the United States, you may have to wait a while before you hear back. If the interview was successful, however, you will be the lucky recipient of a job offer.

Salary

In France, salaried foreigners have the same rights as French citizens, though there are different rules for different categories of employees, that is, managers, professionals, and general employees. Temporary workers have few rights, and illegal workers or workers without contracts have no rights at all.

Salaries in France tend to be rather high for Europe, though lower with respect to the United States. It is important to keep in mind, however, that the benefits can make a lower salary worth more. When considering an offer be sure to take into consideration whether the salary will be paid in France and in francs or in another country in a different currency, how regularly the salary will be reviewed, and how overtime will be calculated and paid. It is also important to ask if the annual salary includes a thirteenth or fourteenth month and bonuses. Salaries in France tend to be paid monthly but you should also ask specific information about the number of weekly working hours and whether you can take time off in lieu of being paid for overtime.

The Contract

Almost all employees in France have a *contrat de travail* or employment contract. These contracts will list information about salary, benefits, the length of the workweek, your job title, obligations and responsibilities, and the length of employment. If you are an employee, you will need to produce your contract when you apply for your *carte de séjour*. Contracts must be written in French but you should always attempt to obtain an English translation—either written or oral—to avoid any unpleasant surprises.

There are two main kinds of contracts: the *contrat à durée déterminée* (term contract) and the *contrat à durée indéterminée* (indefinite term contract). As its name indicates, the term contract expires on a given date and can be issued for a maximum of two years. It must be in written form and you must receive salary equivalent to a person employed on an indefinite term contract. You are also entitled to a bonus at the end of your contract *(indemnité de fin de contrat)*. An indefinite term contract is the typical employment contract for permanent workers. You should be sure to obtain a written contract. The first three months of your contract are generally considered a trial period and until that time has expired, the contract is not legally binding.

Benefits

The benefits associated with working for a French company or any company operating subject to French law are numerous and very costly to both the employer and the government. You should be sure to investigate thoroughly all the benefits associated with your contract and position, keeping in mind that executives are eligible for an additional series of benefits.

A benefits package must include social security. All French employees, foreign employees, and the self-employed must contribute to *la Sécurité sociale*. Social security includes health care (including maternity and sickness), unemployment insurance, insurance for injury on the job, family allowances, and pensions. Contributions are calculated based on your gross salary and are very high both for the employer and for the employee. If you use public transportation, all French companies are obliged to pay half of your monthly transportation subscription.

In addition to the benefits associated with social security, many companies and industries offer additional benefits including supplementary health insurance, a company pension fund, and other benefits like relocation expenses, French lessons, subsidized parking, and a company car.

Unions

At the beginning of the 1990s, the French labor force totaled about 24 million persons. About 10 percent of French workers are members of labor unions. Some 2.4 million workers belong to the Confédération Générale du Travail (CGT), the largest labor organization in France; the Confédératicn Française Démocratique du Travail (CFDT), a Roman Catholic–oriented organization; or the Force Ouvrière. Union membership is required in some industries and as a foreigner you will be subject to the same rules and conditions as the French. Minimum wages are established by government decree, but pay scales are determined by collective bargaining.

While membership dropped off significantly in the 1980s, the force of the unions is not negligible. Attempts to privatize many government-owned industries and, in particular, efforts to reform the social security system led to numerous strikes in the mid-1990s. The business environment in France was gravely damaged in the fall of 1995 by labor unrest. Public employee strikes called by the CGT and the Force Ouvrière unions paralyzed transportation and public services in France's major cities for three weeks in November and December. It is

Paris's immensely photogenic city hall was the backdrop for Robert Doisneau's famous 1950 photograph, "Kiss at the Hôtel de Ville."

estimated that the strike cost employers close to $4 billion. The government was forced to back down and the following months and years, the workers were not averse to flexing their striking muscles.

Public Holidays

According to French law, employers are only required to pay salary on the May 1 Labor Day but most employment contracts include the following eleven public holidays:

Date	Holiday
January 1	New Year's Day
March or April	Easter Monday
May 1	Labor Day
May 8	Liberation Day
May 21	Ascension
May or June	Pentecost
July 14	Bastille Day
August 15	Assumption
November 1	All Saints' Day
November 11	Veterans' Day
December 25	Christmas

When a public holiday falls on a Sunday, employers are not required to give you the following Monday off but in compensation the French have the wonderful tradition of *le pont* or the bridge. *Un pont* takes place when a public holiday falls on a Tuesday or a Thursday. In most cases, employers will grant the included Monday or Friday as a holiday, giving employees a four-day weekend.

A few categories of Americans in France are in a privileged position in regard to employment. These are (1) bearers of a *carte de résident* who have resided in France in that category for ten years, (2) spouses of French citizens, and (3) students who have studied in France two of the preceding years and who have a parent with four years of residence in France.

Business Etiquette

On my first day of work in France, my new boss walked me through the office to introduce me to all of my colleagues. When we reached the glass office of the head of the company I was presented and asked to leave, as the CEO had a matter to discuss with my boss. I barely had an opportunity to close the door behind me when I heard the two of them begin an argument that quickly escalated to a shouting match. Some of my new coworkers saw the shock on my face and laughed. *"Ne vous inquietez pas"* ("Don't worry"), they said. *"C'est normal"* ("It's normal").

Loud arguments were in fact common in my office and in other companies as well. They are just one example of the cultural differences that Americans may face when working in a French office. Cultural misunderstandings and confusion are a normal part of working in a foreign country. Some snafus are unavoidable but the newcomer who wants to follow French business etiquette will do well to observe his or her colleagues and when in doubt ask a trusted French friend or colleague before taking action.

Conversation

The French love and still practice the lost art of conversation. This is one reason why most loud arguments are entirely acceptable. It is a common understanding that if you are in disagreement with a colleague or even your boss, you will use all the skills at your disposal to convince the other of your point of view. Meeting each other half way is usually not good enough. As a newcomer, however, you would do well to follow the lead of those with whom you are conversing and keep your voice as loud or soft and your tone as calm or agitated as theirs. One's ability to speak well and convincingly is important in personal relationships but it is essential to success in one's professional life. The importance the French attach to words is one explanation for their sometime hesitance to speak English. They are aware of their inability to express themselves as well in a foreign language. As a foreigner, one way to impress your colleagues is through regular improvement in your ability to speak their language.

INTRODUCTIONS

Greetings and introductions are a very important part of French business culture. Upon first meeting a person, you should shake hands. Unlike the more American-styled handshake of energetically pumping the other person's hand, the French handshake consists of one strong downward pull. In most companies colleagues and business acquaintances continue to shake hands throughout the duration of their working relationship. Occasionally some female colleagues who are particularly friendly will exchange the traditional double-cheek air kisses known as *la bise*. In some more creative industries (theater, fashion design, the arts, etc.) it is more common for coworkers to greet each other with a *bise* but nowhere in France is it acceptable to hug your colleagues or business contacts.

Unless your French is truly rudimentary, you should try to greet all new acquaintances using the formal *vouvoiement* form until the individual tells you that it is alright for you to *tutoyer* them (address them using *tu*). In many businesses, colleagues never switch to the more informal *tu*, while in others, including journalism or industries with many young people, the switch is almost instantaneous. If a colleague does not ask you to switch to *tu* or continues to address you using *vous*, you should not take it personally. It is not in any way a negative sign of someone's feelings toward you.

THE TELEPHONE

The French have a very different relationship with the telephone than most Americans do. Because even local telephone calls are rather expensive, in their private lives, the French do not generally spend hours talking to friends on the phone, preferring to use the phone to arrange a time to meet. Needless to say, hanging on the phone on personal calls in the office is frowned upon.

When making phone calls for business, it is very important to follow all the same rules for formal conversation, especially when you are calling someone for the first time. You begin a phone call by greeting the interlocutor, being sure to include the title—*"Bonjour, Madame"* for a woman and *"Bonjour, Monsieur"* for a man. It is not acceptable to simply say *"Bonjour"*—the French equivalent of an American "Hello." This is true when greeting employees in public offices as well (the post office, etc.).

You are then expected to introduce yourself by giving your name and the name of your company. One common formula is: *"George Smith de Proctor et Gamble à l'appareil."* Once you have been acknowledged, you may proceed with your phone call.

To close a conversation, again include the title *"Au revoir, Madame"* or *"Au revoir, Monsieur."*

Meetings

American professionals tend to disparage meetings in general as a waste of time. These individuals are often particularly miserable when participating in French meetings, which can drag on for hours and hours seemingly without accomplishing anything. Yet often everyone else leaves satisfied. This is because, in France, meetings are commonly used as a forum for people to air their opinions. Disagreements are common and arguments as well, but in the end professional relationships are often built in precisely these meetings. So if you tend to find long meetings frustrating, at least initially take a deep breath and try to make the most of the time spent with your new colleagues.

Business hours in France run from 8:30 or 9:00 A.M. to 6:30 or 7:00 P.M. Lunch can often last for two hours or more. The best times to schedule meetings are either in the late morning or after lunch. The best meal for conducting business is lunch. In Paris, the French are as

213

punctual as anywhere in North America. In the southern part of the country, however, punctuality may not be taken quite as seriously.

NEGOTIATIONS

Negotiations, a special form of business meetings, are often conducted very differently in France than in the United States. Americans often tend to get right down to business, which can seem a bit abrupt in France. The French are very reserved when it comes to conducting business. It is best not to be informal at least initially. When you are the newcomer, let your hosts take the initiative and follow their lead. If you are not sure about the degree of your fluency in French, do not be proud—bring along an interpreter.

The president of a French company is known as the PDG (pronounced Pay-Day-Zhay), or *président directeur général*. If your negotiating counterparts speak English, it may be helpful to remember that the French often learn British English. For this reason, they may use the British forms of titles, which can lead to confusion in a business meeting or negotiation. It took me several days at my first job to understand that our "managing director" was actually the CEO or president of my company. The "deputy" was the vice president.

PRESENTATIONS

When making a presentation, the most important thing to remember is the language barrier. If you will be making a presentation in English, be considerate to your French listeners and bring translations of important documents. Even if you feel fairly secure with your French, if you will be making a presentation in French, run it by a trusted friend or colleague to be sure that you are not making any major gaffes or using terms in French that might be interpreted differently than you intend.

When making presentations, the French are quite formal initially, though in my experience, the formal nature often dissolves into a more intense examination of the arguments made once the speaker has finished her prepared remarks. You should be prepared to respond to tough questions, especially if you are making a business proposal.

BUSINESS LUNCHES

The lunch break in France commonly lasts up to two hours and it is virtually unheard of to eat a sandwich at your desk (although it is fairly common to see Parisians enjoying a baguette filled with ham or cheese in many brasseries). And although business lunches are a normal part of professional life in France, they do not proceed according to the same rhythms as typical American business lunches.

The French see the business lunch as an opportunity to eat well and to get to know the people they are or will be doing business with, as well as a chance to make a deal. In the end you will get down to business but it will not happen with the appetizer. As with all questions of business etiquette, follow the lead of your French host and do not try to speed ahead and get to the "meat" of the discussion. Typically the person who extended the invitation pays for the lunch, and although there are always exceptions, it is not common to split the bill.

The Corporate Hierarchy

Americans working in France often comment that companies are more formally structured and that employees adhere more rigidly to a predetermined corporate hierarchy. In fact, while in some industries this is changing to promote initiative and for other reasons, most French companies still believe that the most effective action and decision making is done by using a fairly structured hierarchy. When confronted with new problems, junior employees will typically pass them up in the chain of authority to their bosses.

This hierarchy also affects interpersonal relations. When an American moves to a job in a new city, it is common to view colleagues as a first resource for new friendships. Under normal circumstances, relationships among coworkers in France are perfectly friendly but the French tend to draw a very distinct line between their professional and personal lives. The two rarely mix. While socializing outside of work is rare among coworkers of equal status, it is virtually unheard of between bosses and their staff. In any case, the invitations can be extended only in one direction, if at all. For example, as a rule, one would not invite one's boss to dinner.

Sexual Harassment

While friendships may not evolve as easily in the office, relationships between men and women are far more flirtatious than has become acceptable in the American corporate environment. In recent years, however, awareness of the implications of sexual harassment on the working environment has been on the rise—although the French tend to think that the Americans have gone too far. In 1995, when I was working in Paris as a journalist, I was invited to participate in a panel on a French television show that discussed questions of sexual harassment. As a young American woman, I was considered an authority on the evolution of the sexual harassment legislation and culture. Unfortunately, the other women on the panel spent the entire program criticizing Americans for taking things too far, as usual.

Nonetheless, if you feel you are in the unfortunate position of being harassed by a colleague, first try to evaluate whether your feelings could be based on cultural misunderstandings. If you decide this is not the case, there are legal options, although you would do well to try to defuse the situation on your own. Remember, it's almost impossible to be fired in France so it's unlikely that you could lose your job as a result of unwanted sexual advances.

Working in the Public
or Private Sector

As an American, finding a job in the public or private sectors in France is not an easy task, but it can be done. French companies, American companies, the American government, and international organizations make up the realm of employment options in these sectors, for an American looking for a job in France.

For many people, the best way to get work in any of these fields is to be hired in the United States and arrange for a transfer overseas. In this case, the company or organization covers the expenses associated with relocation, handles all the cumbersome paperwork, and in many cases offers lucrative benefits packages that include housing subsidies and tuition for children's education. The one drawback with this strategy for moving to France is that it takes time and patience—ingredients that are often in short supply once you've made the decision to move overseas and are anxious to get going.

The next best option is to conduct a job search from within France. While this is difficult, there are many American success stories. By being in France, you will have the advantage of being able to benefit from networking and will be present for interviews, which can come up at a moment's notice. Unfortunately if you are successful and find a job, you will have to return to the United States to request your work permit (see Chapter 4).

The deck is stacked in more ways than one against Americans job hunting in France. The country already suffers from high unemployment. It is difficult for many French people to find full-time work. By law, before French and foreign companies can hire an American, they must be able to demonstrate that no unemployed Frenchman or woman would be capable of performing the job. As an American, you also fall in line behind any citizens of the European Union, who have precedence over other foreigners who are looking for work in France.

It is essential that you find ways to make yourself stand out as a candidate. As an American, your ability to speak and write as a native English speaker will be one strong selling point. The more specialized your background and training, the better your chances of capturing a position.

Another obstacle you may face in your search for a full-time contracted position is the strict French labor laws that make it nearly impossible for companies to fire employees and therefore make employers reluctant to hire new workers and grant them term *contrats à durée indéterminée*. If you are willing to be flexible and accept part-time work or short-term contract work, you will markedly improve your chances of being hired on a permanent basis. Once you have your foot in the door, your ability to network will help you discover unpublicized openings that become available.

French Companies

In terms of sheer numbers the largest number of available jobs in France will be in French-owned companies. The advantage here is that you have better odds of finding an opening. The disadvantage is that you will be competing directly against the vast pool of French job seekers.

Some of these companies will have openings that are designed specifically for foreign nationals with special language or technical skills. If you discover such a niche position and can convince the employer that you are the right candidate for the job, then you are golden. Generally, the more fluent your French, the more attractive you will seem, but often for these types of positions, your French language skills will not be crucial to getting the job. These jobs are fewer and farther between but can be easier to obtain as an American.

If you decide to take on the native French competition and apply for jobs where the fact that you are a foreigner is a liability rather than an asset, your language skills had better be flawless. You will need to be able to speak and write in perfect French and have a good understanding of French corporate culture and in particular the corporate hierarchy (see Chapter 19).

French corporate culture is very formal and structured. Americans often have a difficult time adjusting to environments where initiative is not usually rewarded—though the times are changing. As an American, you will be expected to adapt to the way the French company does business, rather than striking out on your own. While this can seem confining at times, it is one of the best ways to really understand French culture in depth.

American Companies

While the French have had a love-hate relationship with Americans and perceived American cultural imperialism, they have very little compunction about filling their lives with American consumer goods. French youth wear Levis, Nikes, and Carhart workmen's clothing. They drink Coca-Cola and Budweiser and love to eat at McDonald's and American and Tex-Mex-style restaurants and bars. They listen to American music and watch American movies. In the office they work on IBM computers and love Motorola cellular phones.

It would seem that the omnipresent American firms are the perfect place to begin a job search in France. Yet many Americans looking for work in France are chagrined to discover that, contrary to their expectations, American companies operating overseas are run and staffed primarily by locals. These companies have overseas operations because they are trying to insert their products into a foreign market. The best people to help them reach that goal are locals.

To make things even more complicated, by law, foreign companies are prohibited from hiring a foreigner if a French person could perform the job. Employees from the home office often fill the few positions that are available to Americans. Companies prefer to send current employees abroad, to benefit from the previously accumulated corporate experience and to avoid the hassle of obtaining working papers for an American who would be new to the firm and hired locally.

A view of Biot, a Provençal village

That said, there are definitely opportunities available for Americans who are good at networking and persistent. If working for an American company is your goal, you should make every effort to integrate into the American expatriate network in France (see Chapter 3). I found my first job in journalism in Paris because I had met several journalists through my university's alumni organization, one of whom thought of me when he heard of an opening.

The job seekers who are most likely to end up employed are also those with staying power and endurance. It can take time to bring an intense job search to a successful conclusion.

The U.S. Government

Seasoned diplomats will confess that Paris and London are the two plum posts, usually given as political reward or in recognition for years of exceptional service. They are fiercely competed over and the government has little trouble filling them. While there are more than thirty U.S. government agencies operating in France, unless you or your spouse is a foreign service officer or works for that particular agency in the United States, you have only the slimmest possibility of finding a position as a local hire.

Working for an American agency can be a reassuring experience. You are surrounded by Americans and generally conduct most of your work in English. You have access to American resources and if you are at the U.S. Embassy, you can buy American food and magazines in a commissary. It is the perfect way to transplant an American lifestyle to another environment. There are two categories of positions available to Americans as U.S. government employees in France.

FOREIGN SERVICE

Foreign Service officers (or political appointees in the case of ambassadors) generally fill high-level positions at American overseas posts. If you are patient and are willing to work toward a posting in France ten or fifteen years down the road, this may be the route for you. It takes years of experience before Foreign Service officers are even considered for postings in France. But the life of a diplomat in France has been described as cushy—at worst. There are two categories of Foreign Service employees; for both you must be a U.S. citizen and at least twenty years old. To apply, you must contact the U.S. Department of State (see the Useful Addresses section at the end of this chapter).

Foreign Service Officers   To be hired as a Foreign Service officer, you have to undergo a highly competitive selection process that consists of a written exam, which is offered at U.S. embassies and consulates around the world, and an oral assessment, which is offered at a limited number of assessment centers in the United States. If you pass the oral assessment, you will have to pass an extensive background check to obtain your security clearance and you will be asked to choose from four areas of specialization: administrative, consular, political, or economic. If you sign on to the Foreign Service, you have to agree that you will serve anywhere in the world, which means that to make use of your French language skills, early in your career, you will likely be sent to a post in Francophone Africa.

Foreign Service Specialists   Foreign Service specialists are hired by the State Department and have top security clearance but usually fill positions that are related to security or technical or administrative support. In this category, you will find security guards, information technology specialists, computer programmers, telecommunications experts, administrative assistants, physicians, nurses, and counselors.

Though the application process is not quite as complicated as for Foreign Service officers, you must have the requisite skills to be considered a viable candidate and again you must be willing to work anywhere in the world.

THE U.S. EMBASSIES AND CONSULATES

Finding work at U.S. embassies and consulates is not an easy task. Most of the positions that become available are temporary and administrative in nature. Because they often require a security clearance, the personnel office generally prefers to fill the positions from a roster of Foreign Service officer spouses, who would have already passed a background check. That said, positions do occasionally open up. The American Embassy in Paris has an established application process (some of the consular missions may be a bit more flexible). To be eligible for any position, applicants must possess a valid ten-year French work permit. To apply for embassy employment, you must send a letter describing your area of interest, a current résumé, a copy of both sides of a valid French work permit, a copy of your U.S. passport, and, if applicable, a copy of a current security clearance. The Embassy will contact successful or eligible candidates when an opportunity in their area of interest becomes available. The Embassy's personnel office keeps applications on file for one year.

International Organizations

There are two primary international organizations that are headquartered in Paris: the United Nations Educational, Scientific and Cultural Organization (UNESCO) and the Organization for Economic Cooperation and Development (OECD).

UNESCO is an agency of the United Nations and operates in the areas of education, science, arts, communications, and other cultural concerns. Although the United States is currently not a member of UNESCO, positions are available for U.S. citizens, and the U.S. government is present in an observer capacity. When applying, you should emphasize your ability to speak one or more of the six United Nations official working languages (Arabic, Chinese, English, French, Russian, and Spanish) and demonstrate your interest in education, science, communications, or culture.

The OECD is the successor to the Organization for European Economic Cooperation and Development that administered and implemented the Marshall Plan for European recovery at the end of World War II. The United States, Canada, and Japan are members along with most European states. The organization is dedicated to increasing world trade and improving development and stability in member countries. The OECD's activities are highly specialized and the organization has a preference for advanced degrees (doctorates) in economics, statistics, and finance. Language skills are also an advantage.

It is not easy to come by a position in an international organization but if you find someone willing to hire, you are not required to have French working papers, just to be a national of one of the member countries. There are lots of advantages to working for an international organization, as well, including a tax-free salary.

Useful Addresses

FOR FOREIGN SERVICE

U.S. Department of State
Recruitment Division
P.O. Box 9317
Arlington, VA 22219
(703) 875-7200

THE U.S. EMBASSY AND CONSULATES

U.S. Embassy
2, avenue Gabriel
75382, Paris Cedex 08
Tel: (01) 43 12 22 22
Fax: (01) 42 66 97 83

U.S. Consulate, Paris
2, rue St-Florentin
75382 Paris Cedex 08
Tel: (01) 43 12 49 42
Fax: (01) 42 61 61 40
U.S. Consulate, Marseille
12, boulevard Paul-Peytral
13006 Marseille Cedex
Tel: (04) 91 54 92 00
Fax: (04) 91 55 09 47
U.S. Consulate, Strasbourg
15, avenue d'Alsace
67000 Strasbourg Cedex
Tel: (03) 88 35 31 04
Fax: (03) 88 24 06 95
U.S. Consular Agency, Nice
31, rue du Maréchal-Foch
06000 Nice
Tel: (04) 93 88 89 55
Fax: (04) 93 87 07 38

INTERNATIONAL ORGANIZATIONS
Organization for Economic
Cooperation and Development (OECD)
2, rue André-Pascal
F-75775 Paris Cedex 16
United Nations Educational, Scientific
and Cultural Organization (UNESCO)
7, place de Fontenoy
75352 Paris 07 SP
Tel: (01) 45 68 10 00
Fax: (01) 45 67 16 90

THE TOP 10 FRENCH COMPANIES
OF 1998
(AS RANKED BY FORBES)
AXA-UAP
23, avenue Matignon
75008 Paris
Tel: (01) 40 75 57 00
Fax: (01) 40 75 57 50
Web site: http://www.axa.com/
Elf Aquitaine Group
Tour Elf
92078 Paris–La Défense Cedex
Tel: (01) 47 44 45 46
Fax: (01) 47 44 73 66

Web site: http://www.elf.fr/
Renault Group
34, quai du Point du Jour
92109 Boulogne-Billancourt Cedex
Tel: (01) 41 04 50 50
Fax: (01) 41 04 52 89
Web site: http://www.renault.com/
Total Group
24, cours Michelet
92069 Paris–La Défense
Tel. (01) 41 35 40 00
Fax. (01) 41 35 28 27
Web site. http.//www.total.com/
Suez Lyonnaise Group
72, avenue de la Liberté
92753 Nanterre
Tel: (01) 46 95 50 00
Fax: (01) 46 95 54 17
Web site: http.//www.suez-lyonnaise-des-eaux.co.fr/
Peugeot Group
75, avenue de la Grande-Armée
75116 Paris
Tel: (01) 40 66 55 11
Fax. (01) 40 66 54 14
Alcatel Alsthom
54, rue La Boétie
75382 Paris Cedex 08
Tel. (01) 40 76 10 10
Fax. (01) 40 76 14 00
Web site: http://www.alcatel.com/
Carrefour Group
B.P. 419-16
75769 Paris Cedex 16
Tel: (01) 53 70 19 00
Fax: (01) 53 70 86 16
Web site: http.//www.carrefour.fr/
GAN-Assurances Nationales
2, rue Pillet-Will
75448 Paris Cedex 09
Tel: (01) 42 47 50 00
Fax: (01) 42 47 35 28
Web site: http://www.gan.fr/
Société Générale Group
29, boulevard Haussmann
75008 Paris
Tel. (01) 42 14 20 00

Fax: (01) 42 14 38 28
Web site. http://www.socgen.com/

AMERICAN COMPANIES

Abbott Laboratories
12, rue de la Couture
Silic 233
94528 Rungis Cedex
Tel: (01) 45 60 25 00
Fax: (01) 45 60 04 98
Air Products and Chemicals Inc.
Tour Pleyel Centre Paris-Pleyel
93521 Saint-Denis
Tel: (01) 48 09 75 00
**Allied-Signal Inc.—Allied-Signal
Aerospace Service Corp.**
5, avenue Matignon
75008 Paris
Tel: (01) 43 59 07 69
Fax: (01) 40 74 00 63
American Express Company
Place de l'Opéra
75008 Paris
American Home Products Corp.
11, rue du Château-des-Rentiers
75013 Paris
Tel: (01) 44 06 43 21
Fax: (01) 44 06 43 69
Amway Corporation
14, avenue François-Sommer
92164 Antony
Tel. (01) 46 74 21 80
Fax: (01) 42 37 08 11
Apple Computer, Inc.
Le Wilson 2
92058 Paris
Tel: (01) 49 01 49 01
Armstrong World Industries
Contact via:
International Operations Office
Armstrong World Industries
P.O. Box 3001
Lancaster, PA 17604
Atari Corp.
7, rue Sentou
Suresnes
98150 Paris

Tel: (01) 42 04 10 79
Fax: (01) 42 04 10 79
Atlantic Richfield Co.—ARCP
53–57, avenue Kléber
75016 Paris
Tel: (01) 45 53 59 33
Fax: (01) 45 53 02 26
Avis Rent A Car System Inc.
Tour Franklin
92042 Paris–La Défense Cedex 11
Tel. (01) 49 06 68 68
Fax: (01) 47 78 98 98
Avon Products, Inc.
60331 Liancourt Cedex
Tel: (01) 44 73 07 00
Fax: (01) 44 73 07 09
Bausch and Lomb, Inc.
10, route de Léuvis-St-Nom
78320 Le Mesnil St. Denis
Tel: (01) 30 69 65 00
Fax: (01) 34 61 70 35
Bayer AG—Bayer S.A.
49-51, quai de Dion-Bouton
92815 Puteaux Cedex
Tel: (01) 49 06 50 00
Fax: (01) 40 06 52 19
BMW France S.A.
3, avenue Ampère
78180 Montigny-le-Bretonneux
Tel. (01) 30 43 93 00
Fax: (01) 30 43 35 71
B. F. Goodrich
Corporate Headquarters
140, avenue Paul-Doumer
92508 Rueil-Malmaison Cedex
Tel. (01) 47 32 06 00
Fax: (01) 47 49 11 54
Borden, Inc.
20, rue Auguste-Vacquerie
75116 Paris
Tel: (01) 47 23 71 12
Bridgestone Corporation
ZA de Courtaboeuf
Immeuble Hightec 2
22, avenue de la Baltique
91953 Les Ulis Cedex
Tel: (01) 64 46 13 00

225

Bristol-Meyers Squibb Co.
38 bis, rue des Entrepreneurs
75015 Paris
Tel: (01) 45 75 80 53
Fax: (01) 45 75 46 00
Burston-Marsteller
11, rue Paul-Baudry
75009 Paris
Tel. (01) 40 74 07 08
Fax. (01) 40 74 07 14
Cadbury Schweppes
123, rue Victor-Hugo
92300 Levallois-Perret
Tel: (01) 49 68 70 00
Fax: (01) 49 68 00 04
Campbell Soup Co.—Lamy Lutti, S.A.
36, rue Marcel-Henaux
59202 Tourcoing
Tel: (03) 20 01 92 17
Fax: (03) 20 76 30 77
Caterpillar, Inc.
40, avenue Léon-Blum
B.P. 55x
38041 Grenoble Cedex 9
Tel: (04) 73 23 70 00
CBS, Inc.
8, rue Bellini
75116 Paris
Tel: (01) 47 27 00 73
Coca-Cola, Inc.
Contact via.
Coca-Cola, Inc.
P.O. Drawer 1734
Atlanta, GA 30301
Tel: (404) 676-2121
Colgate Palmolive Co.
55, boulevard de la Mission-Marchand
92401 Courbevoie
Compaq Computer Corporation
4, avenue de la Norvège
91953 Les Ulis Cedex
Data General Corporation
6-8, rue Andras-Beck
Dynasteur 92
92366 Meudon–La Forêt
Tel: (01) 40 94 60 00

Deere and Co.—John Deere
10, rue de Paris (Ormes)
B.P. 211
45144 Saint-Jean-de-la-Ruelle
Tel: (03) 88 80 71 41
Digital Equipment Corporation
91004 Évry
Dow Chemical Co.
49, rue de Billancourt
92016 Boulogne Cedex
Du Pont de Nemours
137, rue de l'Université
75007 Paris
Tel: (01) 45 50 65 50
The Dun et Bradstreet France
345, avenue Georges-Clémenceau
92882 Nanterre Cedex 09
Tel: (01) 41 35 17 00
Fax: (01) 41 35 17 77
Eastman Kodak Company
24, rue Villiot
75012 Paris
Tel: (01) 40 01 35 55
Fax. (01) 40 01 42 84
Eaton Corp.—Eaton Controls S.A.
Avenue des Sorpiers
B.P. 5
74311 Thyez Cedex
Tel: (04) 50 98 68 00
Fax. (04) 50 96 08 80
Exxon Corp. Esso S.A.
6, avenue André-Prothin
92400 Courbevoie
Tel: (01) 49 03 60 00
The Franklin Mint World Headquarters
4, avenue de l'Escouvrier
95200 Sarcelles
Tel: (01) 39 90 54 51
General Electric Co.
8, avenue Franklin-D.-Roosevelt
75008 Paris
Tel: (01) 45 62 62 22
Fax: (01) 45 61 18 16
General Mills, Inc.—Biscuiterie
Nantains
Île Beaulieu

Avenue Lotz-Cosse
44200 Nantes
Tel: (02) 51 72 44 00
Fax: (02) 51 72 44 09
General Motors Corporation
33, quai de Dion-Bouton
92814 Puteaux Cedex
Tel: (01) 46 92 52 08
**The Gillette Company—
Braun Electric France**
22-28, rue Henri-Barbusse
92110 Clichy-Paris
Tel: (01) 47 39 32 03
Fax: (01) 47 39 52 65
Hasbro, Inc.
71, La Plaisse
B.P. 13
73370 Le Bourget du Lac
Tel: (04) 79 96 48 48
Hewlett-Packard France
1, avenue Canada
91947 Les Ulis
Tel: (01) 69 82 60 60
H. J. Heinz Company
13, rue Madeleine-Michelis
92522 Neuilly-sur-Seine Cedex
Tel: (01) 47 45 51 30
Fax: (01) 47 45 16 39
Kimberly-Clark Corporation
7, avenue Ingrès
75016 Paris
Tel: (01) 45 24 43 22
Fax: (01) 45 25 85 24
Levi Strauss & Company
Rue de l'Yser
59480 La Bassée
Tel: (03) 20 29 90 40
Fax: (03) 20 29 90 41
Lockheed Martin Intl. S.A.
4, rue de Penthièvre
75008 Paris
Mattel, Inc.
64-68, avenue de la Victoire
94310 Orly
Tel: (01) 48 92 23 33
Fax: (01) 48 52 73 52

Motorola European Office
1, boulevard Victor-Hugo
75015 Paris
Tel: (01) 53 78 18 00
Fax: (01) 53 78 18 15
Polaroid France S.A.
57, rue des Villiers
92202 Neuilly-sur-Seine
**Quaker Oats Company—Fisher Price
SARL**
B.P. 20
45801 Saint-Jean-de-Braye
Tel: (04) 38 84 42 84
Ralston Purina Company
1, place Charles-de-Gaulle
78180 Montigny-le-Bretonneux
Tel: (01) 30 12 59 59
Fax: (01) 30 12 59 60
Raytheon
326, bureaux de la Colline
92213 Saint-Cloud Cedex
The Reader's Digest Association, Inc.
1-7, avenue Louis-Pasteur
92220 Bagneux
Tel: (01) 46 64 16 16
Fax: (01) 46 64 03 32
Reebok France S.A.
184, rue Tabuteau
78532 Yvelines Cedex
Tel: (01) 30 97 50 00
Sara Lee Corporation—Dim S.A.
6, rue Marius-Aufan
92301 Levallois-Perret Cedex
Tel: (01) 47 59 15 15
Sony Corporation
15, rue Floréal
75017 Paris
Tel: (01) 40 87 30 00
Fax: (01) 47 31 13 57
3M
Boulevard de l'Oise
95006 Cergy-Pontoise
Time Warner, Inc.
25, boulevard de l'Amiral-Bruix
75116 Paris
Tel: (01) 53 64 54 54

Teaching

As an expatriate, you have, by definition, a set of skills and a perspective different from those of the majority of people native to your adopted country. Teaching, therefore, is a vocation that many expatriates find that they are qualified for, even if they have never taught before. And because English language skills are in demand virtually everywhere English is not normally spoken, there is usually a consistent demand for English teachers and tutors. If you're moving to France on a whim, or if you don't have a job lined up before you go, you may find that teaching is a good way to make a buck (or a franc, as the case may be). Teaching English might also be a good option for temporary employment if you've just arrived in France or are between jobs. But the opportunities are not limited to teaching English; you may have skills or talents or experience that enable you to teach a range of other subjects, from business or marketing to computers or other technical skills, or almost anything else in which you might have a particular expertise. Teaching jobs can be found anywhere in the country, on an individual basis as well as in schools, colleges, and other educational institutions and businesses.

A typical Paris street scene

Teaching English

Regardless of any real or perceived language snobbery that exists in France, there is a continuing need and real demand for English language education. Perhaps to the disdain of many French-speaking people, English has become the default global language, and many French businesspeople and professionals find that without basic English skills, they are not able to advance in their careers or do business outside France. Many French businesses have organized corporate education programs that include English language training, and will provide courses free of charge or at minimal expense to their employees. English is particularly necessary in fields of technology and science, where many important texts are published only in English. To fill this demand, there is a bevy of English schools and language centers in all of France's major cities; literally dozens exist in Paris alone.

For those interested in pursuing English language teaching as a vocation, there is a large family of acronyms to learn. ESL (English as a Second Language), EFL (English as a Foreign Language), and ESOL (English for Speakers of Other Languages) are generally interchangeable when referring to teaching the English language to nonspeakers, although some purists will evangelize minor differences in usage. (In some circumstances, ESL refers to teaching English in an English-speaking country to people whose native language is something else; EFL sometimes refers to teaching English in a non-English-speaking country to non-English speakers. Others consider ESOL to be a more politically correct term, as it could refer to individuals learning English as their fourth or fifth language.) TESL refers to Teaching English as a Second Language and TEFL refers to Teaching English as a Foreign Language. TESOL means Teaching English to Speakers of Other Languages, and is also the name of a U.S.-based organization for ESL/ EFL/ESOL professionals. Don't confuse TESL/TEFL/TESOL with TOEFL, which stands for "test of English as a foreign language," a standardized exam given to test the English language competency of foreign students in the United States.

In France, as in most places, teaching English does not always mean teaching English as a foreign language. In many cases, the subject of "English" means a combination of English-language literature, literary history, poetry, and composition. As a subject, English courses of this type are taught at schools and universities, and usually require students to have a high level of English comprehension and fluency. Finding a job as an English teacher, by this definition, can be a difficult endeavor unless you have prior experience and full teaching credentials.

There are also differences in preference for British or American English that you must be sensitive to if you're pursuing a career in teaching English. Most French students of English will have a preference for the type of English that they wish to learn, and many feel strongly about it. Some people believe American English to be an inferior or lower-class language, while others prefer to learn English with an American accent because they feel it is more easily understood. In addition, as many of the texts and teaching materials available in France are produced in the United Kingdom, they use British English. If you have students who prefer to learn American English, you may need to special order materials from the United States and make an extra effort to draw attention to the differences between the two styles.

GETTING CERTIFIED

There are a number of different ways to get a certification in teaching the English language. There are bachelor's and master's degree programs offered at many colleges and universities, as well as professional certification programs sponsored by official TESL/TEFL/TESOL organizations. And there are hundreds of private schools and programs around the world that offer certification programs. If you are interested in pursuing a certificate, you should probably enroll in a school or program before you leave for France, as there are far more TESL/TEFL/TESOL certification programs in the United States than in France. Although a certificate and formal training will open up many more opportunities for you down the road, many people forgo certification altogether and look for teaching positions or take students based entirely on their being native English speakers with college degrees. In addition, there are many volunteer positions available to those willing to teach English, many of which are sponsored by organizations that provide a way for you to become certified.

THE RSA-CAMBRIDGE AND TRINITY COLLEGE CERTIFICATES

Most established certification schools and programs are recognized by one of the two main TEFL certification programs: the RSA-Cambridge certificate and the Trinity College certificate. The RSA-Cambridge program, officially called Certificate in English Language Teaching to Adults, or CELTA (formerly called "RSA Cert" or CTE-FLA), was developed at England's Cambridge University, and offers intensive, short-term instruction in basic language teaching methodology. The course has been offered for more than seventeen years by RSA-Cambridge TEFLA centers located around the world, and is generally taken as a one-month intensive, hands-on program, with actual classroom teaching practice. Most CELTA courses cost about $2,500. A certificate sponsored by Trinity College in England is also available, mostly at schools in the United Kingdom. Although well received by many English language schools abroad, it is not as widely recognized as the CELTA certificate, and Trinity College does not oversee and assess the schools and programs that adhere to its curriculum, resulting in less consistency from school to school.

WORKING

Finding Work

PRIVATE AMERICAN AND BRITISH OVERSEAS SCHOOLS
There are a few American and British schools, most of which are located in Paris, that are fully accredited by the U.S. or U.K. educational authorities and follow American or British curricula. These schools generally cater to the children of American businesspeople, diplomats stationed in France, wealthy French, and expatriates. All classes are taught in English. In addition, most have a full range of extracurricular activities for students that are also conducted in English, such as scouting or sports. Teaching positions at these schools become available infrequently, and generally require you to have full teaching credentials and at least a master's degree in the subject that you wish to teach. These schools sometimes do have unexpected openings, however, and it is possible to secure a steady teaching position if you are well qualified and persistent in your search. Although most teachers are hired locally, there are several U.S.-based agencies that sponsor job fairs and place teachers in overseas positions. See the address section at the end of this chapter for contact information.

BILINGUAL SCHOOLS
The French school system includes a variety of schools that teach classes in both French and English. Some of these schools have special sections for American, British, and other foreign students who have recently arrived in France and are adapting to the French school system. While many of these schools are considered to be private, some are subsidized by the government. These schools and programs vary immensely, so you would do well to research curricula and understand exactly what types of classes are taught, and in what languages. A list of French schools offering bilingual education can also be found in the address section in Chapter 16.

LANGUAGE SCHOOLS
There are hundreds of language schools, large and small, that exist throughout France and cater to French people and other non-English speakers from all walks of life who wish to learn English or improve their language skills. Most structured English teaching opportunities are to be found at language schools. Some language schools are for chil-

dren, others are for adults, and yet others cater to specific types of language skills such as technical English or business English. In addition, many corporations have internal language schools that are offered to their employees for free or for minimal cost as a way to improve their value to the company. If you are looking for a position at an organized language school, you should understand the dynamics and policies of the program they sponsor. Some schools will mandate that you teach a proprietary curriculum that they have developed; others will allow you to make up your own lesson plans and design the course yourself. Most established language schools will only hire teachers with a TESL/TEFL/TESOL certificate or with previous experience teaching English. It is not uncommon, however, for schools to hire you without these qualifications if you have a postgraduate degree or merely present yourself well. If you don't have previous experience or a certificate, you may try taking on individual students for a while before applying for a position at an established school.

PRIVATE STUDENTS

Taking private students or small groups is a great way to gain teaching experience, build a solid curriculum, and make decent money. Sometimes working independently in this way you can actually make more money than if you had a regular job with a language school or other educational institution. It also allows for a greater level of flexibility, as you can make your own hours and teach only when and as much as you wish. Usually, students will come to you with specific needs or desires, and you'll have to adapt your curriculum to them. Often businesspeople or executives search out private tutors or teachers to help with specific business goals or projects that they may have. As an independent English teacher, you may find that you're actually doing more tutoring and editing than traditional teaching, as people come to you with a presentation or speech that they need to perfect before taking it to the public. You should price your services accordingly, and if you find that you're doing a lot of customized work for a particular student, you can ask for more money. Generally speaking, you can earn between FF50 and FF150 per hour as an independent English teacher. Ask for more once you've established yourself and built up a small group of students.

There are many places where you can advertise or post *petites*

Biot

annonces, or classified ads, in order to promote yourself as an English teacher. There are bulletin boards at many schools and universities, and many larger businesses have corporate newsletters that will place your ad. In addition, there are more and more French Web sites emerging that cater to specific localities, or build virtual communities of people with common interests. Several Web sites are listed at the end of this chapter, but as the Web and Internet world is changing rapidly, it makes sense to do additional research on your own. You can also place ads in the two main magazines that are published for non-English speakers who want to improve their language skills. Both *Vocable* and *Today in English* publish in easy-to-read-and-understand English as educational and language aids to non-English speakers.

Teaching

VOLUNTEERING

If you don't need to earn a living, there are many volunteer organizations that will train you and then place you in a teaching position in France. World Teach sends volunteer teachers to France and other countries for one-year terms of service. Although volunteers are expected to pay a small fee, they are provided with room and board. Many of these programs can be found in the magazine *Transitions Abroad*, which focuses on independent travel and teaching overseas. Check the address section at the end of this chapter for more information, and consult Chapter 24, "Internships and Volunteering," for more information on nonpaying teaching positions.

Useful Addresses

TESOL
1600 Cameron Street, Suite 300
Alexandria, VA 22314
Tel: (703) 836-0774
Fax: (703) 518-2535
Fax on demand: (800) 329-4469
E-mail: publ@tesol.edu
Web site. http://www.tesol.edu
Transitions Abroad
Dept. TRA
P.O. Box 3000
Denville, NJ 07834
Tel: (800) 293-0373 or (413) 256-3414
Fax: (413) 256-0373
E-mail: trabroad@aol.com
Web site: http://www.transabroad.com
WorldTeach, Inc.
Harvard Institute for International
Development
14 Story Street
Cambridge, MA 02138
Tel: (800) 483-2240 or (617) 495-5527
Fax: (617) 495-1599
E-mail: info@worldteach.org
Web site: http://www.worldteach.org
IATEFL (International Association of Teachers of English as a Foreign Language)
3 Kingsdown Chambers

Tankerton, Whitstable
Kent, England CT5 2DJ
Tel: +44 227 276528
Fax: +44 227 274415
E-mail: 100070.1327@Compuserve.com
Web site:
http://www.mcc.ac.Uk/~mewcsgm/IATE
FL/IATEFL.html

AGENCIES THAT SPONSOR
INTERNATIONAL JOB FAIRS

International Educators Cooperative
212 Alcott Road
East Falmouth, MA 02536
Tel and fax: (508) 540-8173
International Schools Services (ISS)
15 Roszel Road
P.O. Box 5910
Princeton, NJ 08543
Tel: (609) 452-0990
Fax: (609) 452-2690
Ohio State University
Educational Careers Center
110 Arps Hall
1945 North High Street
Columbus, OH 43210-1172
Tel: (614) 292-2741
Fax: (614) 292-4547

WORKING

Overseas Placement Service for Educators
University of Northern Iowa
SSC#19
Cedar Falls, IA 50614-0390
Tel: (319) 273-2083
Fax: (319) 273-6998
Search Associates
P.O. Box 636
Dallas, TX 18612
Tel: (717) 696-5400
Fax. (717) 696-9500

SOME RSA/CAMBRIDGE
CERTIFICATE PROGRAMS IN THE
UNITED STATES

Center for English Studies
330 Seventh Avenue
New York, NY 10011
Tel: (212) 620-0760
Coast Language Academy
200 SW Market Street, Suite 111
Portland, OR 97201
Tel: (503) 224-1960

English International San Francisco
655 Sutter Street, Suite 500
San Francisco, CA 94108
Tel: (415) 749-5633
St. Giles Language Teaching Centre
1 Hallidie Plaza, Suite 530
San Francisco, CA 94123
Tel. (415) 788-3552
Coast Language Academy
501 Santa Monica Boulevard, Suite 403
Santa Monica, CA 90401
Tel: (310) 394-8618
Georgetown University
3607 O Street, NW
Washington, DC 20007
Tel. (202) 687-4400

A complete list of approved programs can be obtained from:
University of Cambridge Local Examinations Syndicate (UCLES)
Syndicate Buildings, 1 Hills Road
Cambridge, England CB1 2EU
Tel +44 1223 553311
Fax +44 1223 460278

236

CHAPTER TWENTY-TWO

Freelance, Part-Time, and Temporary Work

Some people follow a job with their American company and take a posting in France; others are lucky enough to find a full-time position with a French company immediately upon their arrival. But if you are not one of these lucky few, or if you don't have a *carte de séjour* that permits you to work, chances are that at some point you will end up freelancing or taking a temporary or part-time job.

Freelance, temporary, and part-time jobs are often easier to find than a permanent, full-time position, and, although difficult, it is sometimes possible to find informal or freelance jobs that are "under the table," or *au noir* (in the black), as is said in French. For many Americans and other non–European Union nationals, under-the-table freelancing or informal part-time work may be the only way to make a living because they don't have an easy way to obtain a *carte de séjour* that gives them the right to work legally. It can often be very difficult to get a company to sponsor you for a *carte de séjour*.

Of course, it is also possible to make a living as a legitimate freelancer, or to find legal part-time or temporary work if you have already secured a work permit. All temp agencies in France will require that you have the legal right to work before they allow you to register. And most employers will not consider employing you for any job—part-time, temporary, or otherwise—without proof that you are legally entitled to work in France.

While it is certainly preferable to work as a freelancer legally, the startup costs and taxes associated with working independently can be prohibitively expensive. Most freelancers will forgo the formalities of establishing themselves as an independent contractor, at least while they build a clientele, and look for *travail au noir*, or under-the-table jobs.

The French government has, of late, been more aggressive in its enforcement of employment laws, and has specifically cracked down on businesses or individuals employing illegal immigrants. Under-the-table jobs are still possible to find, but you should have no illusions: these jobs are illegal, and you put your existence in France on the line if you work illegally. If you do not have the legal right to stay in France and you are found to be working illegally, you risk being deported, and your employer could be fined a substantial sum.

That said, freelancing can be rewarding and even lucrative, and temporary, part-time, and freelance work provides benefits and freedoms that are unavailable to people with permanent, full-time positions. You can be your own boss, work on your own schedule, and take only jobs that you want to take. Part-time and temporary jobs are particularly well-suited for students and others who want to have time to study, travel, or pursue other activities. Although you may not have the security or benefits that a regular job provides, freelance, part-time, and temporary work can give you the freedom to explore different vocations—a good idea if you're not sure what kind of job you want. In addition, these types of jobs can be a great way to learn about French culture, adapt to French ways of business, and experiment with various lines of work.

If you're a student or recent college graduate, the Council on International Educational Exchange (CIEE) offers a unique program that enables you to work in France legally for up to three months. The program costs $300, but virtually guarantees that you will be granted an *autorisation provisoire de travail*, or temporary work permit. In addition, CIEE will help you find work and assist you with the required paperwork. CIEE reports that nearly all participants have been able to find work, usually within a few days or a week after arrival in France. Most opportunities are for temp jobs in office environments, as English tutors, or in food service, and pay the French minimum wage or slightly more. In addition, there is usually a two-week trial period in which either you or your employer can back out of the arrangement without penalty, after which there's a month's notification required.

Freelancing

Popular freelancing jobs include modeling; translating; journalism; providing computer services like graphic design, word processing, or Web-related services; domestic help; and handyperson services. The amount of success you find in France depends, among other things, on how much your services are needed, how well you can market yourself and build a client base, how well you speak French, and how well you do your job. As is necessary whenever you move a business, once you arrive in France and adjust a bit to your new surroundings you will likely find that you need to adapt your services to the differences of the French market. If you've already been a freelancer in the United States, you may find that you will either have to offer different services or market yourself differently in order to build an effective freelancing practice in France.

Freelancing also has its drawbacks. The taxes and other charges you will incur as a *travailleur indépendant* can be much more than if you are employed in a regular job. You should set aside at least half your annual income for the government. As is the case with freelancing anywhere, it is necessary to be very organized and keep meticulous records of your work, finances, and interactions with clients in the event that you are audited or get involved in a financial dispute with a client. As an independent worker, you're legally required to register with the Union de Recouvrement des Cotisations de Sécurité Sociale et d'Allocations Familiales (URSSAF), the French social security authority, which will assess your charges each year based on your income.

MARKETING YOURSELF TO CLIENTS

In order to build a successful business freelancing, it is essential to market yourself effectively. The best form of marketing, especially if you're working *au noir*, is word of mouth. In France, perhaps more so than in many other places, networking is of paramount importance. Make sure that your friends and associates know that you are in business for yourself. Have some business cards printed, in both French and English, with your name, title, and line of business. It is also a good idea to have a small brochure produced, also in both French and English, that describes your business offer, talents, and expertise. Be sure to exploit any and all connections that you have.

Advertising in local media can be an effective way to spread the word about your freelancing offer. It can also be a waste of time and money, depending on your line of work. Take the time to research your market position as a freelancer. Are there others offering the same or similar services? How can you differentiate yourself? How can you take advantage of your position as an expatriate to expand your visibility and client base? If you are determined to make a living freelancing, it is important to take your job seriously and be diligent about preparation, marketing, and customer service.

If you do decide that you wish to advertise your services, there are several options. Many expatriate freelancers opt to advertise in the English-language media rather than in the French press. Generally speaking, your ability to offer "cross-cultural" services, or traditional services in English, can be your greatest advantage. Paris is home to a bevy of English-language media, from the well-established *France-USA Contacts*, or *FUSAC*, to *Pariscope*'s Time Out section. The international press, including the *International Herald Tribune*, the *Wall Street Journal Europe*, and the *European*, can also be a venue for advertising. While Paris is certainly home to the largest English-speaking community in France, English-language media can also be found in Marseille, Bordeaux, Nice, and some of the other large metropolitan areas. As the French continue to warm up to Internet technology and the Web, you may also want to set up a Web site that details your freelancing offer, or place ads on various French and international Web sites that cater to the specific market you are trying to reach.

Part-Time and Temporary Work

CONSULTING

It may be possible for you to convince an American company to hire you as a consultant abroad. If they don't already have offices in France, companies may look favorably on the idea of having a representative in a major market and establishing a presence that eventually could turn into a satellite office or foreign bureau.

TELECOMMUTING

As the pace of technology increases, more and more companies are allowing employees to "telecommute," freeing people up to live anywhere in the world. If you work for a company that allows telecommuting, you may be able to move to France while keeping your U.S.-based job. Telecommuting often requires that you create a home office with a computer and high-speed connection to the Internet, a fax machine, and a separate business phone line. See Chapter 11, "*La Vie Virtuelle*: Navigating French Cyberspace," for more information on connecting to the Internet from France and setting up a home office. Keep in mind, however, that this type of work often requires that employees make themselves available during the business hours of the main office. This means that you might have to keep quite irregular hours when time differences are taken into account, especially if your company is based on the West Coast of the United States.

SEASONAL JOBS

Seasonal work in France could include jobs like being a deckhand on a ship along the Mediterranean coast, working as a laborer on a farm, stomping grapes at a vineyard, counseling at a summer camp, or working in a ski resort high in the Alps. Although they often involve hard labor, can be dirty, and may lack certain career objectives, seasonal jobs like these can be found throughout the year, some lasting an entire season, others just a few weeks. Many seasonal jobs require little or no French and some may even provide you with room and board at minimal or no cost. This can be a great benefit because finding temporary accommodations or a place to prepare your own food can often be a challenge, especially in popular resort areas.

Many Americans find work in restaurants or hotels that cater to the mass of tourists that descend upon France year round, but especially in the summer months. The French are enamored with American culture, and there are therefore scores of Tex-Mex and American-style restaurants and diners throughout France, but especially in Paris, along the Côte d'Azur, and in other large cities. Because these restaurants cater largely to American tourists and Anglophiles, your cultural affiliation with the United States can be a big advantage when you walk in the door to ask for a job.

There can often be a lot of competition for seasonal jobs, and most

Much of the skiing in the French Alps is above the tree line, with wide, open spaces and challenging slopes.

employers will hand them out on a first-come, first-served basis. But if you're not picky, and don't mind working hard and getting dirty, they have their advantages. Sometimes you can make quite a bit of money in a short time, literally "cashing in" on the popularity of a holiday resort and the influx of tourists with deep pockets. Jobs of this sort can be a good way to give yourself a taste of France if you're not sure you want to stay for a long period of time. And they can free you up to look for more substantial work later.

TEMPORARY AGENCIES

As in the United States, temporary employment agencies in France (*agences de travail temporaire* or *agences d'intérim*) place workers in companies to compensate for understaffing and fill in for various other reasons. Because of the traditional five-week summer vacations and sixteen-week maternity leaves that French companies routinely grant their employees, temporary workers are often in great demand. Temporary employment agencies such as ECCO, Kelly, and Manpower can be found in all metropolitan areas in France, and may either specialize in employee placement in specific industries or be more general. Most agencies will commonly place people with general administrative or secretarial skills, and it is usually necessary to be fluent in French.

242

Temping has its advantages. Temp jobs can be a good way to learn the particular ins and outs of a company and may eventually lead to being offered a permanent position. They can also be a good way to earn money while looking for a more permanent or lucrative job, a process that can take weeks and sometimes months of research. Temporary jobs can also expose you to a range of different employment situations, helping you make a more informed decision when the time comes to choose a career.

Most temp agencies require that you visit one of their offices for a face-to-face registration process and interview. You will be asked to fill out an extensive questionnaire—that basically mimics your résumé—about your education, experience, and any special skills. If applying for secretarial or administrative work, you will likely be given a test to determine your typing speed (remember: French keyboards do not follow the "qwerty" format of American ones). Your language skills may also be assessed, and you may be required to exhibit fluency in French and at least one to two other languages.

Before you register with a temporary employment agency, be sure that you find out what, if any, industries or fields of work they specialize in and the average length of time of their contracts. Once you have registered, employment agencies will contact you as jobs become available. This could take a matter of days, weeks, or even months. Before you accept a contract, make sure that you are clear about how much, when, and by whom you will be paid. While some agencies consider their obligations fulfilled once a temporary employee is placed in an open position, others pay workers themselves and contract employee services out to corporations in bulk. You may register with as many agencies as you wish; there are no limits.

TRANSLATING AND INTERPRETING

Many Americans find work in France translating or interpreting. These are two distinct fields with different requirements and it is important to know the difference. Translating is the practice of rendering French text into another language or text from another language into French. Interpreting, however, requires a much higher level of fluency, as it refers to the practice of translating in "real time" between speakers of one language and others. A good interpreter understands the nuances of language and can quickly articulate a speaker's meaning from one language to the other. While the requirements for interpreting jobs can be very demanding and positions harder to find, many Americans make a living providing translating services to French authors, journalists, and businesses. If your French is good and you have an expertise in a specific industry or field of study, you may be able to find work translating technical writing from one language to the other.

BEING AN AU PAIR

Working as an au pair has been a popular vocation among foreign workers in France for many generations. It is possible to find work as an au pair anywhere in France—in Paris and the other metropolitan areas, as well as in the provinces and small villages. An au pair, formally called a *stagiaire aide-familiale*, is hired for general child care and light household work, and is given room, board, and a small salary in exchange. Au pair positions can be found once you've arrived in France, or set up via an agency from America or elsewhere in the world. Even today, it is generally easier to find work as an au pair if you are female, although increasingly there are families willing to employ single men. Taking an au pair position can be a great opportunity to improve your French, learn about French culture, and, if you land a position in the right family, you might get some travel thrown in.

The French government has laws and regulations that control au pair employment. Americans wishing to find employment as an au pair will need a long-stay visa, a formal letter from a French family *(déclaration d'engagement)*, and proof that they are registered for classes or enrolled in a French language school. Although it is possible to find less formal or under-the-table au pair jobs once you are in France, most agencies will demand that you meet these requirements.

Most au pairs will work between six and eighteen months in a household, usually for the duration of a semester or school year, but often summer positions can also be found. Legally, au pairs are supposed to work no more than thirty hours per week, no more than six days per week, and no more than five and a half hours per day. In addition, au pairs are not required to baby-sit more than three evenings per week, and are generally allotted time for studying and socializing. As with other types of employment, French law mandates that families pay monthly social security charges to the government to cover their au pair's disability and health benefits. Most au pair positions pay a small salary—about F1,500 per month—as "pocket money." In Paris, you may also get an allotment for public transportation, either as a small stipend or a *Carte Orange* (a monthly pass for the Paris *Métro* and buses).

The work that you are expected to do as an au pair can vary tremendously. Most au pair positions require some amount of light housework such as cooking, washing dishes, doing the laundry and ironing, or vacuuming and dusting. And although it is sometimes possible to find an au pair position in a household without children, your duties will most likely include some amount of general child care. The work and experience can vary tremendously from household to household, so it is generally advisable to meet the family and children with whom you'll be working before you agree to take a position. Often, it is required that au pairs attend language classes or tutoring in French as part of the arrangement. Room and board is always provided. Although traditionally au pair positions have been filled by women, men are increasingly applying for such positions and are sometimes even offered them.

OTHER TYPES OF CHILD CARE POSITIONS

If you're looking for a job with fewer responsibilities than what would be expected of you as an au pair, it is often possible to find work as a demi-pair. Demi-pairs will usually work only twelve hours per week, instead of thirty for au pairs, in exchange for room and board, but are not afforded any salary or spending money. In addition, demi-pair positions can sometimes be for shorter periods of time.

It is also possible to find work as a nanny, which, according to French law, is a proper job with all standard employee rights and benefits. Nannies are usually experienced child care professionals and can be of any age, while au pairs are normally young adults. Nannies generally command a much better wage, but have sole responsibility for children and usually live in the employer's residence.

TEACHING ENGLISH

Your knowledge of English could be one of your greatest assets when you're outside of the United States. There is a great demand for English teachers and tutors throughout the non-English speaking world, and France is no exception. If you don't have the ability to work legally in France, freelance English tutoring is sometimes a good way to make a life for yourself. Although there is a lot of competition—many English-speaking foreigners have the same idea—if you're a good teacher, you will probably be able to find a fair amount of business. For more information on teaching English and other subjects, see Chapter 21, "Teaching."

Useful Addresses

GENERAL INFORMATION

Council on International Educational Exchange (CIEE)
International headquarters:
205 East 42nd Street
New York, NY 10017-5706
Tel: (212) 822-2600
Fax: (212) 822-2699
E-mail: Info@ciee.org
European/French headquarters:
1, place de l'Odéon
75006 Paris
Tel: (01) 44 41 74 74
Fax: (01) 43 26 97 45
E-mail: InfoEurope@ciee.org

TEMPORARY AGENCIES

Drake International
35, rue de la Bienfaisance
75008 Paris
Tel: (01) 42 89 63 63
Fax: (01) 42 89 63 40
ECCO
11, rue La Boétie
75008 Paris
Tel: (01) 40 07 10 60
Kelly Services
13, place de la Défense
92090 Paris–La Défense
Tel: (01) 47 78 13 13
Interim-Nation
Tel: (01) 43 45 50 00
Fax: (01) 42 65 61 26
Web site: http://www.interim-nation.fr
Manpower
9, rue Jacques-Bingen
75017 Paris
Tel. (01) 44 15 40 40

LTD International
47, rue de Ponthieu
75008 Paris
Tel: (01) 45 63 51 67
Plus International
60, rue de l'Arcade
75008 Paris
Tel: (01) 40 08 40 30
Fax: (01) 45 22 49 53
Eliness Travail Temporaire
94, rue St-Lazare
75009 Paris
Tel: (01) 42 80 51 06

AU PAIR AGENCIES IN THE UNITED STATES AND FRANCE

Association for International Training (AIT)
10400 Little Patuxent Parkway, Suite 250
Columbia, MD 21044
Tel: (410) 997-2200
Fax: (410) 992-3924
Alliances Abroad
18 Buena Vista Terrace
San Francisco, CA 94117
Tel: (415) 487-0691
Fax: (415) 487-1164
InterExchange
161 Avenue of the Americas
New York, NY 10013
Tel: (212) 924-0446
Fax: (212) 924-0575
Nurse Au Pair Placement (NAPP)
32, rue des Renaudes
75017 Paris
Tel: (01) 47 64 46 87
Fax: (01) 47 64 48 20
Web site: http://www.oda.fr/aa/napp

Nannies Incorporated
8, rue Dobropol
75017 Paris
Tel: (01) 45 74 62 74
Fax. (01) 45 76 62 74

SEASONAL JOBS

**Centre d'Information et de
Documentation de la Jeunesse (CIDJ)**
101, quai Branly
75740 Paris Cedex 15
Tel: (01) 44 49 12 00
**Centre d'Information de la Jeunesse
Provence-Alpes**
4, rue de la Visitation
13248 Marseille Cedex 04
**Service des Échanges et des Stages
Agricoles dans le Monde (SESAME)**
9-11, square Gabriel-Fauré
75017 Paris
Tel: (01) 40 54 07 08
Club Méditerranée
25, rue Vivienne
75002 Paris
Web site. http://www.clubmed.fr
Service recruitment:
11, rue de Cambrai
75957 Paris Cedex 19
General recruitment information:
Tel: (407) 337-6660

Abercrombie and Kent
1520 Kensington Road
Oak Brook, IL 60521
Tel: (630) 954-2944
Fax: (630) 954-3324
**American Institute for Foreign Study
(AIFS)**
102 Greenwich Avenue
Greenwich, CT 06830
Tel: (800) 727-2437 or (203) 869-9090
Fax: (203) 869-9615
Web site: http://www.aifs.org
Backroads
801 Cedar Street
Berkeley, CA 94710
Tel: (800) 245-3874
Fax: (510) 527-1444
Education First (EF)
Institute for Cultural Exchange
1 Education Street
Cambridge, MA 02141
Tel: (800) 637-8222
Fax (617) 621-1930
Web site. http://www.edtours.com
European Travel Commission
One Rockefeller Plaza
New York, NY 10111
Tel: (212) 218-1200
Web site: http://www.visiteurope.com

CHAPTER TWENTY-THREE

Starting Your Own Business

Traditionally speaking, France has less of an entrepreneurial spirit than the United States. The notion of getting rich quick or the "million-dollar idea" is a peculiarly American concept, and small businesses and startup companies are not nearly as prevalent in France as they are in the United States. Many French small businesses are family-owned shops or services and operate more as a way of life than as the means to tremendous profitability. This idea of running a business as a way of life rather than a profit center may be attractive to many Americans who have moved to France to escape the work-a-day culture and dog-eat-dog business climate of the United States. That said, there are many opportunities for doing business in France and many Americans and other foreigners who have come to France with good ideas and translated them into very successful companies. In addition, the hard-driving American work ethic has increasingly been exported all over the world, and the business environment in France, and Western Europe in general, is becoming more similar to America's as each year passes. Nevertheless, even in the most competitive and hard-driving of French businesses, employees take long lunches and are granted long summer vacations. And no one can deny that French cheese makes life a whole lot more livable, regardless of what business you're in.

The French government encourages foreign individuals and corpo-

*The Roman-style column in Paris's Place Vendôme is
topped with a statue of Napoléon instead of Caesar.*

rations to do business in France. There are many formalities, but the
government has taken steps to reduce bureaucracy and paperwork in
order to help businesses set up shop in the hopes that more businesses
will mean more jobs and a stronger economy. In addition, with the continuing development of the European Union and its monetary and economic unification, scheduled to take place before July 1, 2002, French
companies are increasingly free to do business throughout Europe.

This means that for some businesses, the potential market is not limited to just France. It also means that there is a greater potential for economic stability in France as well as throughout Europe, and that businesses will be less vulnerable to the ebbs and flows of severe economic trends in any individual member nation.

France is the fourth largest economy in the world, and is also the fourth largest in the world in the areas of import, export, and investment. In addition, France is the world's leading country for tourism. Many Americans and other foreigners have started successful companies by extending their "outsider" perspective into a business idea that caters to the demand of tourists. But businesses can take any form, from restaurants and specialty food stores, to technology companies, professional services, and even agricultural businesses. Starting a business anywhere can be exhausting, both physically and financially, but the failure rate of new businesses in France is less than it is in many other European countries: about one-third of new companies will not survive their first five years.

Purchasing an Existing Business

If you're not inclined to invest the financial resources and physical effort required to start a new company, you many want to consider buying an existing business. Many small businesses are family owned and passed from one family member to another, or sold by word of mouth, but there are still lots of opportunity to find existing businesses for sale. It may be possible to breathe new life into a failing or marginally successful company with new energy, specialized expertise, or different ways of doing business. Buying a company usually requires less money, significantly less effort, and is less risky than starting a similar business from scratch as much of the infrastructure and many processes are already in place. There is a variety of specialized publications in France that contain listings of businesses for sale, and you can often find listings or ads in local newspapers as well. See the address list at the end of this chapter for several of these publications and other organizations that provide advice and services for purchasing a business.

Types of Businesses

Companies in France are governed mainly by the Commercial Company Law of 1966 as well as by various other legislation and the French Civil Code. When starting a company, you should thoroughly research the different corporate structures permitted under French law and choose the business type that best suits your individual financial situation, your entrepreneurial idea, the market as you see it, and the concerns of any partners and investors you may have.

REPRESENTATIVE OR BRANCH OFFICES

If you have or are affiliated with an existing company in the United States or elsewhere, under French law it is possible to set up a representative or branch office in France. For example, most major American news organizations have a Paris bureau that they use as a satellite for news and information gathering. Other companies set up branch offices specifically in order to establish a presence or promote a brand in France as they prepare to enter the European market. The branch office is considered part of the parent company, not an individual entity, and its liabilities or debt is the responsibility of the parent company. If you set up a branch or representative office in France, the general manager of the branch must have power of attorney in order to ensure that the office complies with French law, and the foreign head office is responsible for the liability of the French office.

SUBSIDIARIES

A subsidiary is in many ways very similar to a branch or representative office, but maintains a higher level of independence that limits the liability of the parent company abroad. With subsidiaries, the parent company is liable only for its investment in the subsidiary.

COMMERCIAL AGENTS

Import/export companies and other retail corporations generally use a French agent in order to handle contacts with French manufacturers or distributors. One agent is generally responsible for the whole country. Guidelines for this type of business are complex, as are the contracts that are established with companies outside France, so enlisting the help of a French lawyer and accountant is advisable.

Joint Ventures

A joint venture, or *société en participation*, is set up when two or more companies enter into contract to collaboratively provide goods or services in France. Whereas most companies will need to publicly announce their formation and register with the government, joint ventures require neither action and the details of the partnership are often confidential.

Sole Proprietorships

Sole proprietorships are businesses in which the operation is under the control of a single individual who has total liability for its operation. These types of companies do not have the formal legal structure of a corporation and all the assets and liabilities of the company are also those of the individual owner. If you start a sole proprietorship, you report all profits and losses on your personal tax return.

Partnerships

There are three forms of partnership permitted under French law: general partnership, limited partnership, and partnership limited by shares. A general partnership, called a *société en nom collectif*, has a corporate identity similar to that of a commercial company except that the partners have total liability for the company, jointly and individually. There are no minimum capital requirements for setting up a general partnership and all profits and losses are generally shared by the partners in proportion to their individual investment in the company. General partnerships do not have to publicly disclose their financial information and are not subject to taxation unless they choose to be, but each partner must report profits and losses of their share of the partnership on their individual tax return.

There are two types of limited liability partnerships under French law. A standard limited partnership, or *société en commandite simple*, is a partnership that has at least one unlimited general partner (which could be another company), and one or more partners who have limited liability in the company. The limited partners, however, are not permitted to participate in the company's management. The other type of limited partnership is a "partnership by limited shares," or *société en commandite par actions*, and is basically the same as a standard limited partnership, except that the proportion of each member's contribution is counted in terms of shares in the company.

CORPORATIONS

There are four kinds of limited liability corporations permitted under French law. A *société anonyme* (SA) has many investors who share ownership of the corporation using stock, which can be either publicly or privately traded. To qualify as an SA, the company must have a FF250,000 minimum initial capital investment, or FF1.5 million to be publicly traded. Fifty percent of this amount must be paid upon issue of the stock and the remainder over the course of five years. This capital investment can be either in cash or in kind, meaning that corporate assets such as buildings, machinery, or even intellectual property can qualify, but capital in kind is subject to an audit by the French Tribunal de Commerce, or commercial court. SAs will also need to register all of their accounts with the commercial court. An SA is managed by a *président directeur général* (PDG), the French equivalent of a CEO, who has complete managerial responsibility for the company. A board of directors made up of elected shareholders chooses the PDG. There must be at least seven shareholders, all but one of which can be other corporate entities.

A privately owned limited liability company is called a *société à responsabilité limitée* or SARL. SARLs have many fewer formalities than SAs so this is the structure that most small businesses adopt. The minimum initial capital investment for an SARL is FF50,000, all of which must be paid on registration; in-kind capital is also permitted but is subject to a commercial court audit. An SARL must have at least two but no more than fifty shareholders, who can appoint one or more managers. If there is only one shareholder, the company is considered an EURL, or single-shareholder private limited liability company. The rules for EURLs are generally the same as for SARLs, except that EURLs held by an individual are not subject to standard corporate taxes unless expressly requested.

In an attempt to liberalize corporate regulations and encourage business, the French government since 1994 has allowed a type of business that combines the legal status of a corporation with the flexibility of a partnership, called a *société anonyme simplifiée*, or SAS. An SAS has limited liability and must be formed by at least two partners with an initial capital investment of FF1.5 million, or the foreign equivalent. If you have substantial financial resources, this is an ideal structure.

Setting Up Shop

When registering a new business, you need to go to a company for-mality center, or *centre de formalités des entreprises* (CFE), or your local chamber of commerce. Generally, you will need to submit the company's articles of incorporation, in French, a certificate proving that you have no criminal record, a registration form, and the property lease for the place where you intend to do business. Unless you have specific expertise in these areas, you will probably need to enlist the aid of an accountant and a lawyer who are versed in the ins and outs of French corporate regulations and law. It is generally best to ask friends and associates, preferably people who have gone through the process of starting a company, to recommend lawyers *(avocats)* and accountants *(experts comptables)*. Otherwise, your local French chamber of com-merce or CFE can help. In addition, there is a government organiza-tion called Délégation à l'Aménagement du Territoire et à l'Action Régionale (DATAR) that controls the development of business and industry in France. DATAR can provide you with much of the informa-tion you will need in order to navigate through the paperwork and bureaucratic formalities of starting a company. We've listed the contact information for DATAR at the end of this chapter.

PERMITS AND LICENSES

Some businesses will require that you obtain special permits or licenses in order to conduct business. This applies to food service and agricultural companies, companies that deal with chemicals or other hazardous materials, and many professional trade companies, such as plumbers or locksmiths, that need to be approved by various official trade organizations. Check with your CFE or chamber of commerce to find out if the business you wish to start is governed by special regula-tions or licensing controls.

FINANCING, AID, AND LOANS

Any way you do it, starting a new business requires a large amount of capital. Most American banks don't readily grant loans to individuals or startup businesses overseas. French banks are more likely to grant you a loan, but will normally require that you have been a French resi-dent for quite some time and have established a strong banking history and references. You may be able to convince private investors, both in the United States and in France, to invest in your business idea if you have a particularly good idea and can provide a well-thought-out business plan that virtually guarantees profitability. It is unusual, however, for most businesses to be profitable before a period of several years. In France more than in the United States, established businesses are more accepted and respected than startups. Until your business is part of the landscape, finding money can be a challenging exercise. That said, there are many tax incentives and other benefits that are extended by the government to new companies. Tax exemptions of varying amounts are granted to most new enterprises for up to the first five years of operation and business license taxes are usually waived for at least the first year of operation.

HIRING EMPLOYEES

There are many more guidelines and regulations controlling the hiring and firing of employees in France than there are in the United States. Most employees are hired for an initial trial period, lasting up to six months, before they are offered a contract. During the trial period, either the employer or employee can choose to cease employment for any reason. Once a contract is entered into, however, it is generally quite difficult to fire an employee. There is a set of strict guidelines that employers must adhere to when dismissing an employee, and the employee has the right to take the company to court to challenge the decision.

Employers are responsible for paying the employee's wages, as well as the majority of the employee's social security contributions. Female employees are usually allowed up to an eighteen-week maternity leave. Employees are generally granted 2.5 days of paid vacation for every month worked, amounting to about five weeks annually. See Chapter 18, "Job Hunting," for more information on French employment regulations.

Chambers of Commerce and
Other Helpful Organizations

The American Chamber of Commerce in France, located in Paris, can help with many aspects of doing business in France. They also publish a magazine called *Commerce in France* that provides information and success stories of American business in France. There is also a Franco-American Chamber of Commerce in Paris, as well as in many larger American cities, that can provide information and advice on many aspects of cross-cultural business.

You can also find a wealth of information about starting a company and doing business in France at both the Foreign Commercial Service of the American Embassy in Paris, and at the French Embassy in Washington, D.C. Both embassies have libraries of information, much of which is available over the Web.

Small-Business Ideas to Consider

The possibilities for starting a business are endless. There are Americans living and doing business in France in virtually every sector of society. If you're interested in starting a company and are unsure about what type of company to open, you should consider your own individual skills and expertise, what businesses are particularly successful in both the United States and in France, and where areas of opportunity might exist. As an American living in France, you are in the unique position of being able to have insight into both cultures and each country's specific business climate.

Computer Technology As in the United States, technology in France is booming. France has a very advanced technology sector and a long history of early adoption of technology (for example, the Minitel) and innovation. As the Web continues to grow in influence and size in France, there are many opportunities to play a part. See Chapter 11, *"La Vie Virtuelle:* Navigating French Cyberspace," for more ideas.

Tourism France has a bigger tourism industry than any other country in the world. Consider starting a company catering to this

Tourism: Biot

tremendous market by offering guide or travel services, a travel agency, or a bed and breakfast. Adventure travel is big business, both in the United States and in France. There are many other possibilities and ways to capitalize on tourism.

Retail Maybe there is a product or store that you love in the United States that you just can't find in France. While French tastes can be quite different from American, many American retail businesses have been transplanted to France with tremendous success.

WORKING

Real Estate Agents/Realtors   In Paris, there is no shortage of real estate agents catering to the large influx of foreigners each year. But outside the capital, there are few companies that understand American sensibilities and tastes, or can effectively rent or sell property to various markets.

Accountants   There are only a few accountants in Paris who understand the specific requirements of Americans living abroad. If you have an expertise in business in the United States and France, or the regulations governing foreign nationals, you may be able to start a profitable practice.

Attorneys   The market for attorneys never seems to be satiated. If you are an attorney in the United States, you might be able to brush up on the areas of the law that are applicable to foreign nationals and offer your services in France.

Theaters and Art Galleries   There is a long and rich history of theater and art in Paris, which may make the prospect of contributing to this market either daunting or tremendously exciting, depending on your perspective. Regardless, you may find that there are opportunities to open an American cinema or art gallery elsewhere in France.

Restaurants, Bars, and Discos   You probably shouldn't open another Irish pub in Paris, but the French have always had a fascination with all things American, and if the Tex-Mex craze is any indication, this is not likely to diminish anytime soon. In Paris and elsewhere in France, American-style food and entertainment are very popular.

Health and Fitness   Health and fitness have become big markets in France in recent years. Think about opening a gym, health food store, or restaurant, or offering personal trainer services.

Schools and Student Services   There has always been a big market for education in Paris and the rest of France. You might be able to open a successful practice offering tutoring, English teaching,

258

résumé services, or teaching of various other skills. See Chapter 21, "Teaching," for more information.

Useful Addresses

Délégation à l'Aménagement du
Territoire et à l'Action Régionale
(DATAR)
1, avenue Charles-Floquet
75007 Paris
Tel: (01) 40 65 12 34
**The American Chamber of Commerce
in France**
21, avenue George-V
75008 Paris
Tel. (01) 40 73 89 95
Web site: http://www.amchamfr.com
DIRECTORY OF FRENCH
MANUFACTURERS, DISTRIBUTORS,
AND WHOLESALERS.
Annuaires Kompass
66, quai du Maréchal-Joffre
92415 Courbevoie Cedex
Tel: (01) 41 16 51 00
Fax. (01) 41 16 51 69
DIRECTORY OF THE 30,000
LARGEST FRENCH FIRMS:
Dun & Bradstreet
345, avenue Georges-Clémenceau
92882 Nanterre Cedex 09
Tel: (01) 41 35 17 00
Fax. (01) 41 35 17 77
Directory of French Exporters
24, boulevard de l'Hôpital
B.P. 438
75233 Paris Cedex 05
Tel: (01) 40 73 37 83 or 40 73 31 68
Fax: (01) 43 36 47 98
DIRECTORY OF FRENCH FIRMS
EXPORTING TO THE UNITED STATES:
Telefirm/Telexport
Chambre de Commerce et d'Industrie de
Paris
27, avenue Friedland
75008 Paris
Tel: (01) 55 65 55 65

LIST OF FRENCH SUBSIDIARIES IN
THE UNITED STATES:
**Centre Français du Commerce
Extérieur**
10, avenue d'Iéna
75783 Paris Cedex 16
Tel: (01) 40 73 30 00
Fax: (01) 40 73 39 79
FRENCH INDUSTRY ASSOCIATION
DIRECTORY:
CNPF
31, avenue Pierre-1er-de-Serbie
75784 Paris Cedex 16
Tel. (01) 40 69 44 44
Fax: (01) 47 23 47 32
FRENCH IMPORTERS DIRECTORY:
FICIME
25-27, rue d'Astorg
75008 Paris
Tel: (01) 44 51 14 60
Fax: (01) 42 65 39 49
FRENCH ADMINISTRATION DIRECTORY:
La Documentation Française
29-31, quai Voltaire
75344 Paris Cedex 07
Tel: (01) 40 15 70 00
Fax: (01) 40 15 72 30
FRENCH MEDIA AND PERIODICALS
DIRECTORY:
Ecran Publicité
190, boulevard Haussmann
75008 Paris
Tel: (01) 44 95 99 90
Fax. (01) 42 89 08 72

FRANCO-AMERICAN CHAMBERS OF
COMMERCE
PARIS:
104, rue Miromesnil
75008 Paris
Tel: (01) 53 89 11 00

WORKING

ATLANTA:
999 Peachtree Street, NE, Suite 2095
Atlanta, GA 30309
Tel: (404) 874-2602
Fax. (404) 875-9452

BOSTON:
15 Court Square, Suite 320
Boston, MA 02108
Tel. (617) 523-4438
Fax. (617) 523-4461

CHICAGO:
55 East Monroe Street, Suite 3710
Chicago, IL 60603
Tel: (312) 263-7668
Fax. (312) 263-7860

DALLAS–FT. WORTH.
4835 LBJ Freeway, Suite 640
Dallas, TX 75244
Tel: (214) 991-4888
Fax. (214) 991-4887

DETROIT.
P.O. Box 43959
100 Renaissance Tower
Detroit, MI 48297
Tel: (313) 567-6012
Fax: (313) 567-0142

HOUSTON.
1776 St. James Place, Suite 425
Houston, TX 77056
Tel. (713) 960-0575
Fax: (713) 960-0495

LOS ANGELES:
6380 Wilshire Boulevard, Suite 1608
Los Angeles, CA 90048
Tel: (213) 651-4741
Fax: (213) 651-2547

MIAMI.
141 Sevilla Avenue
Coral Gables, FL 33134
Tel. (305) 444-1587

MINNEAPOLIS–ST. PAUL:
Foshay Tower, Suite 904
Minneapolis, MN 35402
Tel: (612) 338-7750
Fax: (612) 334-2781

NEW ORLEANS:
World Trade Center, Suite 2938
New Orleans, LA 70130
Tel: (504) 524-2042
Fax: (504) 522-4003

NEW YORK.
1350 Avenue of the Americas, 6th Floor
New York, NY 10019
Tel: (212) 715-4444
Fax. (212) 765-4650

PHILADELPHIA:
4000 Bell Atlantic Tower
1717 Arch Street
Philadelphia, PA 19103
Tel. (215) 994-5373
Fax: (215) 994-5366

PITTSBURGH:
c/o Reed, Smith, Shaw & McClay
435 Sixth Avenue
Pittsburgh, PA 15219
Tel: (412) 288-4174
Fax: (412) 288-3063

SAN FRANCISCO.
425 Bush Street, Suite 401
San Francisco, CA 94108
Tel. (415) 398-2449
Fax: (415) 398-8912

SEATTLE:
2102 Fourth Street, Suite 2330
Seattle, WA 98121
Tel: (206) 443-4703

WASHINGTON, D.C.:
1730 Rhode Island Avenue, NW,
Suite 711
Washington, DC 20036
Tel. (202) 775-0256
Fax. (202) 785-4604

CHAPTER TWENTY-FOUR

Internships and Volunteering

In France, perhaps more than in other places, it can be very important to make contacts and build networks in order to establish and grow a career. If you've just arrived in France or are moving there without knowing many people, a great way to gain experience and make contacts is to set yourself up with an internship (a *stage*) or take a volunteer position at a company or organization. Although you likely won't get rich as an intern or volunteer, you'll be immersing yourself in France in a unique way that provides benefits both to you and to the organization that you work for, and for your adopted home as well. In addition, an internship or volunteer job can serve as a bridge between your studies and your career. Many organizations that use interns or volunteers offer available jobs to those people first because there is less of a learning curve than if an outsider were hired. If you're a student, you may also be able to get academic credit for completing an internship or volunteer position in France. Many people who complete internships or volunteer jobs say that they were among the most valuable and educational experiences they ever had.

There are hundreds of internships and volunteer programs available in France, existing in nearly every industry and sector of society. Many are sponsored by educational institutions in the United States and in France, and others are sponsored by businesses or other organizations. Whatever field you're interested in, you can probably find an internship or volunteer position that will help you gain exposure to it, learn the details of a job, and make those all-important contacts. The *stage* is an important part of education and career building in France. Most French students spend at least a summer or an academic year, and sometimes more, in a professional environment related to their field of study. Most companies in a wide variety of industries have internship programs that allow young people to make contacts and gain exposure to the vocation, and that sometimes even lead into a regular job. In this way, completing an internship can be a great investment in your future.

For many Americans and other non-EU nationals, finding an internship or volunteer job can be the only way to live in France legally. Because internship and volunteer positions are, by definition, officially unpaid, you generally do not need to secure a work permit or go through many of the other bureaucratic hassles that would be required if you were attempting to work a regular job in France.

Finding the right internship or volunteer opportunity can sometimes be a challenge. While we'll provide you with a list of opportunities and organizations that can help you get started, you should invest some time researching your options and investigate the details of a position before you commit. Before accepting an internship or volunteer position, you should know what you want to get out of the experience and understand exactly what will be expected of you. Positions like these can consist of one job or many; you should get your sponsor to outline your duties and responsibilities in advance. Try to talk to others who have completed similar programs to get an idea of how your internship or volunteer job will be structured. If you're a student, talk to your study abroad office, your guidance counselors, and your instructors about possible opportunities. Some questions you should ask include: What is the duration of the job and how many hours will you be asked to work? What are the job conditions, that is, supervision and atmosphere? Will you receive any form of compensation, for example, a stipend, room and board, or academic credit? And, is this opportunity one that will enable you to make professional contacts, or one that might lead into a job offer?

Types of Internship

MEDIA INTERNSHIPS

Media internships can involve working in journalism or publishing, in public relations or advertising, or, increasingly, in the Web publishing arena. Most media organizations that take interns require that all applicants speak French with a relatively high level of fluency. News organizations including the Paris-based *International Herald Tribune*, *Time* and *Newsweek* magazines, the *Wall Street Journal Europe*, and various American broadcast news bureaus all take a few interns from time to time. There are bureaus for nearly every major U.S. news agency and media outlet in Paris, and many other field offices throughout France. You may be able to land an internship at the Associated Press, Reuters, or even Agence France-Presse, which maintains a sizable English service in addition to its global French news service. Refer to the address section at the end of this chapter for a list of English-language media in France.

INTERNSHIPS IN THE ARTS

Paris is full of opportunity for individuals interested in pursuing arts-related internships. There are organized internships available at most of Paris's museums and many of the capital's galleries. Interns at museums and galleries are sometimes given research duties, or other administrative work.

LAW INTERNSHIPS

The University of the Pacific's Master of Laws program offers graduates of U.S. law schools a chance to work in a private law firm or company legal department in France after completing a six-week intensive course on international law in Salzburg. Participants must have a law degree from a U.S. ABA school or a recognized law school abroad and can earn credit toward a Master of Laws degree in Transnational Business Practice. In addition, there are prelaw internship programs from Michigan's Alma College and Boston University.

INTERNSHIPS WITH INTERNATIONAL ORGANIZATIONS

France is home to two main international organizations—the Organization for Economic Cooperation and Development (OECD) and

263

UNESCO—and many other international organizations have branch offices in Paris. There are offices for the World Bank, UNICEF, and the United Nations, all of which have internship programs available to qualified applicants.

The OECD, based in Paris, does not offer paid traineeships or internships, as a rule. There are, however, a limited number of nonpaid internships that are offered from time to time to graduate students of economics or others whose study is directly related to the OECD's mission. The OECD also has a "Young Professionals" program, which allocates a limited number of junior administrator positions to people between twenty-six and thirty-three who have a background in economics and some work experience in the field. UNESCO, also based in Paris, offers an international development internship that lasts between one and six months, open to postgraduate students with a master's degree or equivalent. There are forty positions available in this program.

Internship Organizations

There are several organizations, based both in the United States and in France, that place willing applicants in internships in a variety of fields. The Carl Duisberg Society (CDS International) places people in business, economics, journalism, political science, and other internships. Educational Programs Abroad, based in Princeton, New Jersey, sponsors a Paris internship for students of a wide range of disciplines including law, politics, health and social sciences, and museums and arts administration. Global Outreach, based in Virginia, places agriculture students in three- to twelve-month internships in France, as well as a number of other European countries. The Institute for the International Education of Students has programs in Dijon, Nantes, and Paris for students of business, science and engineering, music, and fine arts. If you're interested in politics, the Paris-based Internships in Francophone Europe program offers a chance to work in high-level offices of France's most important political and international organizations. Another interesting program is the summer restoration internships offered by La Sabranenque, an organization that has been working for almost thirty years for the preservation of rural habitats. This internship will have participants helping with the restoration of historic buildings somewhere in rural France.

Finding Internships Through Universities
and Creating Your Own

Many American universities sponsor internship programs in France for their students. If you're enrolling in a study abroad program, the organization or institution that sponsors your program may also sponsor corresponding or related internships. Check with your school's study abroad office to find out about internships that may be offered. If your school does not offer an internship option that interests you, there are many other internship programs sponsored by universities that are open to any students. Alma College in Michigan, American University, Boston University, Dickinson College in Pennsylvania, Ohio State University, the University of Minnesota, the University of Illinois, and the University of the Pacific all offer internship programs in France that are open to any qualifying student, not just students at their own campus. The Career Services and Placement Department at Michigan State University publishes an annual directory of international internships, available both in print and electronic versions. See the address section at the end of this chapter for contact information.

If you can't find a suitable internship through one of the organizations we've mentioned here, there are certainly a lot of other options. It is generally possible to dream up your own ideal internship and then seek out an organization or company that you believe might be able to offer it. Many companies or organizations are open to taking on an unpaid intern even if they do not currently have an organized internship program. Selling yourself to a company or organization may take a little bit of effort, but you may be able to convince them that taking you on as an intern will benefit all parties involved. A little bit of Web-based research or even cold-calling at local offices may land you an experience that you'll value throughout your professional life.

Volunteering

As opposed to internships, which are generally career-oriented, volunteer work is usually altruistic and experiential in nature. Volunteer jobs can be difficult and dirty, but they can also be extremely rewarding. If you're not looking to make money, and want to have an interesting experience and help people along the way, then volunteerism is for you. And there are some additional benefits: some charity or volunteer work does pay a small stipend, and most will provide you with decent room and board. There is a wide variety of volunteer jobs available, often taking the form of archaeology or restoration work, other types of conservation, working with children at camps and summer programs, or working with senior citizens, disabled, or poor people. Like many internships, volunteering can also provide you with a chance to meet a wide variety of people and make contacts that can be valuable to you professionally. In France, networking and making contacts is a critical part of many people's professional lives. Volunteering can be one way to get your foot in the door of a French workplace. Most volunteer jobs are organized by one of the literally tens of thousands of volunteer organizations throughout France and others that are based outside the country that place volunteers in France and elsewhere in Europe and the world. In addition, the Council on International Educational Exchange (CIEE) organizes a wide variety of volunteer programs in France in collaboration with three main French partners: Concordia, Solidarités Jeunesses, and UNAREC. Information about the CIEE-sponsored programs can be found on their Web site. Although it is generally helpful to have a working knowledge of French, few volunteer programs require you to be fluent. Volunteering can be a great way to improve your language skills while gaining experience and education in French history and culture.

ARCHAEOLOGY AND ARCHITECTURE

Many people find volunteer work in archaeology or architecture to be an extremely rewarding experience because it provides a unique window on the culture and history of a specific region of France. You might find yourself toiling away in the sun to uncover remnants of Roman civilization or helping to rebuild deteriorating historic buildings. Most of these volunteer opportunities are available in the summer months, and you will sometimes be expected to camp or live in relatively basic accommodations. The Ministry of Culture's Sous-Direction de l'Archéologie, Documentation, publishes an annual list of excavations throughout France that accept volunteers. For more information, consult the address list at the end of this chapter.

Some of the volunteer archaeological and architectural programs that exist include Concordia, Rempart, and Chantiers d'Études Médié-vales. Concordia's program organizes volunteers to renovate footpaths and hiking trails in the Auvergne region of France. Rempart's mission

I. M. Pei's famous pyramids at the Louvre blend ultra-
modern design with classical architecture.

is to preserve French cultural heritage through the restoration of
threatened buildings and monuments and consists of more than 140
autonomous associations that organize work camps. As a volunteer, you
could end up helping in the restoration of medieval towns, castles,
churches, ancient walls, wind/watermills, or industrial sites. Work
includes masonry, excavation, woodwork, stone cutting, interior deco-
rating, and clearance work. Volunteers with Chantiers d'Études
Médiévales also restore and maintain medieval buildings and sites,
including two fortified castles at Ottrott, in the Alsace region. In addition, La Sabranenque employs volunteers to help preserve and restore
monuments throughout France.

ENVIRONMENTAL AND ANIMAL CARE

There is a range of environmental protection and conservation organizations that rely on volunteerism, including the World Wildlife Fund
and Greenpeace, with offices in France. You should contact the U.S.
offices or offices in France to find out more about what types of volunteer programs are available. The address list at the end of this chapter
provides contact information. It is also possible to find a volunteer

position at one of France's many farms, or at an organization that helps maintain the environment. One such organization is Nature et Progrès, which provides a list of organic farmers in France who hire temporary assistants or volunteers to help with harvesting and general farming.

SOCIAL SERVICES AND HUMAN RIGHTS

There are a number of nonprofit organizations that provide aid to the poor, the elderly, and the disabled that regularly rely on volunteers to help with virtually all aspects of their existence, from fundraising and administration to media and public relations. The Fondation Abbé Pierre pour le Logement des Défavorisés is a Paris-based organization that seeks to provide rooms for homeless people throughout France. This organization takes adult volunteers to assist with promotion of the mission through help designing Web campaigns and other public relations. The Fédération Internationale des Petits Frères des Pauvres (International Federation of Little Brothers of the Poor) employs volunteers to provide assistance and companionship for the elderly. The Fédération has eleven centers in France: six in Paris and its suburbs, and one each in Lyon, Marseille, Nantes, Toulouse, and Lille.

Work Camps and Summer Camps

There are many organizations set up to cater to children and young adults who wish to pursue an educational experience though a summer camp or work camp. The organization Volunteers for Peace is a clearinghouse for many volunteer organizations that promote summer work camps. One such organization, Jeunesse et Reconstruction, organizes work camps throughout France and recruits grape pickers for work at vineyards during the annuai harvest. The Fédération Unie des Auberges de Jeunesse (FUAJ) provides short-term work at youth hostels throughout France. Work can take the form of catering, reception, sports, or instruction. FUAJ also organizes work camps to help renovate hostels where volunteers are paid a small weekly stipend. The Paris-based Centre d'Information et de Documentation de la Jeunesse (CIDJ) acts as a general advisory center for young people and provides information about temporary work possibilities. APARE runs volunteer work camps at historic sites in southern France.

The Louvre and pyramid

Useful Addresses

ENGLISH-LANGUAGE MEDIA AND
BUREAUS IN FRANCE

The International Herald Tribune
181, avenue Charles-de-Gaulle
92521 Neuilly Cedex
Tel. (01) 41 43 93 00
Fax: (01) 41 43 93 70

Time Magazine
14, rue de Marignan
75008 Paris
Tel: (01) 44 01 49 99
Fax: (01) 44 01 49 29

Business Week
11-13, avenue de Friedland
75008 Paris
Tel: (01) 40 75 25 00
Fax. (01) 42 89 04 00

Life Magazine
(Time, Inc.)
14, rue de Marignan
75008 Paris
Tel: (01) 44 95 70 31
Fax: (01) 45 63 01 10

Newsweek
162, rue du Faubourg-St-Honoré
75008 Paris
Tel: (01) 53 83 76 10

People
28, rue du Temple
75004 Paris
Tel: (01) 48 87 30 14
Fax: (01) 48 87 60 89

The Wall Street Journal Europe
3, rue de Surènes
75008 Paris
Tel: (01) 40 17 18 19
Fax: (01) 40 17 18 18

The New York Times
3, rue Scribe
75009 Paris
Tel: (01) 42 66 37 49
Fax. (01) 47 42 88 21

The Associated Press
162, rue du Faubourg-St-Honoré
75008 Paris
Tel: (01) 43 59 86 76
Fax: (01) 40 74 00 45

WORKING

Reuters
19-21, rue Poissonnière
75083 Paris Cedex 02
Tel: (01) 53 40 24 00
Fax: (01) 42 33 00 50
Agence France-Presse
13, place de la Bourse
75002 Paris
Tel: (01) 40 41 46 46
Fax: (01) 40 41 46 32
ABC News
3, rue de l'Arrivée
75749 Paris Cedex 15
Tel. (01) 40 47 80 81
Fax: (01) 40 47 66 58
CBS News
37, rue Marbeuf
75008 Paris
Tel: (01) 53 83 80 90
Fax: (01) 45 61 49 76
CNN
Washington Plaza
29, rue de Berri
75004 Paris
Tel. (01) 44 95 55 10
Fax: (01) 44 95 55 11
NPR
28, rue St-Paul
75004 Paris
Tel: (01) 42 77 68 30
Fax. (01) 48 87 66 60
Radio France Internationale (RFI)
116, avenue du Président-Kennedy
75786 Paris Cedex 16
Tel: (01) 42 30 12 12
Fax. (01) 42 30 44 81

LAW INTERNSHIPS

University of the Pacific
Master of Laws Program
McGeorge School of Law
International Programs
3200 Fifth Avenue
Sacramento, CA 95817
Tel: (916) 739-7195
Fax: (916) 739-7111

Alma College
614 West Superior Street
Alma, MI 48801
Tel: (517) 463-7247
Boston University
International Programs
232 Bay State Road
Boston, MA 02215
Tel: (617) 353-9888
Fax: (617) 353-5402
Web site: http://www.web.bu.edu/abroad

INTERNATIONAL ORGANIZATIONS

**Organization for Economic
Cooperation and Development (OECD)**
2, rue André-Pascal
75775 Paris Cedex 16
**United Nations Educational, Scientific
and Cultural Organization (UNESCO)**
7, place de Fontenoy
75352 Paris 07 SP
Tel. (01) 45 68 10 00
Fax: (01) 45 67 16 90

INTERNSHIP ORGANIZATIONS

Institute of International Education
U.S. Student Programs Division
809 United Nations Plaza
New York, NY 10017
Web site: http://www.iie.org
Internships in Francophone Europe
26, rue du Commandant-René-Mouchotte,
J 108
75014 Paris
Tel: (01) 43 21 78 07
Fax: (01) 42 79 94 13
Web site: http://www.ifeparis.org/
La Sabranenque
Centre International
25, rue de la Tour-de-l'Oumme
30290 Saint-Victor-la-Coste
Tel. (04) 66 50 05 05
Institute of European Studies (IES)
223 West Ohio Street
Chicago, IL 60610
Tel: (800) 995-2300
Fax: (312) 944-1448

**Worldwide Internships and Service
Education (WICE)**
303 South Craig Street
Pittsburgh, PA 15213
Tel. (412) 681-8120
Fax: (412) 681-8187
Internships International, LLC
1116 Cowper Drive
Raleigh, NC 27608
Tel: (919) 832-1575

Michigan State University
Career Services and Placement
Department
113 Student Services Building
East Lansing, MI 48824
Tel: (517) 355-9510, ext. 371
Fax: (517) 353-2957

**Council on International Educational
Exchange (CIEE)**
International Headquarters
205 East 42nd Street
New York, NY 10017-5706
Tel: (212) 822-2600
Fax: (212) 822-2699
E-mail: Info@ciee.org
Web site: http://www.ciee.org
Ministry of Culture
Sous-Direction de l'Archéologie
Documentation
4, rue d'Aboukir
75002 Paris
Tel: (01) 40 15 73 00
Rempart
Union des Associations pour la
Réhabilitation et l'Entretien des
Monuments et du Patrimoine Artistique
1, rue des Guillemites
75004 Paris
Tel: (01) 42 71 96 55
Fax: (01) 42 71 73 00
World Wildlife Fund
151, boulevard de la Reine
78000 Versailles

Tel: (01) 39 24 24 24
Fax: (01) 39 53 04 46
Greenpeace France
21, rue Godot-de-Mauroy
75009 Paris
Tel: (01) 53 43 85 85
Fax: (01) 42 66 56 04
E-mail: greenpeace.
france@diala.greenpeace.org
Amnesty International
4, rue de la Pierre-Levée
75553 Paris Cedex 11
Tel: (01) 49 23 11 11
Fax: (01) 43 38 26 15
Médecins Sans Frontières
8, rue St-Sabin
75544 Paris Cedex 11
Tel. (01) 40 21 29 29
Fax: (01) 48 06 68 68
E-mail: office@paris.msf.org
Nature et Progrès
1, avenue Général-de-Gaulle
84130 Le Pontet
Tel: (04) 66 03 23 40
**Fondation Abbé Pierre pour le
Logement des Défavorisés**
B.P. 205
75624 Paris Cedex 13
Tel: (01) 53 82 80 30
Web site. http://www.fondation-
abbe-pierre.fr
**Fédération Internationale des Petits
Frères des Pauvres**
33, avenue Parmentier
75011 Paris
Tel: (01) 49 23 13 00
Fax: (01) 47 00 94 66
Web site: http://www.petits-freres.org/
Jeunesse et Reconstruction
10, rue de Trévise
75009 Paris
Tel: (01) 47 70 15 88
**Fédération Unie des Auberges de
Jeunesse (FUAJ)**
27, rue Pajol
75018 Paris
Tel: (01) 44 89 87 27

WORKING

Centre d'Information et de
Documentation de la Jeunesse (CIDJ)
101, quai Branly
75740 Paris Cedex 15
Fax: (01) 44 49 12 00
APARE
41, cours Jean-Jaurès
84000 Avignon
Tel: (04) 90 85 51 15
Fax: (04) 90 86 82 19

Earthwatch International
680 Mt. Auburn Street
P.O. Box 9104
Watertown, MA 02272
Tel: (800) 776-0188
Fax: (617) 926-8532
E-mail: info@earthwatch.org
VFP International Workcamps
43 Tiffany Road
Belmont, VT 05730-0202
Tel: (802) 259-2759
Fax: (802) 259-2922

For Further Study

For the most current information about living, studying, and working in France, visit the Web site complement to this book at **www.liveinfrance.com.**

EXPATRIATE TRAVELOGUES AND LITERATURE SET IN FRANCE
Paul Auster, *Hand to Mouth: A Chronicle of Early Failure*
Marti Cranford, *Travels: A Personal Journey Through the United Kingdom, France, and Switzerland*
Charles Dickens, *A Tale of Two Cities*
M. F. K. Fisher, *Long Ago in France: The Years in Dijon*
F. Scott Fitzgerald, *Tender Is the Night*
Janet Flanner, *Paris Was Yesterday: 1925–1939*
Françoise Gilot, *Life with Picasso*
Ernest Hemingway, *A Farewell to Arms*
Ernest Hemingway, *The Garden of Eden*
Ernest Hemingway, *A Moveable Feast*
Ernest Hemingway, *The Short Stories*
Ernest Hemingway, *The Sun Also Rises*
Henry James, *Collected Travel Writings*
Diane Johnson, *Le Divorce*
Harvey Levenstein, *Seductive Journey: American Tourists in France from Jefferson to the Jazz Age*
Peter Mayle, *Chasing Cézanne*
Peter Mayle, *Hotel Pastis*
Peter Mayle, *Toujours Provence*
Peter Mayle, *A Year in Provence*
Mary Davies Parnell, *Plateaux, Gateaux, Chateaux*

For Further Study

Anne Rice, *The Vampire Armand*
Mort Rosenblum, *The Secret Life of the Seine*
Ruth Silvestre, *A House in the Sunflowers: Summer in Aquitaine*
Danielle Steel, *Five Days in Paris*
Gertrude Stein, *The Autobiography of Alice B. Toklas*
Amanda Vaill, *Everybody Was So Young: Gerald and Sara Murphy, A Lost Generation Love Story*
Edith Wharton, *A Motor-Flight Through France*

NONFICTION BOOKS ABOUT FRANCE

General
David Applefield, *Paris Inside Out: The Insider's Guide for Visitors, Residents, Professionals and Students on Living in Paris*
David Applefield, *Paris Anglophone: Print and Online Directory*
Ann Barry, *At Home in France: Tales of an American and Her House Abroad*
James Bentley, *The Most Beautiful Villages of Burgundy*
Edward Berenson, *The Trial of Madame Caillaux*
Robert W. Cameron and Pierre Salinger, *Above Paris*
Ina Caro, *The Road from the Past: Traveling Through History in France*
Raymonde Carroll, *Cultural Misunderstandings: The French-American Experience*
Robert Gilpin and Caroline Fitzgibbons, *Time Out: Taking a Break from School to Travel, Work and Study in the U.S. and Abroad*
Handbook of Commercial French
Michael Jacobs, *The Most Beautiful Villages of Provence*
The Junior Service League of Paris, *At Home in Paris*
Alex Karmel, *A Corner in the Marais: Memoir of a Paris Neighborhood*
Eric Kocher, *International Jobs: Where They Are, How to Get Them*
Michelin Travel Publications, *France Green Guide*
Michelin Travel Publications, *France Red Guide*
Michelin Travel Publications, *Paris Green Guide*
Nancy Mitford, *The Sun King*
Miles Morland, *A Walk Across France*
Jean-Marie Perouse de Montclos, *Châteaux of the Loire Valley*
Carol Pineau and Maureen Kelly, *Working in France: The Ultimate Guide to Job Hunting and Career Success à la Française*
Polly Platt, *French or Foe? Getting the Most out of Visiting, Living, and Working in France*
Milena Ercole Pozzoli, *Castles of the Loire: Places and History*
Roger Price, *A Concise History of France*
Louis-Bernard Robitaille, *And God Created the French*
Harriet Welty Rochefort, *French Toast: An American in Paris Celebrates the Maddening Mysteries of the French*
Ross Steele, *The French Way: Aspects of Behavior, Attitudes, and Customs of the French*
Earl Steinbicker, *Daytrips France: 45 One-Day Adventures by Rail, Bus, or Car*
Sally Adamson Taylor, *Culture Shock: France*

274

For Further Study

Gordon Wright, *France in Modern Times*
Herbert J. Ypma, *Paris Flea Market*

Art
Françoise Cachin, *Manet*
Jean-Marie Chauvet, Christian Hillaire, and Eliette Brunel Deschamps, *Dawn of Art: The Chauvet Cave: The Oldest Known Paintings in the World*
Pierre Daix, *Picasso*
Nicholas d'Archimbaud and Bruno De Cessole, *Louvre: Portrait of a Museum*
Slvi Dos Santos, *Provence: The Art of Living*
Paul Gauguin, *Noa Noa: The Tahiti Journal of Paul Gauguin*
Amy Handy and Nancy Grubb (editors), *Treasures of the Louvre*
Robert L. Herbert, *Impressionism: Art, Leisure, and Parisian Society*
Robert Rosenblum, *Paintings in the Musée D'Orsay*
Hilary Spurling, *The Unknown Matisse: A Life of Henri Matisse, 1869–1908*
Daniel Wildenstein and James N. Wood, *Monet's Years at Giverny: Beyond Impressionism*

Cuisine
Barnaby Conrad, *Absinthe: History in a Bottle*
Linda Dannenberg, *Paris Bistro Cooking*
Alain Ducasse, *Ducasse Flavors of France*
Sandra A. Gustafson, *Cheap Eats in Paris*
Pierre Hermé, *Desserts by Pierre Hermé*
Kermit Lynch, *Adventures on the Wine Route: A Wine Buyer's Tour of France*
Kazuko Masui and Tomoko Yamada, *French Cheeses*
Richard Olney, *Provence the Beautiful Cookbook: Authentic Recipes from the Regions of Provence*
Robert M. Parker, *Bordeaux: A Comprehensive Guide to the Wines Produced from 1961 to 1997*
Robert M. Parker, *The Wines of the Rhône Valley*
Marilyn Piauton, *How to Eat Out in France: How to Understand the Menu and Make Yourself Understood: Dictionary and Phrase Book for the Restaurant*
Patricia Wells, *Patricia Wells at Home in Provence: Recipes Inspired by Her Farmhouse in France*
Daniel Young, *The Paris Café Cookbook: Favorite Recipes from the Fifty Best Cafés in Paris*
Tim Zagat (editor), *Zagat Paris Restaurant Survey, 1999*

War
Stephen E. Ambrose, *D-Day, June 6, 1944: The Climactic Battle of World War II*
Stephen E. Ambrose, *Pegasus Bridge*
Lucie Aubrac and Konrad Bieber, *Outwitting the Gestapo*
Larry Collins and Dominique Lapierre, *Is Paris Burning?*
Gregory Maguire, *The Good Liar: A Dramatic Story Set in Occupied France During World War II*

For Further Study

Conor Cruise O'Brien, *The Long Affair: Thomas Jefferson and the French Revolution, 1785–1800*
Josephine Poole, *Joan of Arc*
Douglas Porch, *The French Foreign Legion: A Complete History of the Legendary Fighting Force*
George F. Rude, *French Revolution*
Cornelius Ryan, *The Longest Day: June 6, 1944*

FRENCH LITERATURE
Honoré de Balzac, *Cousin Bette*
Honoré de Balzac, *Lost Illusions*
Honoré de Balzac, *Père Goriot*
Ludwig Bemelmans, *Madeline*
Ludwig Bemelmans, *Madeline's Rescue*
Albert Camus, *L'Étranger*
Albert Camus, *La Peste*
Alexandre Dumas, *The Count of Monte Cristo*
Alexandre Dumas, *The Man in the Iron Mask*
Alexandre Dumas, *Marguerite de Valois*
Alexandre Dumas, *The Three Musketeers*
Gustave Flaubert, *Madame Bovary*
Wallace Fowlie, *French Stories/Contes Français: A Dual-Language Book*
Victor Hugo, *The Hunchback of Notre Dame*
Victor Hugo, *Les Misérables*
Victor Hugo, *Ninety-Three*
Eugène Ionesco, *La Cantatrice Chauve*
Eugène Ionesco, *La Leçon*
Albert Lamorisse, *The Red Balloon*
Gaston Leroux, *The Phantom of the Opera*
Guy de Maupassant, *L'Ami Maupassant*
Guy de Maupassant, *Selected Short Stories*
Baroness Emma Orczy, *The Scarlet Pimpernel*
Marcel Proust, *Remembrance of Things Past*
Edmond Rostand, *Cyrano de Bergerac*
Antoine de Saint-Exupéry, *Le Petit Prince*
Jean-Paul Sartre, *Essays in Existentialism*
Jean-Paul Sartre, *Existential Psychoanalysis*
Jean-Paul Sartre, *No Exit and Three Other Plays*
Jean-Paul Sartre, *Truth and Existence*
Jules Verne, *Around the World in 80 Days*
Jules Verne, *A Journey to the Center of the Earth*
Jules Verne, *Paris in the 20th Century*
Jules Verne, *Twenty Thousand Leagues Under the Sea*
Émile Zola, *La Bête Humaine*
Émile Zola, *Germinal*
Émile Zola, *Nana*

Appendix:
Technical Information
You Should Know

GENERAL INFORMATION
Capital city: Paris
Official name: République Française
Type of government: Republic
Head of government: Prime Minister
Size: Slightly smaller than the state of Texas
Area: 547,030 square kilometers (211,154 square miles)
Coastline: 3,427 kilometers (2,129 miles)
Geographic highlight: Mont Blanc (highest point, 4,807 meters)
Independent states within French boundaries: Andorra and Monaco
Languages and dialects: The primary language is French. There are several
   rapidly declining regional dialects including Provençal (*Provence*), Breton
   (*Brittany*), Alsatian (*Alsace and Lorraine*), Corsican (*Corsica*), Catalan
   (*southwest*), Basque (*Pays Basqు:3*), Flemish (*northeast*).
Bordering countries: Belgium and Luxembourg on north, Germany on east,
   Switzerland on east, Italy on southeast, Spain on southwest
Surrounding seas and oceans: English Channel, Atlantic Ocean, and the
   Mediterranean Sea
Population: 58,609,285
Religions: Roman Catholic 90%, Protestant 2%, Jewish 1%, Muslim 1%, unaf-
   filiated 6%
GDP: $1.32 trillion (1997 estimate)
GDP growth rate: 2.3% (1997 estimate)
GDP per capita: $22,700 (1997 estimate)
Unemployment rate: 12.4%

277

MAIN POLITICAL PARTIES
There are nearly a dozen political parties in France representing the full range of political and social interests. The most important of these, divided according to the left and right of the political spectrum, are the following:

Right
Rally for the Republic (RPR): The RPR was originally the Gaullist party, united around President Charles de Gaulle in 1958. Current President Jacques Chirac restructured the party in 1975 but it remained dedicated to the Gaullist principles of opposition to big government and socialism as well as strong executive powers.

Union for French Democracy (UDF): This coalition party was initially founded by Republican leader Giscard d'Estaing. The members advocate a move to the center and recently united in a coalition with the RPR and defeated the Socialists in the 1993 parliamentary elections.

National Front (FN): The National Front, led by nationalist Jean-Marie Le Pen, is France's most controversial party. The party platform contains a heavy measure of racism, particularly directed toward France's many North African immigrants. Although the party faces strident criticism from the media and the mainstream political institutions, it has nevertheless succeeded in obtaining a certain measure of political power. It has held from one to three seats in Parliament as well as a handful of mayorships.

Left
Socialist Party (PS): This fairly leftward leaning party has existed since the beginning of the century, but it took the personality of former President Mitterrand to bring it to power. The party's popularity has fallen in recent years as the French economy has faced difficult times and socialist cures have failed to remedy the problems. The party's symbol is a red rosebud.

Communist Party (PCF): Often part of ruling coalitions, France's Communist Party was a major force in French politics until the late 1970s. It still sells itself as the workers' party. Although it continues to obtain a significant number of seats both in the Senate and the National Assembly each election, popularity has plummeted with the general fall of communism.

MAJOR MEDIA
Newspapers: There are three primary national newspapers, published in Paris: *Le Monde* (France's centrist and most respected national daily, considered the newspaper of intellectuals); *Libération* (a rather left-wing newspaper, still considered to have a communist/socialist editorial slant); and *Le Figaro* (considered to have a right-wing slant both in reporting and editorials). *Les Echos* is the national daily financial newspaper. *Le Canard Enchaîné* is a weekly satiric newspaper. Each region has its own newspaper as well. Some examples are *Nice Matin* (southeastern France—Provence); *Sud Ouest* (southwestern France); *Ouest France* (Brittany); and *Les Nouvelles d'Alsace* (Alsace—eastern France).

Magazines: Paris Match (one of the most read weekly magazines, gossipy at times); *L'Express* (a weekly news magazine, akin to *Time* or *Newsweek*); *Le Point* and *Le Nouvel Observateur* (two other news magazines with smaller readerships).

Television Channels: Cable television is becoming quite common but the primary channels that can be seen without cable are as follows: TFI is a private channel and belongs to a BTP Group (Bâtiment et Travaux Publics); it is a rather conservative channel but has a large audience and needs to make profits, which impacts the quality of the programming. The French government still runs two of the major television channels, France2 and France3; both tend to represent the opinion of the state, rather leftist at the time of publication; France3 is specifically for the regions, with regional *informations* (news) each evening at 7. La Cinq joined with Arte to form a single public station and they share the daily programming, with Arte showing French and German cultural programming—movies, documentaries, theme nights; La Cinq has more of an educational slant to its programming and broadcasts during the afternoons. M6 was intended to be a musical channel, but now combines music with a lot of movies and situation comedies. Canal+ is in a separate category with some pay-per-view programming and some *en clair* programming, visible without payment, usually during the day.

THE FOUR BRANCHES OF THE FRENCH POLICE
In the United States there are very clear boundaries between the roles of civilian police and the military. In France those lines are a bit fuzzier. The French police has three *gendarmeries* and the municipal police, which is the force closest to the American police. The *gendarmerie* is a national police organization, with national jurisdiction, which constitutes a branch of the armed forces. The three primary *gendarmeries* are the Riot Police, the Presidential Guard, and the Supplemental Police. The supplemental *gendarmerie* force provides regular policing services in areas where the population is too small to merit a municipal police force.

HOLIDAYS
In France there are eleven national holidays and a number of local festivals. On the national holidays, schools, businesses, and government offices are all closed. The national holidays are as follows:

January 1	Jour de l'An (New Year's Day)
March or April	Lundi de Pâques (Easter Monday)
May 1	Fête du Travail (Labor Day)
May 8	Victoire de 1945 (French Liberation Day)
May 21	Ascension
May or June	Pentecôte (Pentecost)
July 14	Fête Nationale (Bastille Day)
August 15	Assomption (Assumption, a major summer holiday)
November 1	Toussaint (All Saints' Day)

November 11   Armistice 1918 (Veterans' Day)
December 25   Noël (Christmas)

TIME

In France, the twenty-four-hour time system (what we commonly call "military time" in the United States) is used not only for train and movie schedules but also in common speech for setting up appointments. For example, someone might say to you, *"On déjeune à treize heures."* Unless it is early in the morning and you are making an appointment for an hour later, it is safer to use military time. It may be difficult for foreigners to get used to this, so we have supplied an easy table below to help you remember.

Late Night and Morning   Afternoon and Evening

English	French	English	French
1:00 A.M.	1,00	1:00 P.M.	13,00
2	2,00	2	14,00
3	3,00	3	15,00
4	4,00	4	16,00
5	5,00	5	17,00
6	6,00	6	18,00
7	7,00	7	19,00
8	8,00	8	20,00
9	9,00	9	21,00
10	10,00	10	22,00
11	11,00	11	23,00
12 P.M. (noon)	12,00 (*midi*)	12 A.M. (midnight)	24,00 (*minuit*)

Time Differences between France and the United States

France is in the Central European time zone. There is no time difference among French cities. Daylight Savings Time is implemented on the same weekend as in the United States in the spring and ends on the same weekend in the fall. France is six hours ahead of New York and the rest of the East Coast, seven hours ahead of Chicago, eight hours ahead of Denver, and nine hours ahead of California.

1:00	2:00	3:00	4:00	10:00
Los Angeles	Denver	Chicago	New York	France

GENERAL MEASUREMENTS

Distance

General English-Metric Conversions

To Convert	Multiply	By
Inches to millimeters	No. of inches	25.4
Inches to centimeters	No. of inches	2.54
Inches to meters	No. of inches	0.0254
Centimeters to inches	No. of centimeters	0.39
Feet to centimeters	No. of feet	30.48
Feet to meters	No. of feet	0.3048
Meters to feet	No. of meters	3.28
Yards to meters	No. of yards	0.9144
Meters to yards	No. of meters	1.09
Miles to kilometers	No. of miles	1.61
Kilometers to miles	No. of kilometers	0.62

Specific English-Metric Conversions

United States	France
0.394 inch	1 centimeter
1 inch	2.54 centimeters
1 foot	30.48 centimeters = 0.3048 meter
1 yard (36 inches)	91.4 centimeters = 0.9144 meter
39.4 inches	1 meter
0.6214 miles	1 kilometer
1 mile = 5,280 feet	1.6093 kilometers
0.5 mile	0.8 kilometer
1 mile	1.6 kilometer
5 miles	8.0 kilometers
10 miles	16.0 kilometers
50 miles	80.4 kilometers
100 miles	160.9 kilometers
1,000 miles	1,609 kilometers

Square Measurements (Rooms, Houses, and Land)
Rooms are measured in square meters in France. Also, remember that:

144 square inches	= 1 square foot
9 square feet	= 1 square yard
1 acre	= 4,840 square yards or 4,047 square meters

To Convert	Multiply	By
Square inches to square centimeters	No. of inches	6.452
Square inches to square meters	No. of inches	0.000645
Square centimeters to square inches	No. of centimeters	0.1550
Square feet to square meters	No. of square feet	0.0929
Square yards to square meters	No. of square yards	0.836

Appendix: Technical Information You Should Know

To Convert	Multiply	By
Square meters to square yards	No. of meters	1.196
Square miles to square kilometers	No. of square miles	2.59
Square kilometers to square miles	No. of kilometers	0.386
Acres to hectares	No. of acres	0.4047
Hectares to acres	No. of hectares	2.47

Weight

When dealing with weights and measures, there are a few key points to keep in mind. First of all, dry weights and liquid weights are different. Second, the United Kingdom and the United States use many of the same terms for measurements, but they represent different amounts. You will find that many English-language cookbooks you buy in France are published in England, which means you should consult the British conversion scales, not the American ones (see Liquid Measurements). Last, there are probably many conversions that you just never learned in English. For people who need some refreshers, we have included the basic U.S. conversions as well.

General U.S.-French Conversions

To Convert	Multiply	By
Ounces to grams	No. of ounces	28.35
Grams to ounces	No. of grams	0.035
Liters to quarts	No. of liters	1.06
Quarts to liters	No. of quarts	0.95
Pounds to kilos	No. of pounds	0.45
Kilos to pounds	No. of kilograms	2.21

Specific U.S.-to-French Conversions

United States	France
1.00 ounces	28.35 grams
3.53 ounces	100 grams
¼ pound	113 grams
½ pound	227 grams
1 pound (16 ounces)	453.60 grams
5 pounds	2.27 kilograms

Temperature and Weather

In France, temperature is measured in Centigrade or Celsius. To you 40 degrees may sound cold, but that actually means it's *HOT*. The actual calculation for making the conversion is complicated to do without a calculator, so the second table below should come in handy.

To Convert	To	Step 1	Step 2	Step 3
Fahrenheit	Centigrade	Subtract 32	Multiply by 5	Divide by 9
Centigrade	Fahrenheit	Multiply by 9	Divide by 5	Add 32

Common Weather Temperatures

Fahrenheit	Centigrade
104	40.0
90	32.2
70	21.1
60	15.6
50	10.0
32	0
14	−10.0
0	−18.0

BODY MEASUREMENTS

Height

United States	France	United States	France	United States	France
4 ft	122 cm	5 ft	152.40 cm	6 ft	182.88 cm
4'1"	124.46	5'1"	155.94	6'1"	185.42
4'2"	127	5'2"	157.98	6'2"	187.96
4'3"	129.54	5'3"	160.02	6'3"	190.50
4'4"	132.08	5'4"	162.56	6'4"	193.04
4'5"	134.62	5'5"	165.10	6'5"	195.58
4'6"	137.16	5'6"	167.64	6'6"	198.12
4'7"	139.70	5'7"	170.18	6'7"	200.66
4'8"	142.24	5'8"	172.72	6'8"	203.20
4'9"	144.78	5'9"	175.26	6'9"	205.74
4'10"	147.32	5'10"	177.80	6'10"	208.28
4'11"	149.86	5'11"	180.34	6'11"	210.82

Body Temperature

Unless you bring your own thermometer that has measurements in Fahrenheit, you will have to get used to the French thermometer when you're sick. For some people it is more consoling to have the familiar sight of the thermometer from home. In addition, most French thermometers are designed to be held under your armpit or are rectal. Children have slightly different standards from adults.

Adults, Oral Temperature

Fahrenheit	*Centigrade*
96.8°	36.0°
97.5°	36.4°
98.6° (normal body temperature)	37.0°
99.5°	37.5°
100.4°	38.0°
101.3°	38.5°
102.2°	39.0°
103.1°	39.5°
104.0°	40.0°

Children

Placement	*Normal Temperature*	*Fever*
Oral	98.6°F (37°C)	100°F (37.8°C)
Rectal	99.6°F (37.6°C)	100.4°F (38°C)
Under the arm	97.6°F (36.4°C)	99°F (37.2°C)

Body Weight
The key calculations to remember are:

1 pound = 454 grams

No. of pounds × 0.45 = No. of kilos

No. of kilos × 2.21 = No. of pounds

Pounds	*Kilos*	*Pounds*	*Kilos*	*Pounds*	*Kilos*	*Pounds*	*Kilos*
10	4.5	110	49.9	210	95.3	310	140.7
20	9.1	120	54.5	220	99.9	320	145.2
30	13.6	130	58.0	230	104.4	330	149.8
40	18.1	140	63.0	240	109.0	340	154.4
50	22.7	150	67.5	250	113.5	350	158.3
60	27.2	160	72.0	260	118.0	360	163.4
70	31.8	170	76.5	270	122.6	370	168.0
80	36.3	180	81.0	280	127.0	380	172.5
90	40.8	190	85.5	290	131.7	390	177.0
100	45.4	200	90.7	300	136.1	400	181.4

Clothing and Shoe Sizes
Women's Dresses, Skirts, and Pants

United States	6	8	10	12	14	16	18
France	34	36	38	40	42	44	46

Women's Blouses and Sweaters

United States	6	8	10	12	14	16	18	
France	81	84	87	90	93	96	99 (centimeters)	

Men's Shirts

United States	14	15	15½	16	16½	17	17½	18
France	36	38	39	41	42	43	44	45

Men's Suits, Slacks, and Sweaters

United States	34	36	38	40	42	44	46	48
France	44	46	48	50	52	54	56	58

Children's Clothes

United States	2–3	4–5	6–6x	7–8	10	12	14	16
France	2–3	4–5	6–7	8–9	10–11	12	14	14+

Women's Shoes

United States	5	6	7	8	9	10
France	36	37	38	39	40	41

Men's Shoes

United States	7	7½	8	8½	9½	10½	11	11½
France	39	40	41	42	43	44	45	46

Children's Shoes

United States	7½	8½	9½	10½	11½	12½	13½	1½	2½
France	24	25½	27	28	29	30	32	33	34

COOKING AND BAKING

Oven Temperature
When you are baking, be sure to remember that the dial on the French oven
has the temperature in Centigrade.

Definition	*Fahrenheit*	*Centigrade*
Very slow	250°	121°
Slow	300°	149°
Moderately slow	325°	163°
Moderate	350°	177°

Definition	Fahrenheit	Centigrade
Moderately hot	375°	191°
Hot	400°	204°
Hot	425°	218°
Very hot	450°	232°
Very hot	475°	246°

Water Temperature

Water	Fahrenheit	Centigrade
Boiling	212°	100°
Simmering	185°	85°
Freezing	32°	0°

Solid Ingredients (United States Only)

Amount	Equals
1 pinch	A bit less than ¼ teaspoon
1 dash	a few drops
3 teaspoons	1 tablespoon
2 tablespoons	1 ounce
8 tablespoons	½ cup = 4 ounces = 1 dL
2 cups	1 pint = ½ quart
4 cups	2 pints = 1 quart
4 quarts	1 gallon = 128 fluid ounces

Butter

500 grams = ½ kilo

No. of Ounces	Equals	No. of Grams
0.5	1 tablespoon	15
1	2 Tbs. = ¼ stick	30
2	4 Tbs. = ¼ cup = ½ stick	60
4	8 Tbs. = ½ cup = 1 stick = ¼ pound	115
16	32 Tbs. = 2 cups = 4 sticks = 1 pound	450

Sugar

No. of Ounces	Of	Equals	No. of Grams
0.16	granulated sugar	1 teaspoon	5
0.5	granulated sugar	1 tablespoon	15

No. of Ounces	Of	Equals	No. of Grams
1.75	granulated sugar	¼ cup or 4 Tbs.	60
2.25	granulated sugar	⅓ cup or 5 Tbs.	75
6.75	granulated sugar	1 cup	200
16	brown sugar	1 pound or 2⅓ cups	450
16	confectioner's sugar	1 pound or 4 cups	450

Flour

No. of Ounces	Equals	No. of Grams
¼	1 tablespoon	8.75
1.25	¼ cup = 4 Tbs.	35
1.5	⅓ cup = 5 Tbs.	45
5	1 cup	140

*Note: measurements listed here are for unsifted flour, 1 cup unsifted flour minus 1.5 tablespoons = 1 cup sifted flour

Liquid Measurements

Again, make note of the fact that the British and American conversions are different in some cases. They have been listed separately in the table below. Remember, "tsp." is "teaspoon" and "Tbs." is "tablespoon." Small amounts can be written as portions of liters (l) or as centiliters (cl) and milliliters (ml). One liter equals 100 centiliters and 1,000 milliliters. For example, 0.35 liter is equal to 35 centiliters and 0.01 liter equals 10 centiliters. Or, 0.2366 liter equals 236 milliliters and 23.6 centiliters. Also, one U.S. gallon equals 0.833 British Imperial gallons, and 1.201 U.S. gallons equals one British Imperial gallon.

Liquids

Measurement	Equivalent
1 gallon	4 quarts or 128 ounces
1 tablespoon	0.5 fluid ounce
½ pint	1¼ cups
⅛ pint	¼ cup + 1 tablespoon
¼ pint	⅔ cup
1 quart	4 cups or ¼ gallon (U.S.)
1 quart	2 pints (U.K.)
1 pint	2.5 cups or 0.5 quart (U.K.)
1 pint	16 ounces or 2 cups (U.S.)

Specific U.S.-French Liquid Conversions

United States	*France*
⅕ teaspoon	1 milliliter
1 teaspoon	5 milliliters
1 tablespoon	15 milliliters
⅛ pint	75 milliliters
¼ pint	150 milliliters
½ pint	300 milliliters
8.5 fluid ounces	0.25 liter
1 pint	0.4732 liter
1 pint (U.K.)	0.5683 liter
33.5 fluid ounces	1 liter
1 quart	0.9463 liter
1 quart (U.K.)	1.137 liter
1 gallon (U.S.)	3.7853 liters
1 gallon (U.K.)	4.546 liters
3.3 fluid ounces	0.01 liter
1 fluid ounce	29.574 milliliters
1 teaspoon (tsp.)	4.9288 milliliters
1 tablespoon (Tbs.)	14.786 milliliters
1 cup	0.2366 liter

ELECTRICAL STANDARDS AND ELECTRONICS

France and the rest of Europe have a different standard of electrical current than the United States. For this reason, appliances brought from the United States cannot function without a transformer. For smaller machines, a converter is usually enough. For larger ones, a heavy-duty transformer is needed. Some of these converters and transformers have outlets for two-prong American plugs; buy some three-to-two-prong adapters in the United States just to be safe. In addition to the difference in current, the plugs themselves are different. In France, the average plug has two or three round metal tubes where the flat, rectangular metal prongs are on an American plug. In the United States, the standard is 110 volts, and in France it is 220/240 volts and 50 Hz AC cycles (in some areas of France it is 125 or 115 volts). When it comes to phone jacks, modern French homes have the RJ11 jack we use in the United States, but older ones still have three-pronged French jacks. You can easily find an adapter at a local hardware store.

When it comes to videocassette recorders (VCRs), the difference has to do with the speed at which the cassette turns. A videocassette designed for an American VCR will not function in France unless it is first converted using a special machine. There are many stores that specialize in converting such tapes, but the procedure is not cheap. The American VCR standard is "NTSC," while the French one is "SECAM." There are video rental stores (including Blockbuster Video) all over the country.

NUMBERS

One of the problems that plagues expatriates is the use of the decimal point in France. What is a million or billion in English, and what is it in French? This is especially confusing when large amounts of money are written. There is one basic concept you have to get straight: in French numbers the period goes where our comma goes, and the comma goes where our period does. In France, a decimal point is written using a comma and not a period; to separate thousands, the French use the period.

English	French
8.5	8,5
1,300	1.300
1,000,000	1.000.000
1,000,000,000	1.000.000.000

TELEPHONE AND MAIL

The French telecommunications and postal services are both publicly owned and run. Though it can often be costly to make phone calls and ship packages, both France Télécom and *La Poste* have made great strides. To call within France you must dial 0 and the regional code (1 for Paris and the Île-de-France; 2,3,4, or 5 for the other regions), then the local area code and number. To make an international call, dial 00 and then the country code (1 for the United States) and number. Toll-free numbers (or *numéros verts*) are generally indicated by the prefix 0800. It is not possible to dial an American toll-free number in the 1-800 format from France. Most numbers can be dialed (at normal international rates) by replacing 1-800 with 1-888.

Emergency Numbers

Emergency Medical Service	15
Police	17
Fire (*pompiers*)	18
Highway information (CRICR)	(01) 48 99 33 33
Hotline for abused children	119
Hotline for drug abuse	0800 23 13 13
Hotline for AIDS information	0800 84 08 00

Directory Information and Operators

AT&T operator	0800 99 00 11
MCI operator	0800 99 00 19
Local French directory assistance	12
Minitel directory information	3611
International directory assistance	003312 + country code
Minitel international assistance	3617
Phone problems	1013 or 1015

289

Other National Numbers

Time	3699
Wake-up calls	3688
Weather	(08) 36 68 08 08

Area Codes and Postal Codes

France has been divided up into five different regional area codes. The division is more or less as follows. For specific information, consult the beginning of the White Pages:

Region	Area Code
Paris and the Île-de-France	01
Northwestern France	02
Northeastern France	03
Southeastern France	04
Southwestern France	05

French postal codes always have five digits and are generally written before the name of the city or town in an address.

City	Area Code	Postal Code
Aix-en-Provence	04	13090
Alès	04	30200
Annecy	04	74000
Arles	04	13200
Auvillar	05	82340
Avignon	04	84000
Bayonne	05	64100
Bordeaux	05	33370
Brest	02	29200
Cannes	04	06400
Carcassonne	04	11000
Chamonix	04	74400
Clermont-Ferrand	04	64000
Dijon	03	21380
Grenoble	04	38000
La Ciotat	04	13600
La Trinité-sur-Mer	02	56470
Le Havre	02	76600
Le Mans	02	72000
Lille	03	59000
Lourdes	05	65100
Lyon	05	69000
Marseille	04	01300
Metz	03	57000
Nantes	02	44000

City	Area Code	Postal Code
Nice	04	06000
Nîmes	04	30000
Paris	01	75001–75020
Quimper	02	29000
Roubaix	03	59100
Saint-Étienne	04	42000
Saint-Tropez	04	83990
Saint-Quentin	03	02100
Strasbourg	03	67000
Toulouse	05	31000
Tours	02	37000
Verdun	03	55100
Vernon	02	27200
Versailles	01	78000
Vichy	04	03200

Index

Index

American Church (Paris), 34
American culture, 241
American Embassy
 see U.S. Embassy
American Express, 88
American Graduate School of International
 Relations and Diplomacy, 138
American Hospital (Paris), 82
American Library in Paris (ALP), 183, 184
American network, 50, 196
American resources, 50
American School of Paris, 179
American Tax Institute in Europe, SA, 184
American University (Washington, D.C.),
 265
American University Library, 183–84
American University of Paris, 136
Americans
 French perceptions of, 32–33
 love affair with France, 3–4
Amsterdam, 102, 133
Angers, 184
animal care, volunteer work in, 267–68
APARE, 268
apartments
 leasing, 67–71
 listings, 70–71
 renting with other students, 131–32
archaeology, volunteer work in, 266–67
architecture, volunteer work in, 266–67
archives, 184–85
Archives de Paris, 186
art, 111–12
art galleries (business opportunity), 258
arts, internships in, 263
Asia, immigrants from, 8
Associated Press, 263
AT&T, 19
ATMs, 16–17, 54
au pairs, 244–45
 residency and work permits, 46
 special visa requirements, 15

baccalauréat, 147, 148, 177
bakery *(boulangerie)*, 65, 88, 90–91
bank account, 16, 46, 53, 69
bankcard *(Carte Bleue)*, 53–54, 88, 103
bankcard (U.S.), 17, 53, 54
banks/banking, 52, 53–56
 loans to businesses, 254–55
Banque Nationale de Paris, 56
bargains, shopping for, 94–95

bars (business opportunity), 258
bars and restaurants, American, 34
Belgium, 7
benefits checks, 50
benefits package, 207–8
 in transfers, 217
Bentley College
 Business Programs Abroad, 138
Bibliothèque Nationale, 185
bills (American), paying, 17–18
birth certificate, 13, 47, 148
births, registering, 49
bise, la, 31, 212
Bloom Where You Are Planted orientation
 program, 34
bookstore *(librairie)*, 182
 English-language, 35, 182–83
Bordeaux, 102, 179, 240
Boston, 197
Boston University, 263, 265
 Language and Liberal Arts Program, 137
boutiques, 93
branch offices, 251
bridge, the *(le pont)*, 210
British Council Library, 184
Brown University, 137
Brussels, 102
bulletin boards, 35, 110, 161, 234
 student housing, 132
bureaucracy, 32, 42, 44
 and starting a business, 249, 254
buses *(les bus)*, 100–1
business(es)
 financing, aid, loans, 254–55
 hiring employees, 255
 purchasing, 250
 setting up shop, 254–55
 starting, 248–60
 types of, 251–53
business cards, 239–40
business etiquette, 211–16
 conversation, 211–13
 for meetings, 213–16
business hours, 213
business lunches, 213, 214–15
butcher shop *(boucherie)*, 90
buying property, 66, 71–73

call-back services, 19, 74
Cambodia, 5
Canard Enchaîné, Le (newspaper), 123
Cannes, 179

Index

French family(ies)
  employing au pairs, 244
  living with, 131, 136, 176
French government
  centralized, 5
  control of industries, 9
  and economy, 193–94
  enforcement of employment laws, 238
  Web sites, 120–21
French language, 129
  children learning, 178
  immersion in, 180
  importance of, 159
  and Internet, 117
  private instruction in, 161
  in study abroad programs, 127
  see also language skills
French language exam, 148
French law, 87, 107, 207
  regarding corporate structures, 251
  regarding employment, 218, 219, 238, 244
  regarding taxes, 52–53
  visa requirements, 14, 15
  visitor status in, 12–13
French Revolution, 4–5
friendship, 30, 31, 215
Fulbright grants, 139

Gai Pied Hebdo (magazine), 36
gay resources, 36
genealogical research, 186–87
general partnership *(société en nom collectif)*, 252
Geneva, 102, 133
Germany, 7
getting ready, 11–23
Global Outreach, 264
graphology, 202–3
Greenpeace, 267
Grenoble, 179
gross domestic product, 9, 194

Handbook of Commercial French, 202, 204
handshake, 31, 212
handyperson services, 239
Harry's Bar, 34
health/health care, 42, 77–85
  eligibility for, 82
  in social security, 208
  for women, 84

health and fitness (business), 258
health care system, 60, 77, 78–79, 80, 82
health insurance, 13–14, 20, 79, 82
  private companies *(mutuelles)*, 81, 149
  proof of, 12, 45
  for students, 149
Hemingway, Ernest, 3, 193, 196
Hertford British Hospital, 82
highways *(autoroutes)*, 104, 105
highways *(routes nationales* [RN]), 105
Hofstra University, 138
holidays, 209–10
home, closing, 18
home protection, 72
homesickness, 34, 134
hospitals, 82–83
Hotmail, 119
house
  renting/buying, 53
house listings, 70–71
household expenses, 18
housing, 64–76
  prices, 65–66
  students, 130–32, 149
  temporary, 66–67
housing bills, 73–74
hugging, 32, 212
human rights, volunteer work in, 268
hypermarkets *(les hypermarchés)*, 86, 93–94

identification, 43
  for *Métro*, 99
illegal workers, 206
immigrants/immigration, 7, 8, 43, 44
  illegal, 238
Immigration and Naturalization Service (INS), 47
immigration office (Office des Migrations Internationales), 14
income tax, 52–53, 59
independent contractor(s), 238
  health insurance, 82
Indochina, 5
information
  Web sites, 124
information network, 118–19
Institut de Gestion Sociale, 138
Institut Français de Langue et de Civilisation Françaises, 160
Institut Pasteur, 77

Index

institut universitaire de technologie (IUT), 150

Institute for the International Education of Students, 264

Institute of International Education (IIE), 139

insurance
  automobile, 107–8
  unemployment, 208
  see also health insurance

interdit bancaire (banking blacklist), 54

Internal Revenue Service, 49, 57–58
  forms and publications for expatriates (list), 58

International Baccalaureate (IB) exams, 179

International Driving Permit, 104

International Financial Times, The, 35

International Herald Tribune, The, 35, 240, 263

International Monetary Fund, 159

International Olympic Committee, 159

international organizations
  employment with, 217, 223
  internships in, 263–64

international publications, 35

International School of Paris, 179

International Student Identity Card (ISIC), 81

Internet, 117–18, 134, 159, 183, 240, 241
  banking programs, 56
  connecting to, 119–20
  and taxes, 57

Internet service provider (ISP) (*fournisseur d'accès*), 119

internship organizations, 264

internships (*stage*), 261–64
  finding/creating, 265
  types of, 263–64

Internships in Francophone Europe, 264

interpreting, 214, 243–44

interview(s), 196, 206, 217

introductions, etiquette in, 212

Islam, 8

Italy, 7

J'Annonce (newspaper), 73

jardin d'enfants, 177, 178

Jeunesse et Reconstruction, 268

job hunting, 193–210
  preparations for, 196–205

job market, 195

job offer, 206

job search, 217–18, 221

joint ventures (*société en participation*), 252

journalism, 239

keeping in touch, 19–20

landlord (*propriétaire*), 68, 69

language, learning new, 27
  see also English language; French language; language skills

language courses/classes, 197–98
  for au pairs, 244, 245

language schools, 159–74
  teaching in, 232–33

language skills, 29, 32, 233, 234
  and employment, 194, 197–98, 206, 212, 214, 218–19, 222, 223, 239, 242
  housing and, 131, 132
  improvement of, by students, 132–33
  in translating and interpreting, 243–44
  and volunteer work, 266

Laos, 5

Lausanne, 102

law internships, 263

lawyers (*avocats*), 52, 56, 72, 251, 254
  business opportunity, 258

leases, 67–68

Le Pen, Jean-Marie, 8

letter from parent or guardian, 14, 15

libraries (*bibliothèques*), 182, 185–86
  English-language, 183–84

Libération (newspaper), 73, 123

licenses, business, 254

Lille, 99, 102, 179, 268

limited liability corporation (*société anonyme* [SA]), 253

limited partnership (*société en commandité simple*), 252

lines, long, 32

London, 102, 133, 221

Louis XIV, 4

Luxembourg, 7

Lyon, 99, 102, 179

Maastricht Treaty, 7, 194

maid's room (*chambre des bonne*), 66

mail, 18

mairie, 47, 60, 65, 80, 83, 110, 113, 177, 178

manners, 30–31
  see also etiquette

Marie-Antoinette, 4

299

Index

301

Index

United Nations Educational, Scientific
  and Cultural Organization
  (UNESCO), 223, 264
Université de Grenoble, 137
universities (American), 135–45, 147,
  149, 150
  finding internships through, 265
universities (French), 129, 130–31,
  146–58
  costs, 149
  enrollment procedures, 147–48
  les grandes écoles, 147
  student housing office, 131
  traditional, 147
universities, international, 136
university libraries, 186
University of California, 137
University of Illinois, 265
University of Minnesota, 265
  International Study and Travel Center,
  139
University of San Diego
  Institute on International and
  Comparative Law, 138
University of the Pacific, 265
  Master of Laws program, 263
university system (France), 146–47, 148
  degree level and other higher learning
  programs, 151*t*
  language programs, 160
  programs for foreign students, 150–52
  understanding, 150
U.S. Department of State, 221, 222
U.S. embassies
  employment in, 222
U.S. Embassy, 18, 34, 47–50, 82, 134, 221
  Federal Benefits Unit, 50
  Foreign Commercial Service, 256
  IRS office in, 18, 57
  Office of American Services, 48–49, 50
U.S. government
  employment with, 217, 221–22
U.S. Passport Agencies, 11
U.S. Postal Service, 18
U.S. Social Security Administration, 61
USA Today, 35
utilities, 17–18, 73–74

vacations, 242, 248, 255
  "studying," 133
value-added tax (*taxe à la valeur ajoutée*
  [TVA]), 52, 95, 107

Versailles, 4
Vietnam, 5
Vietnam War, 5
visa, 11–16
  long-stay, 244
  long-stay for spouse (*pour conjoint*), 16
  visa de long séjour, 12, 13, 44
  visa de long séjour pour mariage, 16
Visa (card), 17, 54, 88
visa application, 13
Vocable (magazine), 234
vocational studies, 138
volunteering, 235, 261–62, 265–68
Volunteers for Peace, 268
voting, 50

Wall Street Journal Europe, The, 35, 240,
  263
Washington, D.C., 197
Web sites, 118, 119, 120, 162, 234, 240
  CIEE, 266
  commercial and individual, 121–22
  government and official, 120–21
  www.liveinfrance.com, xii
Web 'zines, 123
welfare system, 194
what to bring, 20–22
WICE, 184
window shopping (*la lèche-vitrines*), 86
wine (Web sites), 123–24
wine appreciation courses, 113
women's health care, 84
work
  legal right to, 237–38
  tools for, 21–22
  "under the table," 237, 238, 239, 244
  see also employment
work camps
  volunteer work in, 268
work permits, 42–46, 195, 217, 222, 262
  student, 45–46, 136
  temporary, 238
workers
  cartes de séjour, 45
  visa requirements for, 14–15
work-study programs, 136, 138
World Bank, 264
World Wide Web, 19, 57, 117, 256
World Wildlife Fund, 267
WorldTeach, 235

Yahoo!, 119, 122

304